The Sources of Moral Agency

The essays in this collection are concerned with the psychology of moral agency. They focus on moral feelings and moral motivation, and seek to understand the operations and origins of these phenomena as rooted in the natural desires and emotions of human beings.

An important feature of the essays, and one that distinguishes the book from most philosophical work in moral psychology, is the attention to the writings of Freud. Many of the essays draw on Freud's ideas about conscience and morality, and several explore the depths and limits of Freud's theories. An underlying theme of the volume is a critique of influential, rationalist accounts of moral agency. Rejecting the rationalist thesis that reason alone can originate action, John Deigh shows how moral agency derives from both the cognitive and affective capacities of human beings.

The Sources of Moral Agency
Essays in Moral Psychology and Freudian Theory

JOHN DEIGH

CAMBRIDGE
UNIVERSITY PRESS

Published by the Press Syndicate of the University of Cambridge
The Pitt Building, Trumpington Street, Cambridge CB2 1RP
40 West 20th Street, New York, NY 10011-4211, USA
10 Stamford Road, Oakleigh, Melbourne 3166, Australia

© Cambridge University Press 1996

First published 1996

Printed in the United States of America

Library of Congress Cataloging-in-Publication Data

Deigh, John
    The sources of moral agency : essays in moral psychology / John
Deigh
        p.   cm.
    Includes index.
    ISBN 0-521-55418-7. — ISBN 0-521-55622-8 (pbk.)
    1. Ethics—Psychological aspects.   2. Freud, Sigmund, 1856-1939—
Ethics.   3. Moral development.   4. Social values—Psychological
aspects.   I. Title.
    BF47.D45   1996
    155.2'32—dc20   95-47292
                                                                CIP
A catalog record for this book is available from the British Library

ISBN 0-521-55418-7 hardback
ISBN 0-521-55622-8 paperback

Contents

v

Preface

The essays collected here concern the psychology of moral agency. They focus largely on the origins and operations of moral feeling and moral motivation. These phenomena have always seemed to me to be more puzzling than moral thoughts. A study of the latter, unless it is via metaethics a study of the former, tends to concentrate on their content, and for anyone who disbelieves in innate moral ideas there is no great mystery to the explanation of this content. It is found in the moral instruction people begin to receive as children and so in the norms by which a society organizes its life. By contrast, the peculiar feelings that surround those thoughts and the motivation to act in keeping with the norms they reflect do not have a similar explanation. Feelings and motivation cannot be implanted in a person's mind in the same way as ideas and beliefs can. At the same time, moral feelings and moral motivation are signs of acculturation. Susceptibility to them is one of the chief ways in which we distinguish the psychology of men and women from that of beasts and babies. It is one of the chief ways in which we define ourselves as moral agents in contradistinction to the utterly animal and the very young. Being neither implanted in the mind like the ideas and beliefs of the instructed nor native to it like the instinctual responses of beasts and babies, moral feelings and moral motivation are a puzzle that invites both philosophical and psychological investigation.

The puzzle has been particularly baffling for modern moral philosophy. Its jural character together with its requirement of rational and ultimately secular foundations has introduced into the project of making sense of these phenomena problems that did not trouble the ancients or the medievals. This point was made nearly forty years ago by G. E. M. Anscombe, and she made it with such great force that it still resounds in contemporary work. Her proposal, however, that we go back to Greek conceptions of human psychology and use them to reconfigure our understanding of moral agency offers no solution to philosophers and psychologists interested in understanding the acculturated feelings and motivation of people who grow up in the modern world. Even supposing that the puzzle were more easily solved within a moral psychology suitable to Greek ethics, one has little reason to expect a solution within that psychology to be applicable to ours. The divisions and conflicts that characterize moral feeling and moral motivation in our lives correspond to a tension between duty and interest that is of much less importance in Greek ethics than in modern ethics. Whether or not achieving harmony of the soul or a well-integrated personality was an easier undertaking for the Greeks than for us, it was different.

Modern ethics proceeds from the idea of a highest or supreme authority. Its leading systems depend on such an authority to certify the truth of moral judgments. To be a moral agent a person must be capable of comprehending such truth and of matching his or her conduct to it. This capability has traditionally been located in a faculty of the mind that serves as the instrument or agent of the authority that certifies moral truth and, at least since Butler, this faculty has commonly been identified with conscience. Accordingly, the tension between duty and interest that is of primary importance in modern ethics appears in the soul as opposition between the constraints of conscience and the inclinations of natural desire. The prevailing view has been that disciplining the latter to conform to the former brings proper order to one's life. One achieves harmony of the soul when such conformity becomes second nature. A stable allegiance to or identification with the highest authority consolidates one's personality.

In the oldest systems, those of the seventeenth century, the faculty was included as part of reason. Men and women were understood to be subject to God's laws, and a sound mind and mature intellect were taken to guarantee knowledge of those laws. Perhaps because of Hobbes's radical views or the general rise of interest in epistemology, questions about the nature of this faculty became central to moral philosophy. A series of theoretical answers dominated the next century. They included Butler's principle of reflection, Hutcheson's moral sense, Smith's impartial spectator, Rousseau's general will, and Kant's pure practical reason. Each preserved, in its own way, the idea of conscience as an authoritative source of moral knowledge. In the following century, however, the idea of conscience as disconnected from knowledge of moral truth, as instead a mechanism for producing strong, inhibitory feelings in the face of temptation to violate what one regarded as one's duty and intensely painful ones in response to one's succumbing to such temptation, took hold. J. S. Mill's doctrine of the internal sanction that attached to the bare idea of duty and so operated regardless of the content of the standards people regarded as defining their duties is representative. Similar views were common among evolutionists, whose influence spread with the growing acceptance of Darwin's theory. Indeed, Darwin himself offered an account of conscience as a mechanism for producing feelings of regret and remorse that evolved in social animals who possessed powerful mental capacities. Conscience, according to these later conceptions, was no longer an authoritative source of moral knowledge.

In the main, I agree with these later conceptions. Conscience, I believe, is best understood as a psychological mechanism for maintaining social order rather than as an intellective power for attaining truth. Such an understanding requires that one focus in the study of moral agency on feeling and motivation. It is through their operations in the adult members of a society that such order is realized. No conception, however, would be adequate to the phenomena if it did not include among the principal properties of a conscience that its dictates and reproaches appear to its possessor as the precepts and judgments of a supreme authority. Butler's observation of the manifest superiority of conscience to all other principles of action must be given its due as a sound bit of moral phenomenology, even if it does not have the epistemological consequences that he drew. The later conceptions of Mill and the evolutionists fell short in this regard. They leave unexplained the peculiarities of the moral feelings and motivation distinctive of modern life and crucial to modern ethics. And insofar as they seem unable to explain these peculiarities, there is a basis for the older conceptions.

How then can one accept a conception of conscience like Mill's and the evolutionists' and at the same time retain the phenomenology of moral experience on which the older conceptions were based? How can one continue the advance in our understanding of human beings that the empiricist movement in psychology and the Darwinian revolution in biology represent, free from the temptation to fall back into belief that we humans, in view of our moral capacities, possess special, higher powers untraceable to anything in our animal nature? To me the most promising answer is to be found in Freud's later works. The general theory of personality that Freud developed in the last phase of his career contains the synthesis necessary for a satisfactory answer. It at once explains conscience as a psychological mechanism for maintaining social order and as an internal agent that appears to its possessor as being invested with supreme authority. While other twentieth century theories surpass Freud's in explaining the development in human beings of moral judgment or the disposition to act altruistically, none does as well in achieving this synthesis. Freud's theory thus goes farther than any of its competitors toward solving the puzzle about how human beings come to be susceptible to the peculiarly moral feelings and moral motivation distinctive of modern life and crucial to modern ethics. The essays that follow, except for the last two, are rooted in this idea and influenced to various degrees by Freud's thought.

The first three deal with questions on which consideration of the nature and workings of conscience throws direct light. The question with which the opening essay deals is that of whether morality consists of rules that override

PREFACE

all other reasons for action. Understanding how morality, through the workings of conscience, functions to maintain harmonious personal and social relations enables one, I argue, to see why the demands of conscience in some situations, though consistent with what morality requires, would nonetheless be
unreasonable, its claims to supreme authority ignorable. Accordingly, one can
see in these situations that what morality requires does not override the reasons one has to act otherwise. The next essay takes up the curious Hegelian
doctrine of the criminal's right to be punished. In the course of criticizing
two defenses of this doctrine, I show how the second relies on the way conscience works to bring and restore integrity to one's personality as well as harmony to one's social relations. If the demands of conscience were regarded as
supremely authoritative, then this defense would be sound. I conclude, to the
contrary, that the defense fails in view of the tendency of conscience to make
unreasonable demands on its possessor. In these two essays Freud's influence
on my thought goes unnoted. It becomes explicit, though, in the third. This
essay concerns the thesis that the sense of justice and duty in human beings
derives from our capacity for love and friendship. I critically discuss both
conceptual and developmental accounts of the sense of justice that support
the thesis. My aim is to bring out difficulties in these accounts that Freud's
explanation of the nature and acquisition of a conscience seems suitably
equipped to handle.

The next three essays then examine Freud's explanation. The first of these
compares its exposition in *Civilization and its Discontents* with that in *The Ego
and the Id* and argues for seeing the former as more cogent than the latter and
for the coherence of the conceptual scheme on which it rests. The next probes
deeper into the exposition in *Civilization and its Discontents*. It first comments
on the change in the view of morality Freud presented in that work from the
one he presented in *The Future of an Illusion*, and it then explains this change
as a product of the revision Freud made to his theory of instincts and particularly of the way this revision resulted in significant alterations to his explanation of conscience. The third considers how well Freud's theory, as an account of moral agency, stands up to the principal objection that such rationalists as Kant and Reid raised to the naturalist accounts of their day. While
Freud's division of the mind into conscious and unconscious parts promises a
more successful reply than any available to his naturalist predecessors, I argue
that philosophical limitations on his theory leave him without a satisfactory
reply and suggest a failure on his part to appreciate the depth of the rationalist alternative to his account.

The seventh, eighth and ninth essays then critically discuss three different
versions of the rationalist alternative. These originate in the works of Thomas
Nagel, Kant, and Sidgwick, respectively. Each, I argue, fails to establish the key

thesis of rationalism, that reason alone can initiate action. These essays thus constitute a defense of the antirationalism that is basic to Freud's theory. They are also intended as an empiricist answer to the arguments for rationalism that are currently so prominent in debates among moral philosophers.

The last two essays in the collection stand apart from the first nine. The tenth offers an interpretation of Hobbes's ethics as presented in *Leviathan*. There is a remarkable affinity between Hobbes's thought and Freud's. Not only did both subscribe to materialism and pursue the project of bringing human thought and conduct within the scope of the natural sciences, but both also held rather unflattering views of human nature, which included a deflationary view of reason. Both, to be sure, as champions of science, saw reason as a powerful tool for organizing experience. But neither regarded reason as an innate capacity for determining the proper ends of life. In particular, both thought it was what Freud called a secondary process. In the tenth essay I explain how this view of reason is incorporated into Hobbes's ethics through his conception of the laws of nature as rules of reason. Whether Hobbes's program can be extended to Freud's theory, however, remains an open question. The final essay is a conceptual study of shame. It concerns different aspects of our personality from those implicated in the possession of a conscience. Recent, influential work on the emotion has treated it as comparable if not equivalent to what Freud characterized as inferiority feelings. I criticize such treatment and argue for an alternative. The alternative reveals a deeper sense of self-worth implicit in moral agency than that which is presupposed on the treatment I criticize.

I have been fortunate to have received a great deal of help on these essays from many friends. I thanked some when the essays first appeared, and my gratitude remains undiminished. Jonathan Adler, Robert Audi, Cheshire Calhoun, David Copp, Ed Curley, Stephen Darwall, Ilham Dilman, Micky Forbes, Bernard Gert, George Graham, John Hardwig, Barbara Herman, Jim Klagge, Joshua Rabinowitz, Amélie Rorty, Michael Stocker, and Laurence Thomas gave me valuable criticisms and suggestions on one or another of these essays as they were being written. Four of the essays began as comments on work by others: David Brink, Rosamond Rhodes, Susan Wolf, and Richard Wollheim. I profited from our exchanges and am grateful too for the additional suggestions they later made. David Levin, Connie Rosati, and Ira Singer read and commented extensively on several of these essays. Their observations, criticisms, and encouragement were invaluable. Marilyn Friedman and Larry May took an early interest in my ideas about Freud, and I have gained much from our conversations over the years about my work and about issues in moral psychology generally. Richard Kraut has helped me immeasurably in sorting out my ideas and distinguishing those worth retaining and developing from those that were not. He read many of these essays in draft and generously and acutely commented on each. All improved as a result.

I have been interested in questions of moral psychology since I first studied ethics as an undergraduate. I would not have gotten very far in pursuing these questions, however, or thought very fruitfully about them without the guidance and support I later received from Herbert Morris. My ongoing discussions with him about emotions, motivation, psychoanalysis, and moral agency as well as about my work have been of immense benefit to me, and he has been unfailing in his help and encouragement. I owe him my greatest, warmest thanks.

Work on one of these essays was supported by a summer stipend I received from the National Endowment for the Humanities. I began work on two others when I was a fellow for a year at The Hastings Center. There I was supported by a fellowship for independent research, again from the National Endowment for the Humanities. My work that year was also facilitated by a research leave from Northwestern University, and two subsequent one-term leaves from Northwestern also helped to advance my projects. I am grateful to these institutions for their support and to The Hastings Center as well for its wonderful hospitality.

I wrote the oldest essays in this collection using pens, legal pads, scissors, tape, and other simple tools. Only when I had produced a complete and neatly printed draft would I give it to a typist for transformation into a submittable manuscript. I wrote the newer essays with a personal computer and used an attached printer to generate submittable manuscripts. I cannot say that the quality of my thought improved with the change in technology, but I can say that the time and fuss it took me to produce a finished essay was reduced considerably. Lynn Hill knew from long experience how inefficient the rituals of my older methods were, and she engineered my transition to more efficient tools and new rituals of composition. In this and countless other ways she has made my work easier, my life better.

Sources

One of these essays appears here for the first time. The others were published in various journals and collections and are, with one exception, reprinted with only minor changes. The exception is Chapter 6, which is a bit longer than the previously published version and has a different title. I gratefully acknowledge the following sources and thank the publishers for permitting these essays to be republished.

Chapter 1. "Morality and Personal Relations" originally appeared in George Graham and Hugh La Follette (Eds.), *Person to Person* (Philadelphia: Temple University Press, 1989), pp. 106-123. It derives from comments I gave on Susan Wolf's "The Superficiality of Duty" at the 1984 Central Division Meeting of the American Philosophical Association. It is reprinted here by permission of Temple University Press.

Chapter 2. "On the Right to Be Punished: Some Doubts," originally appeared in *Ethics*, 94 (1984): 191-211. A negligibly different version of Part 1 was first presented at Tulane University's 1981 conference on Respect for Persons and subsequently appeared (under the title "Respect and the Right to Be Punished") in *Tulane Studies in Philosophy*, 30 (1982): 169-182. The whole article is reprinted here by permission of the University of Chicago Press.

Chapter 3. "Love, Guilt, and the Sense of Justice," was first published in *Inquiry*, 25 (1982): 391-416. It is reprinted here by permission of the Scandinavian University Press, Oslo, Norway.

Chapter 4. "Remarks on Some Difficulties in Freud's Theory of Moral Development," originally appeared in *International Review of Psycho-Analysis*, 11 (1984): 207-225. It is reprinted here by permission of the Institute of Psycho-Analysis.

Chapter 5. "Freud's Later Theory of Civilization: Changes and Implications" was first published in Jerome Neu (Ed.), *The Cambridge Companion to Freud* (Cambridge: Cambridge University Press, 1991), pp. 287-308.

Chapter 6. "Freud, Naturalism, and Modern Moral Philosophy" is a slightly longer version of an essay that originally appeared under the title "Psychoanalysis as Ultimate Explanation" in D.Z. Phillips (Ed.), *Can Religion Be Explained Away? Claremont Studies in the Philosophy of Religion* (New York: St. Martin's Press, 1996, in press). The earlier version was prepared for and discussed at the 16th annual Claremont Conference in the Philosophy of Religion. The version in this volume was subsequently given at the 32nd Oberlin Colloquium in Philosophy. It is reprinted, with revisions, by permission of St. Martin's Press and Macmillan Press - copyright holder for publication in the United Kingdom.

Chapter 7. "Reason and Motivation" is a substantially revised version of a paper I first gave at the 94th Semi-Annual Meeting of the Conference on Methods in Philosophy and the Sciences. Its core ideas were presented in my comments on Richard Wollheim's "Our Selves and Our Future" at the 23rd Oberlin Colloquium in Philosophy. It is published here for the first time.

Chapter 8. "Empathy and Universalizability" was first published in *Ethics*, 105 (1995): 743–763. It was prepared for and first presented at Washington University's 1994 conference on Ethics and Cognitive Science and has been reprinted in Larry May, Marilyn Friedman, and Andy Clark (Eds.), *Mind and Morals* (Cambridge, MA: MIT Press, 1996). It is reprinted with the permission of the University of Chicago Press.

Chapter 9. "Sidgwick on Ethical Judgment" originally appeared in *Essays on Henry Sidgwick*, Bart Schultz (Ed) (Cambridge: Cambridge University Press, 1992), pp. 241–258. It derives from comments I gave on David Brink's "Sidgwick and the Rationale for Rational Egoism" at the University of Chicago's 1991 conference on Henry Sidgwick as Philosopher and Historian.

Chapter 10. "Reason and Ethics in Hobbes's *Leviathan*," was first published in the *Journal of the History of Philosophy*, 34 (1996, in press). It developed out of comments I gave on Rosamond Rhodes's "Hobbes's Unreasonable Fool" at the 1992 Central Division Meeting of the American Philosophical Association. It is reprinted by permission of the publisher.

Chapter 11. "Shame and Self-Esteem: A Critique," originally appeared in *Ethics*, 93 (1983): 225–245. It is reprinted by permission of the University of Chicago Press.

Abbreviations

All citations of Freud's work refer to *The Standard Edition of the Complete Psychological Works of Sigmund Freud*, James Strachey, trans. (London: Hogarth Press, 1953-1971). Below is a list of the works I cite. Citations will omit titles of individual works and will give year and volume number instead.

(1905). *Three Essays on the Theory of Sexuality*, vol. VII, pp. 130-243.

(1913). *Totem and Taboo*, vol. XIII, pp. 1-162.

(1914). "On Narcissism: An Introduction," vol. XIV, pp. 73-102.

(1915a). "Instincts and their Vicissitudes," vol. XIV, pp. 117-140.

(1915b). "The Unconscious," vol. XIV, pp. 166-215.

(1916-17). *Introductory Lectures on Psycho-Analysis*, vols. XV and XVI.

(1917). "Mourning and Melancholia," vol. XIV. pp. 243-58.

(1920). *Beyond the Pleasure Principle*, vol. XVIII, pp. 7-64.

(1921). *Group Psychology and the Analysis of the Ego*, vol. XVIII, pp. 69-143.

(1923). *The Ego and the Id*, vol. XIX, pp. 12-66.

(1924a). "The Economic Problem of Masochism," vol. XIX, pp. 159-170.

(1924b). "The Dissolution of the Oedipus Complex," vol. XIX, pp. 173-179.

(1926). *Inhibitions, Symptoms, and Anxiety*, vol. XX, pp. 87-175.

(1927). *The Future of an Illusion*, vol. XXI, pp. 5-56.

(1928). "Dostoevsky and Parricide," vol. XXI, pp. 177-194.

(1930). *Civilization and Its Discontents*, vol. XXI, pp. 64-145.

(1933a). *New Introductory Lectures on Psycho-Analysis*, vol. XXII, pp. 5-182.

(1933b). "Why War?" vol. XXII, pp. 199-215.

(1940). *An Outline of Psycho-Analysis*, vol. XXIII, pp. 144-207.

For Maish and Dotch

1

Morality and personal relations

Is morality a system of rules to live by? Many philosopher think so and regard ethics as the discipline that formulates, systematizes, and justifies such rules. Yet this approach to ethics can make living a decent, upstanding life seem a matter of living according to formulae. The culprit is almost always an excessive rationalism, which takes morality to be an abstract system of principles whose truth no fully rational soul who gave them a complete and impartial hearing could deny.[1] On the most ambitious of these rationalist views, the relation of the system to the customary morality of this or that earthly society is understood to be like the relation of a Platonic form to each of its exemplifications in the world. Just as each exemplification resembles imperfectly the form, so the customary morality of each earthly society resembles imperfectly the system. And just as according to Plato's theory of education one arrives at knowledge of the forms by stages that begin with acquaintance with their exemplifications, so according to a well-respected rationalist theory of moral education one arrives at moral knowledge, knowledge of the abstract system of principles, by stages that begin with the inculcation of the mores of one's society.[2] The rationalist will tell us that those who attain such knowledge come to understand themselves as having realized fully their rational nature and achieved true freedom and that this final advance in self-knowledge gives a special meaning and value to their use of and adherence to the system's principles. But to one who has trouble seeing why such individuals are any more rational or free than a ruthless businessman who knows what he wants and has the brains and determination to get it, moral judgments and moral decisions, *as the rationalist characterizes them*, will seem like so many computational or legalistic exercises. What this approach obscures and distorts, when it runs to such abstraction, is morality's social function, its role in defining and regulating people's personal relations and their more distant social relations.

---

1. Recent works of ethical rationalism include Alan Donagan, *The Theory of Morality* (Chicago: University of Chicago Press, 1977); Alan Gewirth, *Reason and Morality* (Chicago: University of Chicago Press, 1978); and Stephen Darwall, *Impartial Reason* (Ithaca: Cornell University Press, 1983).
2. Lawrence Kohlberg, *Essays on Moral Development* (San Francisco: Harper & Row, 1981, 1984), vols. I & II.

A different approach focuses on this social function. In any communal group of people, peaceable relations among them will not last for long if they do not share an understanding of what forbearances and positive services each owes the others. The customary morality of a society is to a large extent a shared understanding of this sort, and its function, then, is to foster and maintain peaceable, stable relations among the society's members. This idea, to be sure, is far from new. It can be attributed to Protagoras for instance, if Plato, in the dialogue he named for Protagoras, accurately represented his views.[3] And among modern philosophers, Hume is widely recognized as its most powerful exponent.[4]

Now the customary morality of any society, if it is to foster and maintain peaceable, stable relations among the society's members, must include certain prohibitions and requirements. It must include prohibitions on the use of violence, requirements of honesty and respect for others' property, and prohibitions and requirements that regulate sexual conduct. This much is plain from the common conditions of human life: that men are mortal; that they are prone to hostile and belligerent action when their survival is threatened; that some scarcity in the necessities of life exists; that in men benevolence is limited in its range and weaker than self-love; and that competition for sexual favors is a source of such jealousy and insecurity that it can abruptly turn fierce and vicious. It is not surprising then to find in different societies many similar prohibitions and requirements, and these similarities among the prohibitions and requirements of different societies have seemed to some to be the reflection of a true morality, a system of supremely rational principles of which all civilized people are, however dimly, aware and which, through their awareness, guides their conduct or would guide it if other influences and considerations did not interfere.

Belief in such a morality, however, is not necessary for understanding why different societies have similar prohibitions and requirements. Other explanations, which make no reference to a true morality, are available. Thus, different societies have similar prohibitions and requirements because their customary moralities have the same social function and because the above-listed conditions of human life are true of human beings the world over. Still, the tempta-

---

3. Plato, *Protagoras*, C.C.W. Taylor, trans. (Oxford: Clarendon Press, 1976), 322a–d.
4. David Hume *A Treatise of Human Nature*, 2nd ed., L. A. Selby-Bigge and P. H. Nidditch (eds.) (Oxford: Clarendon Press, 1978) bk. 3, pt. 2; *Enquiries Concerning Human Understanding and the Principles of Morals*, 3d ed., L. A. Selby-Bigge and P. H. Nidditch (eds.) (Oxford: Clarendon Press, 1975), sec. 3 of the second *Inquiry*. Recent works that develop this idea include P. F. Strawson, "Social Morality and Individual Ideal," *Philosophy*, 36 (1961): 1–17; G. J. Warnock, *The Object of Morality* (London: Methuen, 1971); and J. L. Mackie, *Ethics: Inventing Right and Wrong* (Hammondsworth: Penguin, 1977).

tion remains to regard these similar prohibitions and requirements as prefiguring moral principles that are valid for all rational souls, and yielding to this temptation, many philosophers have sought to uncover these principles and to reconstruct the system they constitute. As a result, these philosophers have tended to discount morality's social function as either an uninteresting fact about customary moralities or a by-product of the universal acceptance among human beings of that system of principles whose content and logic these philosophers have made it their project to explicate. They have, in other words, been led to consider questions of content and logic in abstraction from social function. And a useful antidote to the allure of this rationalist project is to consider social function in abstraction from questions of content and logic.

A good way to proceed is to focus on personal relations, relations between friends and among the members of a family. On this way of proceeding, we should first consider the natural dynamics of such relations as determined by the mutual love and affection that bind friends or the members of a family together, and we should then consider how their mutually accepting certain moral prohibitions and requirements on their conduct toward one another, that is, their having a shared understanding of what they owe each other in the way of forbearances and positive services, affects these dynamics. The idea of this second step is to bring out both how a morality can serve to reinforce the bonds of friendship and family that mutual love and affection establish and how it can help to restore harmony to these personal relations when they have been strained or ruptured. This idea, once developed, can then be readily extended to social relations more distant than those of friendship and family, social relations that arise from joint membership in a society. It can thus be made to yield an account of how a morality serves to foster and maintain social stability generally. With this way of proceeding in mind then, let us turn to the natural dynamics of personal relations.

We can spare ourselves the diversion of imagining a state of nature, arcadian or harsh, whose human inhabitants live either without the need of an organized society or without the benefit of one. It will suffice to describe abstractly how some natural feelings and attitudes work to bring and keep people together while others drive and keep them apart. I have already mentioned affection and love as representative of natural feelings and attitudes of the first sort. To these we should add feelings of dependency – those of young children toward their parents of course, but also those of spouses, of intimate friends, and of aging parents toward their adult children. And we should add as well the complementary feelings of protectiveness – those of parents toward their children, and also those of spouses, of intimate friends, and of adults toward their aging parents. Where these natural feelings and attitudes are strong and mutual or complementary, friends and family are close-knit.

3

At the same time, underlying tensions may exist. A man may be insecure in his relations with a friend, say, or harbor unconsciously hostile attitudes towards him. This insecurity or hostility may be traced to past differences between them, or it may have only superficially to do with his friend, its roots going back to disappointments and injuries he suffered long before they first met. Be this as it may, these underlying tensions represent structural weaknesses, so to speak, in their relations. Hence, irritation and anger that a friend's thoughtlessness or selfishness provokes are more likely to cause a rift in the relations, and the suspicion and enmity that may then set in will impede renewal of good relations. These are natural feelings and attitudes of the sort that drive and keep people apart. Of course, if a friendship is structurally sound, then anger and irritation that can quickly erupt between friends will just as quickly die down. No suspicion of the other's motives or lack of attachment will take hold. No enmity, with its characteristic desire to strike back, will occur. Only a serious betrayal of friendship would severely strain or rupture such relations. Few of our friendships, though, ever achieve this ideal.

At the heart of good relations is trust. Trust cements a friendship, so we say, and correspondingly its erosion or destruction, whether due to an accumulation of harms and hurt feelings or a single act of betrayal, commonly causes friendships to falter and break up. These points apply readily to the natural dynamics of personal relations. For trust can develop directly from mutual affection and love. Thus, when mutual affection brings two people together, when mutual love unites them, each cares about the other's welfare and has concern for his happiness, and each realizes that his own welfare and happiness likewise matter to the other. Trust then develops when this realization gives one confidence in the other, confidence that he will act with one's interests at heart. And this trust is shown in one's engaging with him in cooperative activities, relying on him for help and support in one's own activities, and sharing with him something of oneself: one's plans, hopes, concerns, fears, and the like. Confident that he will not act against or in disregard of one's interests, one does not take precautions or remain watchful or alert in one's relations with him as one would when dealing with someone whom one took to be potentially or actually opposed or indifferent to one's interests. Moreover, one's trust in him need not be total like a child's trust in its parents, and it need not be blind like the trust of innocent love. Trust can be limited by recognition of the normal boundaries that separate adult lives, and it can be made wise by experience so that one comes not to expect too much of friends and loved ones, to allow for their foibles and personal imperatives. A reasonable trust, which develops out of mutual affection and love, is therefore possible. Its elements are the realization that the person one trusts cares and

4

has concern for one and a resulting confidence that he will not act against or in disregard of one's interests.

What damages such trust, then, are acts that harm or put one in danger. Needless to say, one's trust in a friend would remain intact so long as one was unaware of his having harmed or endangered one. But the recognition that he has should lessen one's confidence in him. It should give one reason to question how much he cares and has concern for one. In the worst case, his act will exhibit false friendship and thus undermine completely one's trust. However, it may only indicate a susceptibility to thoughtlessness or selfishness or an inability to resist temptation or persevere in hazardous circumstances. In any of these latter cases the damage to one's trust will be limited, though of course repeated acts of this kind or retaliatory measures of one's own would worsen the damage.

At the same time, repair is possible. Realizing what he has done – that he has harmed one or upset one through endangerment – he may express sorrow and regret. Perhaps it was unintentional or necessary under the circumstances, in which case he might try to put one's mind at ease through explanation and reassurance and might also offer compensation for any harm. But even if it were indefensible, he could still try to set things right. He could renounce the satisfaction he got from the action and offer to make it up to one in kind. And seeing the depth of his feeling and the sincerity of his desire to preserve the friendship, one may in turn show oneself willing to forget the harm or distress one suffered and not to hold it against him. In these ways hard feelings can be assuaged, suspicions removed, and trust restored. In these ways, ruptured relations can be made once again whole.

This trust, whose development, loss, and restoration I have been tracing, is to be understood as a wholly natural attitude, one that the best of friends, for instance, have toward each other. That is, one can understand it without assuming anything about either friend's having accepted moral prohibitions and requirements on his conduct. And indeed, my intention is that it be so understood. The basis for this understanding should be clear enough. The care and concern that each friend has for his friend's welfare and happiness, being aspects of his affection and love, are direct. They are unmediated by his having accepted any such moral requirements as the requirement to look out for the welfare of his friends. Consequently, since trust in this case arises from a realization that one's friend has such care and concern for one's welfare and happiness, it arises without regard to his having accepted any moral prohibitions and requirements on his conduct.

The model for such trust, as you might expect, is the earliest form of trust in a human life: the infant's trust in its mother. Trust in this case develops in response to the mother's love. It arises from the infant's recognizing in its mother's attention to its wants and needs, in the actions she takes to satisfy them, and in her accompanying facial and vocal expressions, a constant, benevolent desire for its happiness. The confidence in her that the infant thereby acquires amounts then to trust that obviously develops without the infant's having regard to its mother's acceptance of moral requirements. After all, even your brightest infant does not yet comprehend the moral duties of parents that custody of their children entails. In other words, we plainly understand an infant's trust in its mother as a wholly natural attitude in the sense previously specified.

This trust, it is important to note, is a matter of the infant's having confidence in its mother in view of her devotion to its happiness. It is not or not merely a matter of its having such confidence in view of her reliability as a provider of food, comfort, and warmth. That she regularly provides for her infant's wants and needs may explain its great attachment to and rudimentary love for her, but it cannot explain its trust. For trust, unlike attachment and love, necessarily looks to the will.[5] A good will is what qualifies a person as trustworthy. Mere regularity in her behavior that is due entirely to competence and a steady interest in what she does qualifies her as dependable or reliable and nothing more. Thus the infant's trust in its mother is explained by its recognizing her good will as manifested in the love and care she bestows. And analogously for other forms of natural trust: one's recognizing another's good will, as it is manifested in her affection and concern for one, explains such trust.

Let us now introduce moral prohibitions and requirements into the circumstances of personal relations. Specifically, let us add to our account of friendship and family that friends and the members of families - infants, toddlers, and others too young or senile to have or still have a conscience excepted - understand and accept these prohibitions and requirements as binding on their conduct toward one another. Friends, we are now supposing, have a conscience about how they treat each other as well as a natural inclination to treat each other well, and each, so we are further supposing, believes about the

---

5. I am here adapting Rousseau's important observation that the child's love for its parents develops from its recognizing in the benefits it receives from them their love and affection for it. See J. J. Rousseau, *Émile, or On Education*, Allan Bloom, trans. (New York: Basic Books, 1979), p. 213; see also John Rawls, *A Theory of Justice* (Cambridge, MA: Belknap Press,1971), pp. 463-464 and 490-496. To fit the observation to my account, I suggest that the child becomes attached to and develops a rudimentary love for its mother before it recognizes itself as the intended beneficiary of its mother's attention and care and that Rousseau's observation applies to a later developmental stage at which the child's trust in its mother arises. In other words, I suggest that Rousseau's observation concerns not the onset of love but rather the development of a maturer love that includes trust. For extensive discussion of factors determining the child's attachment to its mother, see John Bowlby, *Attachment and Loss* (New York: Basic Books, 1969), vol. 1.

other, sees in his conduct, that he too possesses a conscience. In other words, their acceptance of moral prohibitions and requirements on their conduct toward each other is mutual. And similarly for the members of families.

This mutual acceptance by friends and family members of moral prohibitions and requirements on their conduct furthers the ends of friendship and family unity. The point is not hard to see. Take, for example, a friendship. While friends are inclined to treat each other well, they are also only human. Each therefore is subject to temptations, pressures, and impulsive and selfish desires that, if yielded to, would lead him into action that would harm or endanger his friends. That is, they invite or prompt thoughtless and selfish actions, which, as we noted before, can damage or rupture good relations. Of course, his affections and concern for his friend counter to some degree these temptations, pressures, and desires, but rarely to a degree that would remove them as threats to the friendship. The threats they represent, however, are significantly reduced by his acceptance of moral prohibitions and requirements as binding on his conduct. For such acceptance, which in an individual's psychology is shown by the possession of a conscience, increases his ability to check the motivational force of these temptations, pressures, and desires. His conscience puts him on guard against the unwanted consequences they lead to, and it strengthens his will to resist them. It monitors his thoughts and intentions, and it acts as a break against inconstancy, pliancy, and self-indulgence. In these ways, acceptance of moral prohibitions and requirements, when mutual, reinforces the bonds of friendship, and it likewise reinforces the bonds of the family unit.

Again, trust is a key element in these, now moralized, relations. But the trust that cements these relations is not a wholly natural trust and, correspondingly, acts that cause or risk harm to a friend or relative are not the only kind of act that can damage or destroy it. Friendships and families, as we are now conceiving of them, are governed by moral prohibitions and requirements and, consequently, trust between friends and among the members of a family is sustained not only by their mutual affection and love but also by their mutual acceptance of these prohibitions and requirements. That is, the trust one has in a friend, say, is grounded both in a belief that one's friend cares and has concern for one's welfare and happiness and in a belief that he is sensitive to moral prohibitions and requirements and has a conscience about fulfilling the duties they define. To be sure, such trust draws much more of its strength from a friend's affection and concern than from his conscientiousness. But it would be a mistake to exclude the latter altogether from being a source of trust. In a civilized society, the good will that qualifies a friend as trustworthy consists partly in his benevolence towards one and partly in his having a conscience about how he treats one.

7

This distinction between being benevolent and having a conscience is by no means nominal. Indeed, we have already implicitly acknowledged its reality in noting how conscience importantly supports the benevolent attitudes and feelings that friends and the members of families have toward one another. But we can establish the distinction's reality more clearly by pointing out a realm of action that conscience, independently of benevolence and sometimes in opposition to its influence, governs.

Broadly speaking, conscience moves its possessor to conform his conduct to moral prohibitions and requirements. Thus it directs him to give to others what he owes them. Typically what one owes another would benefit him, whereas withholding it from him would harm or endanger him. Typically then, conscience and benevolence agree in the actions they prompt. Sometimes, however, what one owes another would not benefit him and could even harm or endanger him. For instance, one might owe another the truth on some matter in circumstances in which he would be better off not knowing it. In this instance, conscience and benevolence oppose each other. Conscience would direct one to tell him the truth while benevolence, unrestrained by conscience, would move one to withhold it from him and to lie, if this were necessary, to keep him ignorant of it. The duty to tell the truth is therefore one example of a moral requirement that conscience at times enforces when benevolence is silent and even at times enforces against benevolence's wishes. Additional examples are the duty to respect the property of others, the duty to respect their privacy, and the duty to forbear making false promises. The occasional conflicts between these duties and the urgings of benevolence make clear that conscience and benevolence are distinct sources of motivation.

Correspondingly, then, trust that cements friendships and families, conceived of as moral relations, can be damaged or destroyed in two distinct ways. Since such trust develops from mutual acceptance of moral prohibitions and requirements as well as from mutual affection and love, it can be damaged or destroyed by acts that violate those prohibitions and requirements as well as by acts that harm or endanger a friend or relative. In particular, it can be damaged by acts of the former kind that are not also acts of the latter kind. A mother, anxious about her daughter's social life, illicitly reads her daughter's diary. It may contain only the most tame and reassuring descriptions of a normal teen-age girl's life, nothing the girl wouldn't openly tell her mother. Nevertheless, if the girl discovered this invasion of her privacy, trust between mother and daughter would be damaged. The invasion would undermine the girl's confidence in her mother as a respecter of her privacy. Similarly your trust in a roommate could easily be damaged if you discovered that while you were at work or school and without your consent, he took your new car for afternoon drives. "No harm done," he might say, "I always refill the tank." And he could be right: no harm was ever done or risked. Still, his actions would likely undermine your confidence in him as a respecter of your personal property. In this way the failure to observe a duty that one has to a friend or relative, even when unattended by any harm or risk of harm to him, can strain and perhaps even rupture one's relations with him.

At the same time, if one sees that one has in this way damaged relations with a friend, one can attempt to repair the damage. One can express sorrow and regret, offer explanations, ask forgiveness, and make apologies and further amends. By these actions one disowns, as it were, one's transgression, seeks to regain the trust one lost, and signals a desire to renew good relations. Indeed, having invaded a friend's privacy or property or violated some other duty to him, one owes him an explanation, apologies, and perhaps additional reparations. One's reparative acts therefore fall within the province of the moral prohibitions and requirements that govern one's relations with him, and with friends and family generally. In other words, these prohibitions and requirements not only define the duties of forbearance and positive service performance of which helps to maintain trust between friends and the members of a family but also define a duty of reparations, which one incurs upon violating one of these duties and through the discharge of which one seeks to restore the trust one breached by that violation. Compliance with moral prohibitions and requirements thus serves both to maintain harmonious relations with friends and family and to guide passage back to harmony when those relations have been damaged.

Obviously, though, fulfilling a duty of reparations one has incurred will not automatically restore harmony to the relations one has damaged. Harmony is restored when mutual trust and goodwill are reestablished, and their reestablishment is not automatically or even assuredly accompanied by the performance of this duty. For one thing, the friend to whom one had the duty one violated may not, despite one's expressing regret, asking forgiveness, and offering apologies and other reparations, be willing or ready to trust one again or to let the resentment he has toward one subside. Consequently, he may not accept one's apologies or grant forgiveness. Or though he outwardly accepts them and grants it, he may not truly forgive. His distrust and resentment continue, perhaps unconsciously. For another, one's reparative acts may themselves be insincere. One may perform the duty of reparations one has incurred but have no sense of guilt or bad conscience about the act for which one is offering reparations. One may make apologies and further amends but not regret or repent it. If evident, one's insincerity will impede one's regaining the trust one lost. Within friendships and families especially, perfunctory apologies and amends-making only harden ill-feeling. And even if one successfully masks one's insincerity, one's own, presumably complicated, feelings

9

about one's actions and one's friend are likely to interfere with the renewal of harmonious relations. Thus, on either side of the friendship, suspicions and bad feeling or self-doubt and anxiety can impede the reestablishment of mutual trust and goodwill that offering and accepting reparations normally accomplishes.

The foregoing, in effect, warns against confusing reparative acts so called because they fulfill the duty of reparations with reparative acts so called because they succeed in restoring harmony to damaged personal relations. To avoid this confusion let us call the former formally reparative and the latter effectively reparative. Formally reparative acts, as we've seen, are not necessarily effectively reparative. Yet the connection between them should be clear. A violation of a moral prohibition or requirement is liable to arouse in its victims resentment at being denied what was owed them and to bring into doubt the strength of the violator's conscience. It tends to create in the victims illwill toward the violator and to lessen their confidence in his having accepted moral prohibitions and requirements on his conduct toward them. It tends, that is, to undermine their goodwill toward and trust in him. Now, if his action is defensible, then he normally needs only to express regret and to offer an explanation and perhaps also an apology to appease any ill-will or resentment he may have aroused and to reassure the victims that he has a conscience about how he treats them. If, on the other hand, his action is indefensible, then to achieve the same results he normally needs to offer at least an apology and often additional reparations besides. Thus, in either case, his formally reparative acts serve to restore the victim's goodwill toward and trust in him or to forestall their losing that goodwill and trust, a loss that would normally occur if no such acts were performed. And if he is sincere in performing them and if their recipients are understanding and forgiving, then these acts should be effectively reparative as well.

Of course, the mutual love and affection and the complementary feelings of dependency and protectiveness that unite friends or the members of a family also motivate them to mend their differences and renew good relations when those relations have been strained or ruptured. The pain of disaffection and the desire for union are themselves strong motives to reconciliation. A sense of guilt and a stricken conscience are, then, not the only springs of reparative action. Indeed, it is reasonable to assume that within friendships and families the workings of conscience normally have a secondary role in bringing about such action. Their role is nonetheless important. For conscience not only guides one to perform those actions that, because formally reparative, conventionally facilitate reconciliation but also provides motivation to attempt reconciliation. And this additional motivation is sometimes needed; for despite the strong motivation that love, affection, and feelings of

10

dependency or protectiveness provide, anxiety over rekindled anger, fear of rejection, and especially pride can stand in the way of one's making the attempt. Conscience, in other words, not only counsels but prods. It tells one about the moral path one should take back to good relations and helps, when help is needed, to start one down that path.

To summarize, then, while mutual love and affection and complementary feelings of dependency and protectiveness naturally bind friends and the members of a family together, their having mutually accepted moral prohibitions and requirements on their conduct toward each other reinforces these natural bonds. In particular, while mutual love and affection and complementary feelings of dependency and protectiveness form the natural basis for the trust that cements friendships and families, mutual acceptance of moral prohibitions and requirements broadens and makes firmer that basis. It contributes both to the maintenance of that trust and to its restoration when it has been damaged. Relations between friends and among the members of a family, in being governed by moral prohibitions and requirements, are thus made more stable. What I earlier called morality's social function is clearly exemplified in these personal relations.

It is exemplified as well in more socially distant relations, specifically those that arise from joint membership in a community. For social cohesion in a community depends on its members' sharing an understanding of what each owes the others, both individually and collectively, in the way of forbearances and positive services. That is, in a community, the prevalence and constancy of harmonious social relations depend on its members' mutually accepting moral prohibitions and requirements on their conduct toward each other. To be sure, most every member will have some affection and fellow feeling for and towards the others, but in the absence of widespread acceptance of moral prohibitions and requirements throughout the membership, such affection and fellow feeling would be either too limited or too weak to hold the community together. Alone they would not effectively counter the narrow interests, including especially self-interest, and the emotions and impulses that motivate actions harmful to others. The frequency of such actions would breed fear and distrust among the members, making their relations acrimonious and hostile. To check the spread of acrimony and hostility throughout the community, to create conditions for social harmony, most every member then must accept moral prohibitions and requirements as binding on his conduct toward the others. That is, he must develop a conscience, which both works to restrain him from yielding to those narrow interests, emotions, and impulses that, if acted on, would harm others and moves him to reparative action when he has violated one of its strictures and consequently damaged or risked damaging harmonious relations he has with others. In other words, widespread ac-

11

ceptance of moral prohibitions and requirements among the members of a community is necessary for peaceful, friendly relations to prevail among them.

Here too trust is a key element. Widespread acceptance of moral prohibitions and requirements makes possible a climate of trust in which fellow feeling and a general affection for others can survive and grow. It forms the basis for trust among acquaintances and strangers, and this basis is then broadened and made firmer by the spirit of fellowship that a community in which such trust is established fosters and that normally informs relations among its members. Thus trust that stabilizes these social relations is similar to trust that cements friendship and families. In either case it is based on both natural and moral attitudes and dispositions. At the same time, the two differ in that trust among the members of a community is normally established through mutual acceptance of moral prohibitions and requirements and strengthened by mutual goodwill and fellow feeling, whereas trust between friends and among the members of a family is normally established through mutual love and affection and strengthened by mutual acceptance of moral prohibitions and requirements. Consequently, while the account of how the workings of conscience contribute to the maintenance of trust among the members of a community and to its restoration when that trust is damaged will be similar in general respects to our earlier account of how the workings of conscience contribute to the maintenance and restoration of trust between friends and among the members of a family, the two accounts will differ importantly in specifics. Put summarily, conscience normally has a much more important role in bringing stability to the social relations to which joint membership in a community gives rise than it does in bringing stability to personal relations.

This summary difference is reflected, for instance, in the much greater rigidity that moral prohibitions and requirements have in their application to one's dealings with strangers and acquaintances. After all, it would be a sadly wooden family whose members dealt with each other as punctiliously as they dealt with strangers and acquaintances, and similarly punctilious dealings between friends would be a sure sign that their friendship was withering. Friends and family, as a rule, are more understanding and accepting of certain acts of noncompliance with moral prohibitions and requirements, certain failures to fulfill duties one owes them, than are strangers and acquaintances of parallel acts of noncompliance, parallel failures to fulfill duties one owes them. They are more understanding because the greater reserves of good feeling on which their trust in one is staked makes one's complying strictly with moral prohibitions and requirements less important in a wider range of cases to maintaining that trust, and they are more accepting because the greater concern they have for one's welfare implies a greater concern that their rights not stand as ceremonial obstructions to one's efforts at avoiding harm or making gains. Consequently, in one's dealings with friends and family one has greater latitude to act in disregard of a moral prohibition or requirement than one has in one's dealings with strangers and acquaintances. In many cases, reasons that one could not expect strangers or acquaintances to accept as excusing one's having disregarded duties owed them one can expect friends and family to accept.

A good source of examples is the duty to respect another's property. Thus the roommate who took your car for afternoon drives without your consent, though a friend, did not have a good enough reason to excuse his failure to respect your property. But had he taken your car to fetch a sister of his who was stranded in a strange part of town, you would, I presume, have accepted this reason as excusing his action. Indeed, if the two of you were close enough friends, he would no doubt have assumed more or less automatically that you would understand. By contrast, you would have to be a person of singular magnanimity to be equally understanding when a mere acquaintance - the super of the large apartment complex in which you live, say, or a new roommate whom you only just met the day before - takes your car without your consent for the purpose of fetching his stranded sister. He might leave you a note explaining the disappearance of your car, but he could not reasonably expect you to accept this explanation as excusing his action. What he appears not to appreciate is the greater rigidity that moral prohibitions and requirements have in their application to a person's dealings with strangers and acquaintances, a greater rigidity that reflects the greater dependency of trust between strangers or acquaintances on mutual acceptance of moral prohibitions and requirements.

That the rigidity of moral prohibitions and requirements varies in this way is then an explicable fact on an approach to ethics that focuses on morality's social function. By contrast, on rationalist approaches that focus on morality's content and logic in abstraction from its social function and that take morality to be a system of rules whose validity is universal and ascertainable by reason, it is a fugitive fact. The hallmark of such rationalism is the thesis that the rules of morality are the supreme rules of practical reason: when these rules apply to one's situation, they yield prescriptions that reason requires one to follow above all others.[6] Yet this conception of morality as an abstract system of supremely rational rules implies, if anything, that the rigidity of moral prohibitions and requirements is invariant across social contexts. For to allow that the rigidity varies according to social context is to allow that in social contexts of less than maximum rigidity certain extramoral considerations,

---

6. See, e.g., Gewirth, passim and Darwall, pp. 201-239.

which give way to the prescriptions of morality in social contexts of maximum rigidity, can override those prescriptions and so lead one rationally to act in disregard of whatever moral prohibition or requirement applies. It is, in other words, to allow that sometimes one has more reason to put morality aside than to follow its prescriptions, and this result would appear to conflict with any conception of morality that represents it as an abstract system of supremely rational rules.[7]

One might, of course, question whether the conflict is real. After all, the fact that is alleged to be fugitive on these rationalist approaches is a fact about customary moralities, and these approaches are not immediately concerned with explaining such facts. Their immediate concern is with explicating the content and logic of morality, conceived of as a system of rules that is distinct from every customary morality, and therefore what is generally true about customary moralities may have no bearing on these approaches. Still, the particular fact in question cannot be so easily dismissed as irrelevant to them. For any rationalist explication of morality will include a duty to respect the property of others, and surely the assumption that your close friend and roommate was neglecting this duty rather than the duty the customary morality of our society includes, when he took your car to fetch a stranded sister, does not negate the implication of the above example. Surely, even if your roommate had attained a true understanding of his duty to respect the property of others, whatever this may come to, it would not be more rational for him to forbear from taking your car than to take it in the circumstances he faced. Someone who, however reflective and deep his understanding of morality, does not see the greater tolerance in certain circumstances for disregard of moral duty that his friendships and family relations allow is someone in whom the workings of conscience in those circumstances are not elevating but crippling.

So the difficulty this fact poses for these rationalist approaches is real.

---

7. Rationalists will no doubt object that in taking your car your roommate is not putting morality aside but rather acting on his judgment that the duty to help his sister is *in these circumstances* (as I described them) more urgent than the duty to respect your property. One reply to this objection is to point out that our example retains its force even if we explicitly assume that in fetching his stranded sister your roommate acts from simple sibling love and not from a sense of duty. But a more telling reply, perhaps, is to produce a cleaner example, which is not hard to do. Your roommate's sister, who lives far away and whom he hasn't seen in years, calls unexpectedly from the airport. An unscheduled landing . . . a layover of two hours . . . could he come out to visit? He can't take just anyone's car without its owner's consent, of course, but he might take yours if the two of you were close enough friends. In this example, I would hope, there is no temptation to suppose that your roommate, in taking your car without your consent, is answering the call of a more urgent duty than his duty to respect your property.

Nonetheless, it may not seem very great. After all, even the most doctrinaire rationalists recognize exceptions to moral rules. They recognize, for instance, that in self-defense one may sometimes use lethal force against others.[8] Such exceptions, these rationalists will explain, are part of morality itself. They are built into the rules of morality much as tax exemptions are built into our tax laws, and so one no more puts morality aside when in self-defense one uses lethal force against others than one puts the tax laws aside when one takes advantage of a tax exemption. Similarly, then, these rationalists might go on to argue, that the rigidity of moral prohibitions and requirements varies according to social context is part of morality itself, for morality includes along with the rules that define its prohibitions and requirements, which are its main rules, certain auxiliary rules that guide one's application of the main rules, and these auxiliary rules regulate how rigidly the main rules are to be applied. Accordingly, one would not be putting morality aside when, in the context of a friendship and for reasons one expects one's friend to accept, one acts in disregard of a moral prohibition or requirement that applies in one's situation. Hence, these rationalists would conclude, that we regard moral prohibitions and requirements as applying less rigidly in our dealings with friends and family is consistent with a conception of morality that represents it as an abstract system of supremely rational rules.

This argument, however, this attempt to save the rationalists' conception of morality, serves only to flush out the difficulties that underlie the rationalist approach. For one thing, it manifests the general tendency of those who take this approach to formularize the judgment- and decision-making acts of human beings, and this tendency becomes a liability in cases of judgment and decision making that are highly sensitive to context and consequently not reducible to simple formulae. The point is that, while a rationalist can always reinterpret generalizations that accurately describe the habits of thought people exercise in making judgments and decisions as formulae they use in making those judgments and decisions, such rationalist interpretations do not always yield plausible explanations of those acts of judgment and decision making.[9] What is more, these interpretations are most liable to yield implausible explanations in cases in which, because what judgment or decision a person makes depends on small or subtle differences in context, how he makes it is not reducible to some simple formula. And a little reflection should show that

---

8. Donagan, pp. 71-74.
9. Frege's distinction between induction as a formal procedure and induction as a "mere process of habituation" suggests a similar point concerning how in everyday life we form beliefs about the empirical world. *The Foundations of Arithmetic*, 2d ed., J. L. Austin, trans. (Evanston, IL: Northwestern University Press, 1974), pp. 16-17.

the case at hand – the decision to disregard a duty owed to a friend for reasons one expects the friend to accept – is precisely the kind that is most troublesome for rationalist interpretations.

Admittedly, it is hard to prove the charge of excessive rationalism in any particular case. But even if the charge cannot be proved in the case at hand, the rationalist explanation of this case that is given in the argument above reveals a further difficulty in the rationalist approach. For on this explanation, not only do we use some formula in deciding that we may disregard a duty owed to a friend, but the formula we allegedly use is also part of morality, one of morality's auxiliary rules. And granting for the sake of argument that we do use some formula in making such decisions, we can then skeptically ask what makes this formula part of morality, what qualifies it as a moral rule. It is obvious why rationalists would characterize it as a moral rule. They would do so in order to preserve their conception of morality as comprising the supreme rules of practical reason. Rationalists want it to be morality that permits us to disregard a duty when it is rational to do so and, consequently, they find in morality a rule that authorizes our disregarding a duty in this case. But their desire to secure morality's authority in this matter is ill-conceived. When we disregard a duty to a friend for reasons we expect our friend to accept, we do so not because we recognize that morality permits it, but because we recognize limits to morality's governance of our lives and, in particular, in that part of our lives that our relations with friends and family fill.

Consideration of how we would respond if we misjudged our friend's reaction makes this clear. For if our friend, instead of being understanding and accepting of our reasons for disregarding the duty, reacted with anger at the liberty we had taken, we would not think to defend our action by invoking a moral rule that supposedly permitted it. Rather we would recognize that, having invaded our friend's rights for reasons insufficiently strong to defeat his claim of right (which he would now, in effect, be pressing), we owed him an apology and perhaps additional reparations. We would incur, in other words, a more burdensome duty of reparations than any we would have incurred if morality had permitted our action. Our mistake, then, would not be a mistake about what morality permits. Rather it would be a mistake about the liberties our friendship tolerates. We had mistakenly thought that the friendship was close enough, the mutual trust between us strong enough, to make strict compliance with moral prohibitions and requirements in this case unnecessary, and this is a mistake about the extent to which morality governs our relations.

Rationalists who assume that morality comprises the supreme rules of practical reason, who conceive of morality as an abstract system of such rules, and who seek to explicate morality's content and logic in abstraction from its social function, therefore face the following dilemma. If they do not acknowledge as relevant to their approach the fact that the rigidity of moral prohibitions and requirements varies according to social context, they will misdescribe morality's logic. If they acknowledge this fact as relevant and then proceed to explain how it is consistent with their conception of morality, they will misdescribe morality's content.

2

On the right to be punished: Some doubts

I

Some doctrines outlive the systems of philosophy that bear them. Such is the doctrine that a criminal has a right to be punished for his crime. Born of Hegelian social philosophy, it still finds adherents and sympathizers long after the death of its progenitor.[1] The reason for its independent life is not hard to make out. The doctrine captures for many the uplifting thought that human society owes even its most inimical members respect as responsible, moral agents. Punishment is part of any institution of social control that treats persons as responsible, moral agents, and thus punishment becomes a sign of respect. To those attracted to moral theories whose shibboleth is respect for persons, the doctrine has immediate appeal.

At the same time, talk about a criminal's right to be punished is bound to perplex. What manner of right is this? A right to suffer the deprivation of some good or to be visited with some evil? What could ever possess a person to want to assert such a right? The perplexity that these questions engender thus checks any inclination to embrace the doctrine. Looked at in one way, the doctrine is appealing; looked at in another, it is a morass of confusion. What better spur to philosophic inquiry!

The questions in the last paragraph prefigure one standard objection to the doctrine, an objection any of its defenders must answer.[2] Spelled out, the ob-

---

1. Recent expressions of support include: Herbert Morris, "Persons and Punishment," *Monist* 52 (1968): 475-501; Jeffrie G. Murphy, "Moral Death: A Kantian Essay on Psychopathy," *Ethics* 82 (1972): 284-298, pp. 291-292; Joel Feinberg, "Voluntary Euthanasia and the Inalienable Right to Life," *Philosophy & Public Affairs* 7 (1978): 93-123, pp. 104-110: David Hoekema, "The Right to Punish and the Right to Be Punished," in *John Rawls' Theory of Social Justice: An Introduction*, ed. H. Gene Blocker and Elizabeth H. Smith (Athens: Ohio University Press, 1980), pp. 239-269, esp. pp. 264-255; Martin R. Gardner, "The Right to Be Punished – a Suggested Constitutional Theory," *Rutgers Law Review* 33 (1981): 838-864; Martin Perlmutter, "Punishment and Desert," in *Morality and Moral Controversies*, ed. John Arthur (Englewood Cliffs, N.J.: Prentice-Hall, 1981), pp. 396-406, esp. pp. 403-406. The classic statements of the doctrine are in G. W. F. Hegel, *The Philosophy of Right*, trans. T. M. Knox (Oxford: Oxford University Press, 1942), pp. 70-71; and Bernard Bosanquet, *The Philosophical Theory of the State* (London: Macmillan, 1965), pp. 201-211.
2. See Anthony Quinton, "On Punishment," *Analysis* 14 (1954): 133-142, p. 136; S. I. Benn, "An Approach to Problems of Punishment," *Philosophy* 33 (1958): 325-341, p. 329; and Walter Moberly, *The Ethics of Punishment* (London: Faber & Faber, 1968), p. 158.

18

jection is that a right to be punished is otiose; no one would ever have good reason to assert it. Punishment, because it is an evil, is not something a person of sound mind would want to claim as his due. Sheer obstinacy or some other perversity of will is the only motive that could lead someone to demand that he be punished, and a demand that springs from such a motive does not reflect a claim worthy of our respect. Clearly, the principal thought behind this objection is that a right serves essentially to secure for its possessor certain benefits or to protect him from certain harms. This thought, when coupled with the conventional view of punishment as an evil benefiting its recipient only accidentally if at all, implies directly that punishment is not among the things to which one can intelligibly be said to have a right.

To answer this objection a defender of the doctrine must either attack the conventional view of punishment by maintaining that punishment more than accidentally benefits its criminal recipient or challenge the principal thought behind it by arguing that rights serve essentially different purposes from the ones attributed to them in that thought. The most sustained defense in recent literature and the one that throws the most light on the doctrine's appeal takes the latter approach. I refer to the defense Herbert Morris gives in his widely read article "Persons and Punishment." His arguments are both persuasive and instructive. Close examination of them, and of the points at which they break down, will, I believe, prove equally instructive. Morris has shown us the depth of the doctrine's appeal. I aim to show that, though deeply appealing, it remains seriously problematic.

In answering the objection, Morris invites us to imagine circumstances in which a sane and self-respecting person would have reason to claim punishment as his due, without making it part of these circumstances that the punishment benefits its claimant. Hence, while not disputing the conventional view of punishment on which the objection rests, he counters its principal thought. In particular, he brings out that a criminal concerned with maintaining his dignity as a human being would have reason to demand that he be punished in circumstances in which relieving him of that punishment would constitute an affront to his dignity, would insultingly convey to him that he was regarded as less than a person. Morris's answer, therefore, implies that our dignity as human beings confers on us rights irrespective of any benefits those rights secure for us or any harms they protect us from suffering. And this goes directly against the objection's major premiss.

The persuasiveness of Morris's position has its source, I believe, in this view of rights. It captures an intuition we share that in ascribing rights to ourselves we conceive of ourselves as having dignity, a special status or worth.[3] We find

---

3. Other writers have made similar suggestions about rights. See, e.g., Joel Feinberg, "The Nature and Value of Rights," *Journal of Value Inquiry* 4 (1970): 243-257; and Murphy, pp. 292-296.

this idea attractive inasmuch as we sense that, on those occasions when we assert our rights or demand that they be respected, we are not or not merely insisting that we be given certain benefits we have come to expect or that we be spared from certain harms we have come to expect not to suffer. Rather, we are insisting on recognition, deference, and respect due us as persons. Similarly, when we are denied our rights, we do not or do not merely suffer some positive evil or the deprivation of some good, but rather we suffer indignity that comes from conduct disrespectful of our status as persons. This general view Morris expresses by ascribing to each of us the fundamental human right to be treated as a person and by taking this right as implicit in all other human rights.[4]

Yet however convinced we may be that Morris has successfully answered this objection, we may still ask about his argument in support of the doctrine. For even if we accept his view of human rights as grounded in human dignity rather than human welfare, he must still show us that this view yields a right to be punished. His general view of rights, as I said, is quite persuasive, but his argument that this view entails a right to be punished is not similarly compelling. Problems in the doctrine emerge once this argument comes under scrutiny.

The argument we are to examine occurs early in "Persons and Punishment." At the close of Section 1 Morris writes: "I want also to make clear in concluding this section that I have argued, though very indirectly, not just for a right to a system of punishment, but for a right to be punished once there is in existence such a system. Thus, a man has the right to be punished rather than treated if he is guilty of some offense. And, indeed, one can imagine a case in which, even in the face of an offer of a pardon, a man claims and ought to have acknowledged his right to be punished."[5] Plainly, then, Morris intends to be arguing in this section for two conclusions: (a) that we, as persons, have a right to a system of punishment; and (b) that given the existence of a system of punishment, we, as persons subject to this system, have a right to be punished assertable whenever we are guilty of some offense. I will call the right mentioned in (a) the right to punishment, letting "punishment" abbreviate in this phrase "a system of punishment." I will call the right mentioned in (b) the right to be punished, understanding that talk about this right presupposes that a right to punishment has been secured.

Now I propose to waive criticism of Morris's argument for (a). The difficulties I am interested in exploring occur in connection with his argument for (b). At the same time, we cannot ignore the argument for (a) because the argu-

4. Morris, "Persons and Punishment," pp. 489–490.
5. Ibid., p. 476.

ment for (b) depends on it in some way. Let us begin then by setting out the strategy he uses in presenting the former. This strategy involves comparing alternative systems of social control: a system of punishment and a system in which social miscreants are regarded as sick and responded to therapeutically. Through this comparison, Morris intends to bring out circumstances in which there would be a point to claiming a right to punishment.[6] His idea is that in recognizing the point to claiming this right we shall see that there is a fundamental right to be treated as a person which would be denied if this claim were disregarded and which, therefore, entails a right to punishment. Thus, he aims by this strategy to induce us to accept (a). The argument throughout is persuasive rather than demonstrative.

We need not rehearse all the details of this comparison. A general outline will suffice. A system of punishment, Morris maintains, has as its aim to see that justice is done to both the victims and the perpetrators of injustice, where doing justice under such a system requires punishing those whose voluntary behavior violates the rules general conformity to which is necessary for social harmony. Such a system, then, if well designed to achieve its aim, entails an understanding of the behavior to which it responds as behavior that proceeds from choice. In this regard, the system reflects respect for human beings as creatures capable of making choices and determining the conduct of their lives accordingly. Doing justice under such a system thus means treating human beings as persons. This is the system's special virtue. By contrast, a system of therapy has as its aims to see that health is restored to those whose antisocial behavior indicates ill health and to protect the healthy from the danger the unhealthy pose. Such a system, then, if well designed to achieve its aims, entails an understanding of the behavior to which it responds as behavior symptomatic of some malady with which the actor is afflicted. Antisocial behavior is thus assimilated to a nervous tic or sniffles. It is understood on a model of cause and effect that has no room for the idea that the actor determines his conduct through choice. In this regard, Morris contends, a thoroughgoing system of therapy denies human beings their status as persons and is generally indifferent to treating them as such.

Morris thus uses this comparison to show how a system of punishment, given its regard for those subject to it as responsible, moral agents, respects those individuals' choices, while a system of therapy, given its indifference to treating human beings as persons, accords them no such respect. Accordingly, he brings out how the latter system degrades the status of those subject to it, causing them to suffer a variety of insults and indignities, while the former

6. For Morris's detailed comparison of the two systems, from which this outline is constructed, see ibid., pp. 477–485.

upholds their status as persons, thereby making comparable insults and indignities anomalous. In this way, he makes clear that someone whose society instituted a system of therapy to deal with miscreants would have reason to claim a right to punishment. These are circumstances in which the claim would have a point. And reflection on these circumstances and the injustices they entail, when compared with the circumstances defined by a system of punishment, should lead us to see that the virtue special to a system of punishment is unique to that system and so to affirm that we have a right to punishment.

How does this argument advance the case for (b), that we have a right to be punished? Clearly, it should not lead us immediately to affirm (b). What it does do is to teach us several things about a system of punishment, about the role of justice in the design of that system and about the significance of inflictions of punishment within it. Morris's idea, presumably, is that, once we fully learn these lessons, we shall see how in some circumstances claiming a right to be punished would not be pointless and thus, by reflecting on these circumstances, come to affirm that such a right exists. But all of this Morris leaves as an exercise for his reader. We would do well to work through the exercise.

What circumstances, then, might we imagine to convince ourselves that claiming a right to be punished could have a point? The natural answer is to describe circumstances analogous to those Morris describes in arguing that claiming a right to punishment could have a point. Thus, we should imagine someone who lives in a society in which the prevailing system of social control is a system of punishment and who is guilty of some offense and so liable to be punished. Further, let us imagine that those who have authority to mete out the punishment to which this offender is liable place him instead in the custody of some therapist for the purpose of curing him of an illness they believe is responsible for his criminal behavior. These authorities may acknowledge that the more hidebound traditionalists among their brethren would consider the offender guilty and thus deserving of punishment, but they believe, to the contrary, that the root cause of his behavior is some curable illness and that, consequently, therapy is the appropriate response.

Now, we should have no trouble seeing how someone in such circumstances could justifiably react with righteous anger at being declared sick and ordered to undergo, in lieu of the punishment he expects, a regimen of therapy. To be treated as sick because of an act one chose to do is demeaning. The authorities, by ordering such treatment, display an attitude of indifference to the offender as a being capable of determining his conduct through choice, which attitude matches the one made institutional in the system of therapy Morris describes. Thus, just as that system shows a lack of respect for the choices of those subject to it, so the authorities we have imagined show no respect for the choice to do wrong our offender made. He may then, in recognizing their lack of respect, take their order as an affront to his dignity, and if he protested, it would be natural for him to give voice to this protest by asserting a right to be punished. These, it would appear, are circumstances in which claiming such a right would have a point.

Again, as with the argument for the right to punishment, we should assume that a strategy of persuasion operates in this argument. Thus it is through reflection on the single set of circumstances just described that we are to see that denying an offender the punishment to which he is liable because guilty constitutes *in itself* an injustice done to him. This injustice would then readily translate into a violation of a right to be punished. Yet plainly, however successful this strategy is in the argument for the right to punishment, it runs into difficulty here. For we need not construe the injustice done to an offender in circumstances like those just described as a violation of some right to be punished. We can see it instead as a violation of his right to liberty, and this greatly weakens the persuasive force of the description.

That it counts as a violation of a right to liberty is evident once we remind ourselves that in a system of punishment, as Morris characterizes it, the authority to invoke punitive sanctions does not license other interferences with liberty except, of course, those necessary for investigating alleged offenses and prosecuting suspected offenders. Consequently, in such a system those responsible for meting out punishment would be exceeding their authority, trespassing on a guilty offender's liberty, if in lieu of punishment they placed him in the custody of therapists, just as a creditor, to use an analogy Morris endorses, would be exceeding his authority, trespassing on the liberty of those indebted to him, if he compelled them, in lieu of paying their debts, to join a self-help group in the belief that this would cure them of profligacy. The one has authority to mete out punishment, the other to exact what is owed him, but if either, under the guise of this authority, uses coercion against others for different purposes, he violates their right to liberty.

This, to be sure, does not refute the contention that we have a right to be punished. And if we had such a right, it, as well as our right to liberty, would be violated in the circumstances just described. The point is that such circumstances, because they cannot be interpreted unequivocally, do not argue for our having this right. The offender's claim to a right to be punished may actually be an oblique assertion of his right to liberty, rhetorically forceful but literally false, or it may be a straightforward and true assertion of a right. Either is consistent with the circumstances described.

Are there, then, any circumstances in which such a claim would be clearly true? Are there any to which Morris could appeal to show unequivocally that denying a criminal the punishment to which he is liable counts as a violation of a right to be punished? One possibility is the situation in which a criminal receives a pardon against his wishes, for in this case he is denied the punishment he wants just by being released from his liability to it. That is, we need not suppose that the authorities subsequently interfere with his life or liberty. What is more, whether or not there are other possibilities, a defender of the doctrine that there is a right to be punished will have to maintain that in such a situation the criminal is wronged. And this, it would seem, is a hard case – let us say a test case – for the doctrine. Morris himself is prepared to argue that the doctrine passes the test. He holds that pardoning a criminal against his wishes constitutes a wrong done to him.

Initially, we should be puzzled at this. A pardon, after all, is given to the guilty. Like punishment, it would be a false response to innocence. Hence, pardons no less than punishment presuppose that their recipients are responsible, moral agents inasmuch as they presuppose guilt. In pardoning a criminal no less than in punishing one, the authorities acknowledge, as it were, that the criminal's offense was the product of his will, his choice to do wrong, which is to say, they respond to him as a person, someone capable of determining his conduct through choice. Thus pardoning a guilty offender against his wishes does not demean him in the way that compelling him to undergo therapy in lieu of punishment does.

The defender of the Hegelian doctrine, however, has a ready reply.[7] The criminal, in choosing to do wrong, chooses to be punished, and therefore to pardon him against his wishes is to fail to respect that choice: it is to fail to accord him the respect he is owed as a person. Yet this familiar point about the criminal's oblique choices is surely too strong. At most, one who chooses to commit a criminal offense chooses to place himself in jeopardy of being punished or, if determination of his guilt is a foregone conclusion, to incur a liability to punishment. But even one who has incurred a liability to punishment is not thereby assured of being punished, for the decision whether or not to carry out the sentence rests with those who have the authority to mete out punishment. Or so we would have thought. To put the problem succinctly, to hold, as Morris does, that pardoning a criminal against his wishes constitutes a wrong done to him is to deny that the authority of those responsible for meting out punishment includes discretion to forgo the sanction. And this should strike us as rather odd.

Moreover, Morris further embeds this oddity into his position by taking pardoning to be the analog, in a legal system, of forgiveness and then construing the latter on the model of forgiving a debt.[8] Surely the creditor forgives a

7. See, e.g., ibid., pp. 479, 485, 491-492.
8. Ibid., p. 478.

24

debt at his own discretion. After all, he holds against the debtor the right to payment in virtue of which the debtor has a duty to pay. Hence, the creditor as right-holder can demand at the time the debt comes due what is his by right, or he can waive or relinquish that right. Either is an option. Forgiving a debt is one way of relinquishing the right. And if he exercises this option, then he frees the debtor from his duty. Thus there is a marked incongruity in any view that both takes forgiveness of guilt on the model of forgiving a debt and denies that the former can be accomplished without the consent of the guilty offender. The view seems to run afoul of the familiar logic of rights and their correlative duties.

Yet we might be judging too hastily if we dismissed the view as fundamentally confused. Morris, as I mentioned, is prepared to argue for this view. He sees forgiveness as involving more than relinquishing a right. "Forgiveness," he writes, "may be viewed, at least in some types of cases, as a gift after the fact, erasing a debt, which had the gift been given before the fact, would not have created a debt."[9] In this remark we can find material for his argument. A person, we would grant, always has the right to refuse an uninvited gift. Consequently, if a criminal were forgiven against his wishes, it would be as if he had been forced to accept a gift and so denied this right of refusal. In effect, then, it constitutes a wrong done to him. That Morris intends this or some argument like it is plain from the following passage. "We treat a human being as a person provided, first, we permit the person to make the choices that will determine what happens to him and, second, when our responses to the person are responses respecting the person's choices. . . . When we give a person a gift we are neither treating or not treating him as a person, unless, of course, he does not wish it, chooses not to have it, but we compel him to accept it."[10]

The passage suggests the general theme running through Morris's argument: one can affront another's dignity, treat him as less than a person, even when one acts so as to benefit him. Gift giving is typically a beneficent act and, moreover, one that springs from goodwill. Yet this does not make it immune to being derogatory. Charity, to take one obvious case, can, especially when uninvited, offend the dignity of those who receive it. Thus, supposing forgiveness to be, at least in the relevant cases, a kind of gift giving, it would have this liability of being derogatory. And this, it would seem, makes evident that pardoning a criminal against his wishes wrongs him. At work here is the same forceful idea that is at the core of Morris's general view of rights, that they serve essentially to uphold human dignity rather than to protect and advance

9. Ibid.
10. Ibid., pp. 492–493.

human welfare. Having been won over to his general view, we may then be persuaded that forgiveness, because it can show disrespect toward the forgiven when done against their wishes, violates their rights – in particular, their right to be punished. This is, in effect, their right of refusal, assertable even when what they refuse is of benefit to them.

The argument moves along to its conclusion rather quickly, and if we had not already noted the oddity in Morris's position, we might feel no inclination to slow down and retrace our steps. That oddity appeared most striking when we considered the analogy he invoked between forgiveness of guilt and forgiveness of a debt. This suggests that we examine the argument as it applies to the latter.

Thus, imagine a young man of affluent and overprotective parents. They, by providing for all his wants, have made for him a life of comfort and ease. But in comparing himself with less-advantaged friends, who have since late adolescence had to fend for themselves, he comes to admire their independence and to despise his own parent-made life. The desire to make his own way in the world grows stronger, and he becomes increasingly uncomfortable with accepting his parents' largess. At some point he hits upon the idea of a commercial venture, and an acquaintance agrees to lend him a large sum of money to advance his plan. When his parents hear of his debt, they become alarmed, as they imagine all sorts of risks their son is running. They approach the creditor, purchase from him their son's note, and then tell their son that they have erased the debt and that, if in the future he needs money, he should come straight to them.

Their act, well-intentioned though it be, is derogatory. In purchasing the note and then canceling the debt, they treat their son as someone not yet fully capable of taking responsibility for his life. Certainly this is how he will regard their actions. Thus we can easily imagine him becoming irate and indignant, berating them for treating him as their dependent child instead of respecting him as a responsible adult. And he might in the course of venting his anger declare that he had a right to pay his debts, a right that they by their actions denied him.

Plainly, he would be making an important point in declaring that he had a right to pay his debts. He would be pointing out to his parents that he was no longer their ward, that they were no longer his guardians. They, by their actions, indicate a failure to appreciate this change in status. They act as if he were not morally competent to assume financial liabilities, as if they still had the responsibilities of guardians. Naturally, such action humiliates. In ascribing to himself a right to pay his debts, he would be implying, to the contrary, that he was morally competent to assume positions of responsibility and trust

26

much as the ascription of a right to vote implies competence to participate in the electoral system of one's community.

But because his declaration has this point by virtue of what it implies and not by virtue of its being true, the question remains whether it is true. Does he in fact have a right to pay his debts? One would be hard pressed, I think, to maintain that he does, for one can point to no substantive wrong his parents, in erasing his debt, do to him. They have not prevented him from incurring debts, and they have not interfered with his carrying out the business venture he began. Nor can it be said that they have compelled him to accept a gift against his wishes. He no more has to accept the gift of additional wealth their act created than someone who holds elective office has to accept unsolicited campaign contributions from disreputable donors. Divestiture counts as refusal in either case.

It will be useful to note here a distinction that parallels the one Morris draws between the right to punishment and the right to be punished, the distinction between the right to a system of indebtedness and the right to pay one's debts. Recent events in Iran serve to remind us that a society could outlaw moneylending institutions and practices, specifically, the practice of lending money at interest, and such a society, one could argue, presents us with circumstances in which asserting a right to a system of indebtedness would have a point. Moreover, we can imagine someone's arguing, analogously to Morris's argument for the right to punishment, that we *in fact* have this right to a system of indebtedness. Here we need only think of an alternative system such as a patronage system, which a society might institute and in which certain members would act as protectors of groups of others, to see how this argument would go.

The argument, like the Morris original it would follow, would thus draw our attention to a system that in its design and operation showed no respect for the choice-making capacities of those subject to it. It would describe a set of practices and institutions that placed all but a select few individuals in positions of dependency and treated them as, like children, weak-minded and impulsive, beings for whom faith and obedience rather than reason and practical judgment were the most suitable traits to be developed. Each of the substantive wrongs the description made evident would reflect the derogation in status that those kept in positions of dependency suffered, the lack of respect for them as responsible agents. Then, by comparing this system with a system of indebtedness, the arguer would bring out how the latter, because it enables individuals to pursue a wide range of enterprises and fosters a conception of man as independent and self-reliant, showed respect for the capacities of human beings to make and act on choices. And if the comparison persuaded us that this was a virtue unique to a system of indebtedness, then we should also be persuaded that we had a right to such a system.

In this argument, the institutional disrespect that provokes assertion of a right to a different institution corresponds to substantive wrongs in view of which we acknowledge the existence of that right. By contrast, the disrespect the parents in our example show their son corresponds to no substantive wrong in view of which we would acknowledge the existence of the right he asserts. Their action conveys to him that they still regard themselves as his guardians, and given his circumstances and sensitivities, this act insults. But it does not in fact reduce his position, which, after all, is determined by his society's institutions and not by the paternalistic attitudes toward him his parents betray. Indeed, to forgive a debt no less than to exact it implies the legitimacy of the debt and so the moral competence of the debtor. Hence, indignity to a debtor inheres neither in the act of forgiving his debt without his consent nor, as I argued above, in its upshot, the creation of additional wealth. The indignity the son suffers, even if it counts as a violation of his right to be treated as a person, does not establish that he has a right to pay his debts.

Our dignity as human beings may ground rights to certain institutions. Morris's argument for the right to punishment gives credence to this thesis. But the further thesis that, once such institutions are in place, our dignity also grounds rights to the burdens those institutions impose, which rights one may assert whenever one is relieved of some such burden, is not likewise credible. We can state the difficulty it faces generally. We normally understand one's being relieved of a burden by those having authority to do so as a legitimate exercise of their office. And this holds even when they act for reasons of their own including those that, if made known, would make their act an affront to one's dignity. Consequently, to show that within a specific institution such action nonetheless violates a right to the burden one is relieved of requires considerations beyond those that argue for the thesis that human dignity grounds the right to that institution.

It is on this account that Morris's argument for the right to be punished breaks down. For though he advances an additional consideration, namely, that pardoning a criminal without his consent is like compelling him to accept an uninvited gift, this consideration does not ring true. He fails, therefore, to show that such a pardon constitutes a wrong done to the criminal.

None of this, however, detracts from Morris's observation that claiming a right to be punished can have a point. Its point lies in what it implies, that one is a responsible, moral agent. This implication explains the deep appeal of the Hegelian doctrine. Criminals too are responsible, moral agents. But the doctrine, as I have tried to bring out, has other implications that make its acceptance, at least on the grounds Morris presents, problematic.

II

The problems we have turned up in Morris's argument do not, of course, close off all possibility of successfully defending the Hegelian doctrine. In particular, certain reform theories of punishment suggest a line of defense rather different from Morris's. Let us dub this line the Scottish defense, after McTaggart, who to my knowledge was the first to construe Hegel's as a reform theory.[11] Those who take human rights to be ultimately grounded in considerations of human welfare as opposed to human dignity will find this the more appealing line. Moreover, in view of this grounding, it represents the main alternative to Morris's. Hence the necessity for examining it.

To introduce this line let me recur to the standard objection I described at the outset. Recall that Morris answers this objection by attacking its major premiss (that rights serve essentially to secure for their possessors certain benefits and to protect them from certain harms) while leaving undisputed the conventional view of punishment, on which the objection also rests. Now the Scottish defense proceeds in reverse. It attacks the conventional view of punishment while accepting the objection's major premiss. Thus, contrary to the conventional view that at most punishment accidentally benefits its criminal recipients, the Scottish defense, appealing to a reform theory, holds that punishment benefits them by design. Specifically, it holds that punishment renders a criminal benefits in that it provides him with the means necessary for his moral regeneration. The criminal's guilt implies diminished stature, and by submitting to punishment he expiates that guilt and so regains the stature he lost. One then completes this defense by arguing that the harm a criminal would suffer if he remained in his diminished condition, if, in particular, he were denied the means necessary for expiation, suffices to establish his right to be punished, much as the harm a diseased person would suffer if he were denied medicine that would cure him suffices to establish his right to medical treatment.

To be sure, the entire argument needs to be fleshed out. For one thing, we have to explain in more detail the reform theory on which it relies. This means further specifying the benefits the theory maintains a criminal derives from being punished. Here one may be tempted to wax metaphysical. But one may also characterize these benefits more concretely. Thus, as background, we recognize that a criminal has by his act violated one or more of the requirements on conduct, general conformity to which is necessary for preserving peace and harmony in his community. These requirements, let us say, bind the members of the community together into social relations. Consequently, the

11.   J.M.E. McTaggart, "Hegel's Theory of Punishment," *Ethics* 6 (1895-1896): 479-502.

criminal has by his act and by the fact of his guilt ruptured the social relations that exist between him and the other members of the community and so put himself at odds with them. Punishment, understood as expiatory, is then beneficial in that it facilitates reconciliation, a renewal of good relations. By submitting to punishment, the criminal restores to good order the social relations he ruptured and so becomes at one with those with whom he was formerly at odds.

This shows how the criminal derives social benefit from being punished. He may also derive psychological benefit. The onus of restoring the relations he ruptured lies with him. That is, the criminal, by virtue of his guilt, carries a burden of reparations, which he discharges by submitting to punishment. Accordingly, if he is sensitive to his guilt, he will feel the weight of the burden. And the greater the guilt, the more oppressive the weight. He will be plagued by bad conscience and crippled in his dealings with others. Punishment, as a means of making reparations, thus offers a remedy for these ills. It relieves the weight of one's guilt and quiets one's conscience.

Of course, the criminal may at first be insensitive to his guilt. Indeed, it is reasonable to suppose that this is more likely to be the rule than the exception. Assuming such insensitivity then, the reform theorist will argue that punishment, owing to its expressive or communicative function, can render the additional benefit of reawakening in the criminal recognition of and respect for the authority of the requirements he violated and appreciation of the values those requirements uphold. Punishment, in other words, can engender in a criminal who initially felt no guilt or remorse over his act contrition and repentance, attitudes that imply a renewed commitment to the norms and values of one's community and so a revitalized moral personality. In sum, the reform theorist holds that punishment brings about moral regeneration in that it makes once again upstanding one whom guilt had laid low.[12]

The reform theory is built on the postulation of two basic, human goods: the good of harmonious social relations and the good of a well integrated moral personality. These goods are basic in the sense that a person's welfare normally if not necessarily depends on his having them. As the reform theorist sees things, it would be exceptional if not impossible for an individual to live a life free of misery or meanness though he lived in complete isolation from others or only on acrimonious terms with them, and, similarly, such a life would be exceptional if not impossible for one who lacked any commitment to the norms and values of his community or who, though committed to those norms and values, frequently acted on desires and emotions the aims

---

12. On this point, see Herbert Morris, "A Paternalistic Theory of Punishment," *American Philosophical Quarterly* 18 (1981): 263-271, pp. 264-266.

of which conflicted with them. Guilt, then, according to a reform theorist, is not only a condition of diminished stature but also one that involves some loss of these two basic goods. The guilty have damaged the social relations existing between them and others, and they have set themselves against norms and values to which they are presumably committed, suffering from bad conscience or moral blindness as a result. Consequently, unlike the retributivist, who sees the criminal as deserving punishment by virtue of his guilt, the reform theorist sees him as in need of punishment by virtue of that guilt. Punishment restores to him the basic goods he lost. It serves to make whole the social relations he damaged and to reduce inner conflict so that the fractures in his moral personality can mend.[13]

One might, at this point, object that the reform theory has little to do with the systems of punishment operating in modern states. For these systems, because they aim chiefly at discouraging crime and incapacitating criminals, operate without serious regard to the criminal's moral regeneration. But this objection rests on a mistake about the reform theory. The theory is not offered to describe how actual systems of punishment work. Rather, it is offered to describe how they ought to work. And this it does by showing how the practice of punishment can serve values inherent in a moral community. The theory is more a tool of the social critic than of the social scientist; and, indeed, one point social critics might make, if they adhered to the theory and to the view of human rights discussed below, is that insofar as a modern state, because of the way its system of punishment operates, makes it harder for criminals to restore social relations and to regain a well-integrated moral personality, it denies them certain basic rights.

The reform theory takes one a good deal of the way toward a full defense of the Hegelian doctrine. All that remains is to add certain propositions about human rights. I will suggest two. The first is fundamental to a welfare theory of human rights, and the second derives from the first. Thus, fundamental to a welfare theory is the proposition that, with respect to each basic, human good, one has a right to that good. From this proposition, then, it follows that when one lacks some basic, human good, one has a right to whatever means are necessary, within the limits defined by the rights of others, to secure that good. The Scottish defense consists of these two propositions in conjunction with the reform theory of punishment presented above and so constitutes a complete argument for the Hegelian doctrine.

To be sure, that some basic, human good may be scarce in one's community makes the first proposition problematic. Does one have a right to that good

---

13. Morris gives a more developed account of what I have here called the good of a well-integrated moral personality; see ibid.

despite its being in such short supply as to make distribution of some to all impossible? But the question represents only a problem of scope. It does not foreclose the possibility of there being a community in which the members have a right to those basic, human goods the existence of which entails a right to be punished. We may interpret the Scottish defense, then, as presupposing such a community, that is, one in which the material conditions necessary for harmonious social relations and for each member's developing a well-integrated moral personality exist.

A more pressing problem for the defense is this. One may wonder whether an individual retains any rights to the basic, human goods in question once he has committed a crime. After all, he is the person responsible for the loss of these goods and, hence, one might argue, has no claim on others to help him regain what he lost. And if he does not retain any rights to them, then he surely cannot invoke a right to be punished. The Scottish defense, it would thus appear, is undone by its own Catch-22.

The problem, however, is much less serious than it appears. If a criminal, by virtue of his crime, no longer retains any rights to these goods, then he has either forfeited these rights or relinquished them. But neither is a plausible effect of his having committed a crime. Consider the case of forfeiture first. About some crimes we might want to say that they were so monstrous or heinous that their perpetrators had shown themselves to be unfit for human society or undeserving of the fellowship society provides and even, perhaps, to be so hardened or callous as to be incapable of remorse and repentance. In such cases we could with some justification hold that the criminals had forfeited their rights to harmonious social relations and at the same time regard the question of their having a right to a well-integrated moral personality as idle. But not all crimes warrant this view of their perpetrators. Indeed, we should be convicted of our own brand of callousness if we maintained that every crime, humdrum or heinous, entailed forfeiture of these rights. That the criminal is the one responsible for the damage done to the social relations existing between him and others and for the division within himself from which he may suffer is beside the point. A failed suicide is the one responsible for those less than fatal injuries he has suffered, but we do not regard him as having thereby forfeited his rights to health.

We might make the same point against the assertion that the criminal, by virtue of his crime, has relinquished these rights. But this would be somewhat misleading. For on the welfare theory of human rights, rights to basic, human goods are not conceived of as subject to transfer, surrender, abandonment, waiver, or any other act by which their possessor might give them up or forswear their exercise. One might want to say, then, that such rights are taken to be inalienable. But this too would miss the mark if one meant by an alien-able right a right that was like a property right except that its holder was denied those powers by which he could, if he chose, dispossess himself of the right or forsake, if only temporarily, some of the ways in which it could be exercised. On the welfare theory, human rights are not conceived of as like property rights. That is, they are not conceived of as artifacts the purpose of which is to preserve in a person's life a domain over which he can rule as though he were, to use Hart's apt phrase, a small-scale sovereign.[14] Such a conception of human rights is consonant with a theory that grounds those rights in human dignity or the inviolability of choice. But a theory that grounds them in considerations of human welfare offers a rather different conception. It conceives of them as instruments that enable a person to secure for himself those goods without which one would expect his life to be mean or miserable. They work, on the one hand, to increase the volume of their holder's voice so that he is more likely to get attention when he speaks up on his own behalf and, on the other, to supply him with weapons, which is to say, remedies, so that he speaks from a position of strength. In other words, they facilitate, where necessary, his demanding as opposed to merely requesting or pleading that he be accorded some basic, human good or at least not prevented from securing it, for a demand, unlike a request or plea, carries with it an implicit threat should the demand go unheeded. Consequently, others cannot as easily ignore him, nor can they with impunity deprive him of what is his by right. Of course, he can, if he chooses, remain silent and so not claim his rights when others act to deprive him of basic, human goods. But having the option of refraining from claiming one's rights is not the same as having the power to relinquish or waive them.[15] And from the welfare theory's point of view, since such power does nothing to improve human rights, that is, to make them better instruments for promoting their holders' welfare, it makes no sense to regard those rights as including that power. Hence, whereas one who advocates that human rights are grounded in dignity or the inviolability of choice must, with respect to each right he takes to be inalienable, give substantive reasons for denying that persons have the power to relinquish or waive it, one who advocates a welfare theory need only make a conceptual point in arguing that, with respect to each human right, persons lack those powers.

Indeed, this allows the Scottish defense to avoid a complication facing Morris's line of defense. For your normal, street-wise criminal, it is safe to assume, would upon learning that he had a right to be punished declare that he waived that right, expecting the law to operate here as it does when he waives his right

---

14. H. L. A. Hart, *Essays on Bentham: Jurisprudence and Political Theory* (Oxford: Clarendon Press, 1982), p. 183. See also Martin Golding, "Towards a Theory of Human Rights," *Monist* 52 (1968): 521–549, pp. 542-544.
15. The distinction is made by Golding, pp. 542-544.

THE SOURCES OF MORAL AGENCY

to trial by jury. To maintain Morris's line, then, one would have to establish that no wrong was done to this criminal when, despite his declaration, punishment was imposed; and here the natural argument would be that the criminal's declaration was without effect because his right to be punished, being a derivative of the fundamental right to be treated as a person, was inalienable. By contrast, on the Scottish defense, no such substantive argument need be put forward. One simply points out that the criminal is under a misconception. He is like the precocious child who declares one night at dinner that he waives his right to vegetables. This youngster's precocity notwithstanding, he has, according to the welfare theory, simply misunderstood his right to a nutritious diet. The ploy he should take, the one a correct understanding would advise, is to sit quietly in hopes of being overlooked when the asparagus he so dislikes is being served.

I hope that by now I have given a fair statement of the Scottish defense, that any doubts about its coherence have been removed, and that it appears at least to be a plausible argument for the Hegelian doctrine, one that would appeal to those who ground human rights in considerations of human welfare. It is time, then, to consider how an advocate of this defense would handle our test case: pardoning a criminal against his wishes. Can he succeed where Morris failed? That is, can he show that a pardon in such circumstances wrongs the guilty offender? I don't think he can. My reasons will become apparent once we see how he would respond to this case.

We already know such an advocate's general response. Pardoning a criminal against his wishes, this advocate would argue, where the pardon occurs before the criminal has received any punishment, denies him the means necessary for securing certain basic, human goods. Since one has, with respect to each basic, human good, a right to whatever means are necessary, within the limits defined by the rights of others, for securing that good, such a pardon violates the criminal's rights. But now we need to get down to specifics. We need to ask whether such a pardon does in fact deprive the criminal of harmonious social relations or seriously impede his progress toward regaining a well-integrated moral personality. We need to ask, in other words, whether punishment is in fact necessary for his securing these basic, human goods.

That it is necessary for his living once again on harmonious terms with others is surely false. Pardons, no less than punishment, have as their formal aim to restore their recipients to good standing in their community. That is, while a criminal has, as I noted previously, the burden of making reparations to his community, the community, acting through its agents, can decide that reparations are unnecessary. Thus, by an act of pardon, they can relieve him of this burden. He is then given to understand that he can take up again the position of full-fledged member.

Of course, this individual may find upon being released that resentment toward him still exists throughout the community and that this creates an impassable barrier to his reestablishing genuinely harmonious relations with others. But this could also happen though he had been punished. After all, meting out punishment and issuing pardons only formally restore persons guilty of criminal offenses to good standing in their community. Neither action can guarantee that the mutual trust and goodwill essential to harmonious social relations will reemerge. One might, I suppose, maintain that punishing a criminal, while not sufficient for his regaining community trust and goodwill, is somehow necessary. But this is not plausible. For we have no trouble imagining a community, in which resentment and ill will toward some criminal is spread widely, changing its feelings toward him owing to his outward expressions of remorse and repentance, to his suffering misfortune or doing good deeds subsequent to his crime, or just to his having the sort of personality that makes ill will hard to sustain. Changes of heart occur for so many different reasons that it strains credulity to make punishment necessary to a criminal's regaining the trust and goodwill essential to harmonious social relations.

The success of the Scottish defense in meeting our test case therefore depends on there being a convincing argument for the claim that a criminal can regain a well-integrated moral personality only by submitting to punishment. And it may then appear that its failure is certain because the claim itself, when taken to be about all criminals, is obviously false. With some crimes, petty crimes especially, there are surely means other than punishment by which the perpetrators can expiate their guilt, just as with moral offenses that the law does not proscribe there are ways to make reparations that do not require submitting to some form of punishment.[16] But though this shows that the claim is false when taken as a universal generalization, it does not defeat the point behind the claim.

Let me try to get at this point through an analogy. To claim that a sick man can recover his health only by receiving treatment from a qualified physician is, when taken to be about all sick men, obviously false. For some illnesses, minor ones especially, can be cured without the help of any physician. Yet as one's illness becomes increasingly serious, treatment by a qualified physician becomes increasingly important and the chances of one's recovering one's health without such help become slimmer and slimmer. At some point along the continuum of serious illnesses I am imagining, we would say that such treatment is of practical necessity. Thus, when in arguing for the right to receive adequate health care as provided by qualified physicians one asserts that such care is necessary for a sick man's recovering his health, one has in mind

16. For this objection, see A. L. Melden, *Rights and Persons* (Berkeley and Los Angeles: University of California Press, 1977), p. 182.

both the illnesses found beyond this point and the practical necessity of such care. At the same time, one does not mean to restrict the right's scope solely to the treatment of these very serious illnesses, not only because of the vagueness inherent in the class but also because of the unreasonable risks and burdens this restriction would impose on many individuals who suffer from illnesses that are not nearly as serious. Rather, one takes the right to be claimable irrespective of a person's illness but holds that the duties correlative to the right are decreasingly stringent as it becomes easier and easier to get adequate health care without the help of a physician.

This then gives us a way to understand the claim in question so that it is not obviously false. Accordingly, when one asserts in presenting the Scottish defense that punishment is necessary for a criminal's regaining a well-integrated moral personality, one has in mind only very serious crimes and the practical necessity, in regard to them, of submitting to punishment in order to make reparations. At the same time, one takes the right to be punished as claimable irrespective of the criminal's offense but holds that the correlative duties are decreasingly stringent as it becomes easier and easier for him to make reparations on his own.

The claim, when so understood, clearly rests on two propositions. First, for certain very serious crimes one cannot, practically speaking, make reparations except by submitting to punishment. Second, concerning someone guilty of wrongdoing and assuming, of course, that he has a conscience, his making reparations is necessary for his regaining a well-integrated moral personality. Now, we can grant the first since little will be learned from challenging it. The second, however, should give us pause for thought. For not only does it imply, when taken in conjunction with the first, that a legal pardon of someone convicted of a very serious crime, if issued before he has been punished, deprives him of a basic, human good, but it also implies that personal acts of forgiveness, if done before the forgiven have made reparations, are likewise deprivative! And the latter is surely an unsettling implication, so much so that we may wonder what could lead someone to purchase this second proposition. The answer is a certain view of guilt. It is the view that, if a wrongdoer is sensitive to his guilt, then that guilt so preys on his mind that, unless he takes responsibility for its removal by making reparations, its traces will continue to haunt him: it will leave him debilitated and without peace of mind. The second proposition follows directly from this view once one assumes that this condition is incompatible with a well-integrated moral personality. And the view itself foretells of the harm one does a wrongdoer if one expressly forgives him before he has made reparations. Nicolai Hartmann expressed a similar view when he wrote: "It is not as if one wanted guilt as such - one would be glad not to have it. But once we are laden with it, we cannot allow it to be tak-

36

en away, without denying our selfhood. A guilty man has a right to carry his guilt. He must refuse deliverance from without. To retain his guilt is valuable for him despite its oppressive load. . . . To surrender it is moral meanness betokening incapacity to be free. He who pardons a guilty person, compromises him spiritually."[17]

We have worked our way down to the nub of the Scottish defense and discovered that it is a certain view of guilt, which I have formulated as a thesis about human psychology. The thesis if true would correspond to a rather deep fact about the workings of conscience. Perhaps it is true. Our understanding of such deep matters of human psychology being what it is, nothing conclusive can be said. Still, I think we have good reason to be skeptical of this psychological thesis and so to remain unpersuaded by the Scottish defense.

A schematic description of the relevant situation brings this out. One person wrongs another, and, given that both are aware of the wrongdoing and that the wrongdoer is guilty, the act causes a breach in their relations. Mutual trust and goodwill break down. Ill will characterizes the victim's disposition toward the wrongdoer. Characteristically, the victim feels resentment. The wrongdoer, on the other hand, is conscience stricken, uneasy with himself. Guilt, characteristically, is the feeling he experiences. There is a correspondence here between the attitudes and feelings of the principals, and this correspondence can be extended. Thus the wrong the victim suffered may prey on his mind. The insult may burn. Relief requires satisfaction, and the wrongdoer, in making reparations, gives satisfaction. This then serves to assuage the victim's ill will and resentment. Likewise, the wrongdoer's guilt may prey on his mind. A bad conscience may plague him. He gains relief through expiation, and reparative acts bring about expiation. They then serve to quiet his conscience as they remove his guilt. Moreover, when easing of the wrongdoer's guilt concurs with assuaging of the victim's resentment, harmonious relations can then be restored. At the same time, it is possible for the victim to forgive the wrongdoer, to give up feeling resentment toward him, though the latter has made no reparations. Correspondingly, then, it should also be possible for the wrongdoer, having made no reparations, to forgive himself, to give up feeling guilt over his wrong.[18] And when another's forgiveness engenders forgiveness of oneself, harmonious relations can then be restored without one's having to make reparations.

17. Nicolai Hartmann, *Ethics*, trans. Stanton Coit, 3 vols. (New York: Macmillan, 1932), vol. 2, p. 145.
18. Morris writes, "It is also part of the good [of a well-integrated moral personality] that one reject the disposition to do what is wrong and commit oneself to forbearance in the future. I assume that this makes possible, indeed that it is inextricably bound up with, one's forgiving oneself, one's relinquishing one's guilt, and one's having the capacity to enter into life" ("A Paternalistic Theory of Punishment," p. 265).

To be sure, many may find it much harder to forgive themselves than to forgive others. Perhaps having a conscience disposes one to be harder on oneself than on others. Here is a psychological thesis to rival the one at the nub of the Scottish defense. But competing psychological theses aside, the immediate point is that, once we acknowledge that corresponding to others' forgiving one is one's forgiving oneself and that the latter attitude as well as the former is possible despite one's having made no reparations, the psychological thesis at the nub of the Scottish defense becomes highly dubious. The more inclined we are to accept forgiveness of oneself as fact and not fiction, the more skeptical we shall be of that thesis.

That forgiveness is an attitude one can, when guilty of wrongdoing, take toward oneself may be obscured by the fact that, unlike forgiveness of another, with which there is an associated act of forgiveness, there is no comparable act associated with forgiveness of oneself. The verb phrase 'forgive myself' has in the indicative mood no standard present-tense use. Indeed, we seem in ordinary conversation to refer to the attitude only obliquely in such remarks as "I would never forgive myself if she were to lose her job" and "He never forgave himself for not returning her call." And one might wonder whether this is a genuine referring expression or just a figure of speech.

Still, the correspondence between the characteristic feelings and attitudes of victim and wrongdoer, the correspondence between the emotions of resentment and guilt, in particular, both in the way each is characteristically aroused and in the ways each can be resolved, places the burden of argument on one who denies that we are ever capable of forgiving ourselves. Hence, the advocate of the Scottish defense cannot advance his psychological thesis as uncontroverted fact or as a truth to be grasped a priori from an understanding of guilt.

When another, whom one has wronged, forgives one and so invites one to renew good relations with him, his forgiveness and the invitation it implies should encourage one to give up the guilt one feels and to regard making reparations or making further reparations as no longer necessary. Yet an overweening conscience can cause one to feel a need to make reparations, to hold on to one's guilt, and so lead one to insist on receiving some form of punishment. And in these circumstances a right to be punished would only serve to further the unreasonable demands of one's conscience. In other words, if the truth of the matter lay not in the psychological thesis at the nub of the Scottish defense but instead in the thesis that having a conscience tends to make one harder on oneself than on others, then a right to be punished would, for the most part, serve to exacerbate this tendency. The irony of the Scottish defense would then be that it provided argument, based on considerations of human welfare, for a right that one would press largely to one's detriment rather than one's good.

3

Love, guilt, and the sense of justice

Freud once wrote that the sense of guilt was "the most important problem in the development of civilization."[1] Presumably, he would have agreed with a parallel statement about the socialization of the child. How a child acquires moral sensibilities, a sense of guilt, a sense of duty, a sense of justice, is one of the main questions of moral psychology. Philosophers interested in moral psychology, to be sure, would start with a different question. They would ask about something called the nature of these sensibilities and follow this with some such series of questions as, how are we to understand the moral motives that spring from them, in what do the emotions and feelings that mark one as having them consist, are they akin to an intellectual sense like mathematical intuition or more like a perceptual sense such as that of sight, or are they yet something entirely different? and so on. These are typical philosopher's questions. They do not, however, set philosophers at any great distance from research psychologists. Freud speaks as much to the one as to the other.

Indeed, the concerns of each overlap in many areas the concerns of the other. In particular, whether one studies psychological concepts or psychological processes, one must consider questions about the connections between, on the one hand, moral sensibilities and the motives and emotions originating in them and, on the other, the intellectual and emotional capacities and dispositions with which human beings are naturally endowed. One will, of course, frame these questions differently according to one's studies. But the internal connections philosophers set out as answers to their questions will set limits to the psychogenetic ones psychologists may propose as answers to theirs, and, conversely, the success of a psychologist's theory in explaining how a child develops moral sensibilities will be an important desideratum for philosophers in choosing among alternative conceptual stories. Here, as elsewhere, philosophers cannot live by intuition alone.

Either set of questions invites answers that testify to one's optimism or pessimism about human nature, and the major attempts to treat these questions theoretically tend to reflect one or the other outlook. The debate between op-

1. 1930, XXI, p. 134.

39

timists and pessimists about human nature is long standing.[2] Freud's views exemplify the pessimistic outlook. And before Freud, Hobbes and Hume are perhaps its most outstanding modern exponents. The latter two represent human beings as naturally dominated by egoistic motives, so much so that whatever native capacity for fellowship either attributes to human beings is too limited and weak to underwrite the peaceable relations among them that are necessary for a stable society. On their theories, civic virtues and the sensibilities they imply contribute importantly – and for Hume crucially – to maintaining social stability, and men and women acquire these virtues as they come to recognize that conformity to certain rules serves their interests and as they develop concurrently a habit of obedience to those rules. For Hobbes, of course, fear is the true source of this obedience, fear of the evil that would be inflicted on one should one disobey. The virtue of justice, the settled disposition to obey, thus develops when active fear is lost to habit.[3] For Hume, by contrast, the virtue entails a special sensitivity to the rules' purview, which is independent of any fear of the evil consequences to which disobedience makes one liable. Hume recognizes what Hobbes seems blind to, that a genuine sense of justice is part of human psychology, and accordingly his account of moral development is a more complex affair. Still he, no less than Hobbes, regards the virtue of justice as the product of an enlightened self-interest, and so too this moral sense.[4] Freud, needless to say, differs greatly from Hobbes and Hume in the particulars of his theory. Resolution of inner conflict replaces formation of habit as the process through which human beings acquire a moral sense, and aggression rather than self-interest is the natural drive that social forces redirect in inculcating that sense. At the same time, though, his views share with theirs a general pessimistic theme: our sense of duty and justice results from society's turning to its advantage asocial and antisocial drives that are part of our natural endowment and that if left untutored and unharnessed would ruin whatever peace and harmony our capacities for goodwill and fellow feeling could establish.[5]

On the optimistic side of the debate, John Rawls's account of the sense of justice, among recent work, is especially noteworthy. Rawls's thesis is that the sense of justice is itself a form of good will toward humanity, a sentiment of the heart, which grows out of the natural sentiments of love and friendship as

2. For discussion of this distinction between optimists and pessimists about human nature see Roger D. Masters, "Human Nature, Nature, and Political Thought," in, *Nomos: Human Nature in Politics*, J. Roland Pennock and John W. Chapman, eds. (New York: New York University Press, 1977), vol. 17, pp. 69–110.
3. *De Homine*, ch. 13.
4. *A Treatise of Human Nature*, bk. III, pt. 2, sec. ii.
5. Freud, 1930, XXI, pp. 123–133.

these mature in the context of a social order. For Rawls, we fully realize in developing this moral sense our native capacity for human fellowship, and so one needn't look beyond this capacity to determine how human beings establish and maintain harmonious social relations. The strength and scope the capacity comes to have when educated to the requirements of a just social order provide sufficient explanation. His account thus challenges the views of Hobbes, Hume, and Freud on two issues: the essential character of the sense of justice and its origin in human nature.[6]

Rawls's account has received endorsement from several philosophers, and others have independently advanced ideas similar to those at its base.[7] Against this apparent increase in support for the optimistic side I will argue that the main grounds for these recent views, of which I take Rawls's as exemplary, are problematic and that behind the views' problems lie reasons that favor the pessimistic side. My argument will proceed as follows. First, I will consider and criticize the conceptual scheme that grounds the thesis that the sense of justice is a form of good will toward human beings generally. This thesis derives from the idea that the sense of justice is linked essentially to love, and this link, as we shall see, is forged by a certain conception of the emotion of guilt. My criticisms will follow from difficulties I will point out in this conception and will, if forceful, undo the link. Second, I will examine critically Rawls's account of how our sense of justice develops from the natural sentiments of love and friendship, this being the clearest and best worked out developmental account on the optimistic side. I will argue in criticism of it that the problems found in the conceptual scheme reappear in this developmental account when the latter is looked at in light of the former. This will complete my critique of the optimists' view. Last, then, I will draw from this critique conclusions that weigh in favor of an account of the sense of justice that reflects an outlook like Hume's or Freud's. My intention in this final section is to show that a pessimistic position has real merit, that it is worth elaborating, though by no

6. See *A Theory of Justice* (Cambridge, MA: Belknap Press, 1971), pp. 453–512.
7. The endorsers include David A. J. Richards, *A Theory of Reasons for Action* (Oxford: Clarendon Press, 1971), pp. 242–278; David H. Jones, "Freud's Theory of Moral Conscience," *Philosophy* 41 (1966): 34–57; and Bernard Boxill, "How Injustice Pays," *Philosophy & Public Affairs* 9 (1979–1980): 359–371. See also Michael S. Pritchard, "Rawls's Moral Psychology," *Philosophical Topics* 8 (1977): 59–72. Philosophers who have advanced ideas similar to those on which Rawls bases his account include Herbert Morris, *On Guilt and Innocence* (Berkeley and Los Angeles: University of California Press, 1976), pp. 89–110; and Laurence Thomas, "Egoism and Psychological Dispositions," *American Philosophical Quarterly* 17 (1980): 59–72 and "Morality, the Self, and Our Natural Sentiments," in *Emotion: Philosophical Studies*, K. D. Irani and G. E. Myers, eds. (New York: Haven Press, 1983), pp. 144–163. Within psychoanalytic theory similar ideas have been put forth by Melanie Klein, whose account of the child's development of a superego corresponds at key points with the views of several of the foregoing authors. See her *Love, Guilt and Reparation and Other Works 1921–45* (New York: Delta, 1975), pp. 262–289.

means do I wish to suggest that elaborating the position should put an end to the debate. Overall, the thrust of the essay is critical. Its intent, however, is constructive.

I

I am construing the term 'the sense of justice' broadly. As I understand it, it denotes the moral sense that concerns matters of right and wrong, duty and obligation, which is to say, justice in that general sense covering whatever we owe others and ourselves as human beings. Understood in this broad way, the sense ranges in its purview over moral requirements on conduct beyond those that derive from concerns of social justice. What is more, this understanding accords with the general idea that having a sense of justice means being liable to feel constrained in certain circumstances to conform one's behavior to moral requirements and to feel guilt over violations of those requirements. Guilt thus becomes a sign of a sense of justice in that failures to feel guilt over an act of wrongdoing, barring excuse, count as evidence against one's having this sense.[8]

This last point figures as a premiss in the main argument for the optimists' thesis that the sense of justice is a form of good will toward humanity or, as I shall sometimes put it, that concern for the welfare of others informs a sense of justice. The other premiss is about love, mature love in particular. It is, specifically, that if one person loves another, then the former is liable to feelings of guilt on those occasions when he ill-treats the latter. The assumption here is that an internal relation exists between love and the emotion of guilt just as one exists between love and the emotions of fear and grief. For to love someone is to be liable to feel fear when one's beloved is threatened with evil and to suffer grief when serious evil befalls him. Both failure to experience fear in circumstances in which the other is in danger and failure to experience grief when he is badly injured count as evidence against one's loving him. So too a failure to feel guilt when one has ill-treated one's beloved creates uncertainty about one's love. All three failures imply a lack of concern for the other's well-being, a lack that is inconsistent with love.[9]

The argument then reaches its conclusion through an extension of this understanding of guilt. Accordingly, a failure to feel guilt when one wrongs an acquaintance or stranger implies a lack of concern for that person's well-being, and given that this would hold regardless of any special affection one had for him, we could say that one's failure implied a lack of concern for others

8. See Rawls, pp. 474–475.
9. Ibid., pp. 486–487.

42

generally. Since the sense of justice is the source in a moral personality of the liability to feel guilt in such circumstances, the conclusion that the sense is informed by concern for the welfare of human beings generally follows immediately.

To be sure, the argument turns on the assumption that the guilt one feels over ill-treating someone one loves is an exemplar of the emotion. But this is a perfectly natural assumption to make. After all, when we think of feelings of guilt, we are as likely as not to think of experiences that occur in the context of close friendship or love, when we have hurt or injured someone for whom we care a great deal. For such experiences display the full range of painful and distressful feelings we associate with the emotion; much more so, given the strength of the attachment between friends or lovers, than experiences we have when dealing with acquaintances and strangers. One suffers in these exemplary experiences pain that, to borrow Herbert Morris's vivid description

derives . . . from antagonism toward oneself because one has acted against what one is attached to, and this antagonism feeds the feeling that one is divided within oneself. There is hostility toward anyone who attacked what is cherished. Feeling guilt is feeling more than sorrow or regret that what one cares for has been hurt or damaged; it is pain mediated by the judgment "I am responsible for the damage." In feeling guilt we turn on ourselves like a scorpion biting its own tail.[10]

From the assumption, then, that such experiences are standard cases of the emotion of guilt, a general understanding of that emotion follows, and this understanding serves as the link between love and the sense of justice.

Furthermore, when we examine this link we see how it establishes the main ground for the optimists' thesis that concern for the welfare of others informs the sense of justice. The experience Morris describes shows us how. The pain the subject suffers is a consequence of his attachment to that which he has hurt or damaged, and the attachment explains the antagonism toward oneself that Morris depicts as central to guilt. In other words, when one becomes attached to another, an attachment exemplified by love, one becomes liable to suffering such pain upon hurting or injuring one's beloved. Hence, given that such guilt also has its source in a sense of justice, given, that is, that this sense makes one liable to such pain, we can conclude that one who has a sense of justice is similarly, though assuredly more weakly, attached to the individuals to whom he owes, by virtue of the moral requirements that sense encompasses, duties. And this means, since it would be absurd to suppose that he was attached to each and every individual to whom he owed these duties, that he is

10. "Guilt and Punishment," *Pacific Philosophical Quarterly* 52 (1971): 312.

similarly though more weakly attached to human beings generally.[11] Let us use the notion of identification to characterize all such attachments. Accordingly, we will say that one who loves another *identifies* with his beloved, and one who has a sense of justice identifies with his fellow man. This characterization thus makes explicit the grounds for the optimists' thesis.

It is important to see, moreover, that guilt alone among the emotions to which one's sense of justice makes one liable forges this link between the sense and love. Consider resentment, for example, understood as the emotion to which one's sense of justice makes one liable when one is the victim of another's wrongdoing. Resentment felt toward someone who has done one an injustice is then the standard case. Of course, one can feel resentment toward a wrongdoer whose victim is someone one loves and, consequently, we should say that love too makes one liable to feel resentment. But this fact does not establish any essential link between love and the sense of justice, for the cases corresponding to it are nonstandard. Resentment is in this respect like fear, a characteristically self-regarding emotion. The standard cases of fear are all cases in which the emotion is felt on account of one's being in danger. At the same time we recognize nonstandard cases in which the emotion is felt on account of another's being in danger because we understand how through love, that is, through identification with another, one becomes liable to experience characteristically self-regarding emotions when something good or something bad happens to one's beloved, when his life prospects improve or when he is threatened with evil. So too with resentment. Hence, that love makes one liable to feel resentment shows only how the sense of justice, as the source of resentment, works with love to extend the emotion's range beyond the standard cases. It doesn't establish any merger between the two. With guilt, on the other hand, we refer to one's identifying with another or others to account for the standard cases and not just certain nonstandard ones. Put differently, guilt, according to the conception sketched above, implies as a precondition that its subject identifies with others. This makes evident how, through guilt, an essential link is established and why guilt alone carries the burden of the optimists' argument. The above conception of guilt, if correct, bears out their thesis that concern for the welfare of others informs a sense of justice.

The question we must ask then is whether this is the correct conception of guilt. Unfortunately, determining the answer is no easy matter, for there may be no one conception of guilt that is correct, at least as regards the use of the word to denote an emotion. Worry on this point arises because this use is rel-

---

11. Indeed, with respect to those much more strongly attached to human beings we could characterize their sense of justice as something more, as a love of humanity, say. See on this point Rawls, pp. 191-192 and p. 476.

atively new and yet quite popular. Four decades ago, to give one indication of how recent its popularity, Gerhart Piers in his widely influential monograph felt it necessary to write, "For brevity's sake we shall in the following frequently say 'guilt', instead of 'guilt feelings' or 'sense of guilt', a semantic inaccuracy for which common psychoanalytic usage pleads legitimacy."[12] Another indication is given in the *O.E.D.* Looking under 'guilt', one finds the following eye-catching entry: "5d) Misused for 'sense of guilt'," which the Supplement does not correct. Of course, this is now accepted usage, and only purists would question its legitimacy. Yet because 'guilt' as a term for an emotion and its cognates 'feeling guilt', 'feeling guilty', and 'guilt feelings' gained widespread currency through popular consumption of psychoanalytic theory and its offshoots, we should expect that these terms are attended with the problems of usage associated with vogue words. Specifically, we should not be surprised to find that they range in their extensions over experiences that properly fall under several distinct concepts, which were once expressed by now less-popular terms. We should not be surprised, that is, to find that we often conflate distinct concepts in our everyday use of 'guilt' as a term for an emotion. Since the pivotal assumption in the optimists' argument is that the same conception of guilt applies to emotions to which love makes one liable and emotions to which one's sense of justice makes one liable, the possibility of conflation threatens the argument.

The possibility suggests that we look closely at experiences of guilt in which the emotion is felt over wrongdoing that is independent of any hurt or injury done to someone one loves. We should consider guilt suffered on account of one's having violated a moral rule or someone's moral rights, where the victims of one's act, if there are any, are people wholly unknown to one or, though known, one cares not the least for, even despises. A man steals cheap jewelry from Macy's and suffers such guilt that, filled with apologies, he returns the goods the next day. Raskolnikov, to test his greatness, murdered a loathsome pawnbroker whom he despised and her pathetic stepsister for whom he had no feeling whatsoever and was then tormented by guilt until confession gave him some peace. Wrongdoing, which here comes to violation of a moral rule or moral right, is central to these experiences. Any evil that the act causes does not come into account, except, of course, indirectly, insofar as preventing such evils is the ground for the rule or right. What troubles the man who dispossesses Macy's of some jewelry is not the loss the store will suffer but his *theft*. He may understand clearly that the evil is negligible, that the store can easily absorb the loss, but this need not ease his guilt. And

---

12. Gerhart Piers and Milton Singer, *Shame and Guilt: A Psychoanalytic and a Cultural Study* (Springfield, IL: Charles C. Thomas, 1953), p. 5.

though the evil Raskolnikov did was great, his contempt for the pawnbroker and her stepsister makes it seem to him slight. He dwells not on this but rather on having done what is not permitted. Clearly, the subjects in these cases do not love and are not concerned for the welfare of those who are the victims of their acts.

From these cases we form a conception of guilt that is distinct from the earlier one. On this conception, an experience of guilt presupposes not that the subject identifies with others, but that he has accepted moral requirements on his conduct that are imposed by a set of moral rules or implicit in a system of moral rights and correlative duties. This presupposition suggests several important points about the conception. First, the experiences that fall under it fit into the context of social relations generally. That is, we recognize as the typical setting for these experiences a society in which the members are bound together through mutual acceptance of a set of moral requirements. These requirements regulate their conduct in that the members of the society exert on one another, through formal agencies of enforcement and informal urgings and criticism, social pressure to comply. Close personal relations, therefore, do not have any greater claim to providing the context for standard cases than the more distant relations in business or government, for example, that the society may also foster. Second, the moral requirements, acceptance of which these experiences of guilt presuppose, set limits on the conduct of those persons to whom they apply. Accordingly, we are to understand wrongdoing that is central to the experiences as transgression of these limits.[13] The limits, therefore, are genuine barriers to conduct and not merely definitional stops.[14] If one fails to stay within them, one becomes liable, in the absence of a defense absolving one of culpability, to harsh treatment in the form of a punitive response that expresses blame and even condemnation for one's act. In contrast, consider the rules that define an office or position of authority in some institution. They stipulate the extent of the power that goes with that office and so set limits to its exercise. If one in the exercise of office goes beyond those limits, one's action is liable to be nullified. Other officeholders will refuse to recognize it as having any institutional force, for it doesn't meet the conditions defining an official act. Yet this in itself does not call for any punitive response. One didn't *transgress* the limits one failed to observe. Third, because human beings are subject to desires and emotions that, if given in to, would move them to transgress limits placed on their conduct by a set of

13. The idea that guilt is characteristically felt over a transgression of a boundary on or barrier to conduct is due to Piers, ibid., pp. 5 and 11. For a similar view see Morris, *On Guilt and Innocence*, pp. 94–96.
14. This distinction is made by H. L. A. Hart. See his *The Concept of Law* (London: Clarendon Press, 1961), pp. 27–35.

moral requirements, the requirements act as restraints on conduct. The image of a barrier is again suggestive. Thus, acceptance of these requirements amounts to acceptance of a burden of self-restraint, which burden one feels whenever such desires and emotions impel one to act in disregard of the requirements.[15] Finally, these requirements are invested with authority over those whose conduct they restrain, and so acceptance of them implies respect for their authority and a corresponding sensitivity to their purview. They originate, as I said before, in a code of moral rules or a system of moral rights, and thus their authority derives from the authority moral rules have or the authority moral rights confer on their possessors. Respect for their authority, then, is one with respect for the code - respect for law - or respect for persons in virtue of their possessing moral rights.

Using these points we can now characterize the experiences of guilt that fall under this second conception. We understand that a person who is liable to these experiences has accepted the moral requirements on conduct that bind members of his society together into social relations and thus lies under a burden of self-restraint. The emotion arises, characteristically, when he breaks the restraints these requirements impose. Recognizing his culpability, that his act is indefensible, he suffers guilt, indicating harsh self-criticism of the kind appropriate to his act, namely, blame or condemnation of oneself. The emotion, in other words, has a specially self-punitive character. Its pain, on this conception, derives from a reprobative attitude taken toward oneself as culpable wrongdoer that matches the attitude one's society formally expresses toward such wrongdoers through its agents' inflictions of punishment on them. The emotional experiences mirror, as it were, the legitimate responses of those entrusted with enforcement of the society's requirements. The attraction of describing this inner state on analogy with outer regulatory forms and activity is unmistakable.

The experiences that fall under the first conception contrast quite sharply with these. To begin with, we understand them to presuppose natural ties between individuals. One who is liable to these experiences loves and cares for others and thus is said to identify with them. However much mutual acceptance of moral requirements on conduct is necessary to make such ties stable, we can nevertheless conceive of them independently of these requirements. That is, we can conceive of people as bound together by love alone. The emotion then arises when its subject hurts, injures, or in some way does evil to a person he loves. Recognizing this, he suffers pain that derives from hostility and ill will he has toward himself. This hostility and ill will come about naturally in the same way that one would naturally bear ill will and be disposed to

15. On this point, see Morris, *On Guilt and Innocence*, pp. 94-96.

behave hostilely toward another, had he been responsible for such hurt or injury. The emotion, on this conception, mirrors the anger one would feel toward anyone who hurt or injured someone one loved. Such anger is naturally expressed by one's lashing out at whoever is the cause of the injury and, correspondingly, the emotion reflects an attack on oneself; one suffers inner torment for being responsible for a like injury.

The contrast between these two kinds of experience is sufficiently striking for us to regard them as distinct emotions. Whether or not we continue to see them as two conceptions of guilt is a matter of choice. I prefer to do otherwise. For convenience, I propose to mark the distinction by calling the one corresponding to the first conception 'remorse' while reserving 'guilt' for the other. 'Remorse', which was once the proper term for many of the experiences we now use the term 'guilt' to denote, has fallen into relative disuse, and this appears to be one way in which it can be usefully redeployed. I choose this way of assigning the terms to concepts because 'guilt' has obvious juridical implications while 'remorse' fits comfortably in a natural setting. That 'guilt' is associated with punishment makes it more suitable for expressing the second concept. Alternatively, I could mark the distinction by introducing modifiers. Accordingly, 'natural guilt' would denote an emotional experience that falls under the first conception, 'moral guilt' an experience that falls under the second. But I prefer finding a serviceable use for 'remorse' to multiplying senses of 'guilt'. In any event, the choice of terminology does not affect the argument against the optimists' view.

Crucial to this distinction between emotions is the distinction between wrongdoing and evildoing. In line with my proposal guilt is the emotion one feels over the former, and remorse is among the emotions one feels over the latter. The distinction between wrongdoing and evildoing is clear-cut. Wrongdoing is a transgression of a limit placed on one's conduct by a moral rule or a duty correlative to a moral right, whereas evildoing is, roughly speaking, an act that destroys or does damage to something of value, where "something of value" denotes persons as well as objects and so destroying and damaging comprehend killing, injuring, and hurting. From this distinction the distinction between the two emotions follows directly. The one is felt over violations of moral rules or moral rights for which or for the possessors of which one has respect; the other is felt over violence one does to things one treasures or persons for whom one cares and for whose welfare one is concerned. This gives us the most general statement of the distinction, though for simplicity's sake I will keep to the restricted understanding of remorse as being felt over evil one does to someone one loves.

We should recognize, of course, that many times when one wrongs another, one also by the very same act injures or hurts him. Here wrongdoing and evildoing coincide. Consequently, we may assume that the two emotions often oc-cur together as indistinguishable constituents of a complex emotional experi-ence. But where someone has no rights or has surrendered the rights that nor-mally protect him from injury, one can injure him without also wronging him. Such situations make possible experiences of remorse that are distin-guishable from experiences of guilt, the clear examples being those in which the evildoer identifies strongly with the victim of his deed. Huck Finn's friendship with Jim provides an example. Because of his affection for Jim, Huck would likely have felt remorse had he been responsible for Jim's suffer-ing a mortal wound or grievous injury. But he would not have felt guilt. Or if he had, Jim's owner, Miss Watson, not Jim, would have been the one to whom Huck would have been moved to make reparations. For though Jim would have suffered the injury, Miss Watson, according to Huck's conscience, would have been the person he wronged.

This points up a collateral difference between wrongdoing and evildoing, which further serves to distinguish guilt from remorse. Coupled with the no-tion of wrongdoing is that of righting the wrong. That is, when one violates moral requirements on conduct, which are understood to bind individuals to-gether into social relations, one breaches those relations and in consequence lies under a burden of reparation, discharge of which facilitates restoring the relations to good order. Discharging the burden is what I mean by righting the wrong. Confession, apology, and submission to punishment are the famil-iar ways in which one makes reparations and so rights one's wrong. Of course, when one's wrongdoing is defensible, an exculpatory explanation may suffice. But when one can't give a satisfactory explanation, one is deemed guilty and expected to give satisfaction in these other ways. At the same time, those to whom one owes satisfaction, that is, those relations with whom one has breached, whether specific individuals or the members of society generally, can take it upon themselves to restore good relations through forgiveness and thus relieve one of the burden one has assumed. All this should remind us that the state of being guilty of wrongdoing, besides being opprobrious, has a logic comparable to indebtedness, the figure of a debt being common to talk of guilt and punishment.

With evildoing, we might think, at least initially, parallels can be drawn. Thus, coupled with the notion of evildoing is that of remedying the evil. Yet unlike righting a wrong, which is itself a moral requirement, arising when one commits a wrong, and so is set by the code of moral rules or system of moral rights from which moral requirements issue, there are no set ways to remedy evil. One simply does what one can to fix the damage, repair the injury, or soothe the hurt. What is more, many evils are beyond remedy: one may have permanently damaged or destroyed what is valued. In such a case, evildoing is coupled with no corrective measure, only with woe. This result leads directly to further separation of guilt from remorse.

Accordingly, guilt is an oppressive emotion. When one feels guilt, one feels weighed down, under a load. The image of a crooked or crippled person, as contrasted with the upright posture of someone free of guilt, may come to mind. These feelings and images we associate with someone who lies under a burden, in this case a burden of reparation. Thus making reparations serves to relieve one of guilt. Feeling guilt one is moved to confess, offer apologies, ask forgiveness, and submit to punishment where punishment is demanded. Through these acts and, moreover, through gaining forgiveness, the burden is lifted. Guilt gives way to a sense of release. Remorse, on the other hand, is not closely tied to the idea of a burden or the logic of indebtedness. It isn't resolved by one's unburdening oneself through confession or one's squaring accounts through punishment. Indeed, where the evil one did is irremediable, where one is responsible for irreparable injury, say, or death, remorse may move one toward no course of conduct that resolves it. In these cases remorse is like grief. Where a person is overcome or stricken with remorse, we may expect, as with the grief-stricken, paralysis of the will to set in. So too, like grief, remorse tends to an exclusive focus on the past. Consequently, ridding oneself of the emotion necessitates a change in focus. One must put one's evildoing out of one's mind, and where the evil one did is beyond remedy, this may take some time.[16] These features of remorse, the possibilities of or, better, tendencies toward paralysis and exclusive focus on the past, are absent from guilt. Paralysis of the will doesn't typically characterize the guilt-ridden. Their emotion directs them toward a course of conduct that offers relief. Hence, though guilt includes focus on the past, since it is felt over a wrong one committed, it also looks toward the future.

So far I have concentrated in distinguishing guilt from remorse on differences that follow from the distinction between wrongdoing and evildoing. But equally crucial to this distinction between emotions is a distinction between motivational states that underlie them. Underlying remorse, on our restricted understanding of the emotion, is the state of identifying with someone in the sense I specified earlier. Underlying guilt is the distinct state of having accepted the moral requirements on conduct implicit in a code of moral rules or a system of moral rights. This second state, to be sure, may develop from the first. One's coming to accept moral requirements as authoritative re-

16. These two features are suggested in an exchange between Robert Rosthal and Irving Thalberg; see Rosthal, "Moral Weakness and Remorse," *Mind* 76 (1967): 576–579; and Thalberg, "Rosthal's Notion of Remorse and Irrevocability," *Mind* 77 (1968): 288–289. That remorse is characteristically felt over an irremediable evil is a thesis David A. J. Richards advances; see *A Theory of Reasons for Action*, p. 256.

straints on one's conduct may depend on a prior identification with those who first laid down or enforced the requirements. But such a developmental nexus is obviously no bar to our distinguishing the two states as concepts. We may then proceed.

One's identifying with others generates care and concern for them. These attitudes indicate appreciation for pleasures and pains that those with whom one identifies feel and for benefits and harms that come their way. A person who cares and has concern for others is not indifferent to their joy or anguish or to their good or ill fortune. He is disposed to take pleasure in their pleasure and happiness and to be pained at the pain and injury they suffer. He wants to protect them from injury and to alleviate their suffering and is willing to do so at some sacrifice. Remorse is nonetheless possible because his being motivated by care and concern is no guarantee that he will be successful at preventing injury or, even, that he will constantly attend to preventing or avoiding it. What is more, though he cares and has concern for others, he may still be subject to desires and emotions that lead him voluntarily to injure them. Remorse would then show that he did care and have concern for the persons he injured. By contrast, if having injured someone, he showed no remorse yet acknowledged responsibility for the act, his lack of remorse would be evidence that he did not care about the evil he did, that he was unconcerned about the suffering he had caused. He would be remorseless, and a remorseless person is heartless, cruel. He is indifferent to the suffering of others, even if he is responsible for it, and may even take pleasure in having caused it.

Acceptance of moral requirements, on the other hand, generates respect for the authority of the moral rules or moral rights from which these requirements derive. Such acceptance means that one is prepared to act in compliance with them when one's conduct falls within their purview, which is to say, to act out of respect for the authority of the rules or rights that impose them. For when one has respect for moral rules or moral rights, one regards as a reason for forbearing from certain acts that doing them would violate the requirements that those rules or rights impose and this without reference to any further end that compliance with these requirements would promote. Such respect for moral rules or moral rights and the consequent willingness to comply with the requirements they impose is reflected in one's acknowledging as warranted, first, demands and urgings of others that one comply with them when one verges on noncompliance and, second, criticism of and reproach for one's conduct when one has indefensibly violated them. Correspondingly, where one has such respect, we speak of one's being moved by duty to comply with moral requirements and of one's being liable to feel guilt over violations of them. Feelings of guilt thus show that, despite one's transgressions, one recognizes and maintains allegiance to the authority of the rules or rights one violated.

The distinction between the motivational states underlying remorse and guilt is clearest in conflictual situations, where one is pulled in opposite directions. Out of care and concern one may be disposed to interfere with another in order to prevent him from ruinous action but at the same time recognize that such interference would be a violation of his rights. One's will may then be constrained, and out of respect one draws back in the direction of forbearance. We have no right to take the bottle away from our alcoholic friend though he would surely benefit from being deprived of liquor. Or once we've gone ahead and acted, the conflict reappears in our troubled mind. Huck Finn felt bad in failing to turn Jim in; this failure, Huck's conscience told him, was wrong. But, as he also realized, he would have felt equally bad if he had been party to his friend's capture.

Then I thought a minute, and says to myself, hold on; s'pose you'd 'a' done right and give Jim up, would you felt better than what you do now? No, says I, I'd feel bad – I'd feel just the same way I do now.[17]

We can now state succinctly the problem imperiling the conceptual scheme on which optimists ground their thesis that the sense of justice is a form of good will toward mankind. The main ground for that thesis is the link between the sense of justice and love that the scheme purports to establish, and the argument for this link proceeds under the assumption that the same conception of guilt applies to emotions to which one's sense of justice makes one liable and emotions to which love makes one liable. We find, however, that 'guilt' in the use it has recently acquired as a term for an emotion applies to such disparate experiences that we are led to distinguish two types of emotion. One is characteristically felt on account of one's committing a moral wrong, that is, a violation of moral requirements on conduct one has accepted, and thus originates in a sense of justice; the other is characteristically felt on account of one's hurting or injuring someone with whom one identifies and thus originates in love or some other natural sentiment that implies identification with another. Contrasting these two types of emotion shows the differentiation between them to be complete, and this makes the pivotal assumption of the optimists' argument problematic. Unless optimists can give sound reason for supposing that one's sense of justice makes one liable to experiences of the second type as well as the first, their argument breaks down. It would then be in order to observe that, though we commonly use the term 'guilt' to denote emotions of either type, this is a source of confusion and not an indication of a link between the sense of justice and love.

17. Mark Twain, *The Adventures of Huckleberry Finn*, ch. 16. For a discussion of this and related passages, which proceeds along similar lines, see Jonathan Bennett, "The Conscience of Huckleberry Finn," *Philosophy*, 49 (1974): 123-134.

II

The force of this criticism naturally turns our attention to the other part of the optimistic view, the thesis that the sense of justice has its origin in the natural sentiments of friendship and love: that it grows out of them as they mature in the context of a just social order. Clearly, if correct, this thesis would entail that the sense is linked essentially to love, and therefore the criticisms of the previous section would be overcome. Of course, to establish the thesis one must give an appropriate and sufficiently detailed account of how one develops a sense of justice, an account confirmable by the researches of developmental psychology. Confirmation would then establish the thesis. The best worked out account that approaches this description is Rawls's, and accordingly we shall need to examine it to see if it makes the optimistic view once again sound. I will argue that it does not, that the problems pointed out in the conceptual scheme reappear in this developmental account when the latter is seen to rest on the former.

Rawls's account comprises three stages.[18] The first is that of early childhood, when one is completely dependent on one's parents. At this stage, one learns through their instruction moral ideas and moral norms that constitute what Rawls terms a morality of authority. Here one acquires one's first moral outlook. At the second stage one advances to an outlook that is less parent-centered as one enters into social relations with siblings, schoolmates, neighbors, and fellow citizens. During this stage one's moral development progresses according as one joins associations of increasingly larger size and greater organizational complexity and acquires through participation in them the corresponding moral ideas and moral precepts. Here one acquires a morality of association and makes further progress as that morality becomes more complex. One then achieves full moral development at the third stage when particular social and personal relations no longer mediate one's moral outlook. Only at this stage, according to Rawls, does one acquire a sense of justice, a genuine *moral sentiment*. For until this stage one does not accept moral principles universal in scope and justifiable without reference to any particular association of human beings, which acceptance is the mark of a truly moral point of view. At this stage one acquires a morality of principles.

Throughout this account Rawls takes the onset and growth of a liability to feelings of guilt as the chief indicator of progress in moral development. He is

18. Rawls, ch. 8, passim, but esp. pp. 462–479. Rawls restricts this account to a well-ordered society whose public conception of justice is justice as fairness - the conception he favors. He makes no claim to its truth or plausibility as a description of moral development in societies with a different conception of justice. All of the criticisms that follow, however, are consistent with his restriction.

careful to distinguish guilt proper, a genuinely moral emotion, to which one becomes liable only at the final stage, from its precursors, authority and association guilt, in his terminology, to which one becomes liable at earlier stages. Nonetheless, all three conform to the understanding of guilt, as distinct from remorse, that we have developed, for each is characteristically felt over violations of moral requirements on conduct, requirements that, depending on the stage, derive from moral principles upheld by one's sense of justice, rules that govern the behavior of members of an association to which one belongs, or the dictates of one's parents. Thus Rawls regards the earliest experiences of guilt, which is to say, of guilt's earliest precursor, authority guilt, as signaling the incipience of a moral sense and later changes in the character of these experiences as marking development in one's understanding of and commitment to the more subtle and complex moral rules and systems of rights and duties that govern participation in the associations one joins. At the same time, to explain this progress toward acquiring a sense of justice, Rawls appeals first to the genesis of love for one's parents and next to the subsequent forging of bonds of friendship and trust with others. In sum, Rawls's account constitutes an argument for the thesis that the sense of justice grows out of love and friendship as these sentiments arise initially in relation to one's parents and later in relation to others more socially distant than they. Plainly, if cogent, the account would give us strong reason to hold that the sense of justice is linked essentially to love and friendship.

The account, however, is not cogent. Rawls relies at crucial places in his exposition on the supposition that there is this link or on the related supposition that the natural sentiments of love and friendship make one liable to moral feelings when these sentiments reach maturity and to their precursors when they have not fully matured, and these suppositions, as the argument of the preceding section has shown, are problematic. Hence, his developmental account inherits the problems. It remains then for us to make good this observation.

Let us start with Rawls's account of the first stage. Rawls takes as the key step in this stage the child's coming to love its parents. He maintains that once this occurs, given a context in which the parents have and exercise authority over the child, the latter becomes liable to feel guilt when it rebels, as it invariably will, against their authority. Thus he writes:

Yet if he does love and trust his parents, then once he has given in to temptation, he is disposed to share their attitude toward his misdemeanors. He will be inclined to confess his transgression and to seek reconciliation. In these various inclinations are manifested the feelings of (authority) guilt. Without these and related inclinations, feelings of guilt would not exist. But it is also true that the absence of these feelings would indicate a lack of love and trust. For given the nature of the authority situation and the principles of moral psychology connecting the ethical and the natural attitudes, love and trust will give rise to feelings of guilt once the parental injunctions are disobeyed.[19]

The question to ask here, of course, is: What are these principles of moral psychology Rawls invokes to secure his points? Unfortunately, he doesn't explicitly formulate them when describing this first stage of moral development. Later, though, he writes of principles that link the moral sentiments to the natural ones and discusses specifically how the sense of justice is linked essentially to love. He argues that the two sentiments are linked because each gives rise to moral feelings, feelings of guilt and indignation in particular.[20] This suggests that he is applying something like the optimists' conceptual scheme that we examined in the preceding section, and in view of the problems we saw in that scheme, we can conclude that his argument for the link is unsound. And since he advances no other argument for these principles, it follows that he has failed to establish the conceptual scheme they suggest. The upshot, then, is that we have no reason to accept his assertion that, given the situation in which the child is subject to parental authority, its love for its parents gives rise directly to feelings of guilt when it disobeys their injunctions. He has not, in other words, accounted for the advance in moral development at this stage.

To be sure, the emotion Rawls supposes the child comes to experience at this stage is not guilt proper, but rather its earliest precursor, authority guilt. But this does not affect our criticism. For we are to understand authority guilt on the model of guilt: its subjects would explain their experiences by invoking concepts of obedience and disobedience to parental authority. The idea in each case is to distinguish an emotion or family of emotions that presuppose that their subjects see the world as including a certain social order and see themselves as members of that order. Guilt, resentment, and indignation, which Rawls regards as the genuinely moral emotions to which a sense of justice gives rise, presuppose that their subjects see themselves as members of a social order regulated by moral principles, the principles of justice and right. Authority guilt presupposes that its subjects see themselves as members of a social order regulated by the dictates and rules of their parents, who have and exercise supreme authority. By contrast, love, understood as a natural sentiment and thus conceived as a higher-order emotional disposition, does not include in itself such a view of the world; nor does Rawls give us reason to incorporate such a view and its associated dispositions to experience moral emotions into this conception of

---

19. Ibid., p. 465.
20. Ibid., pp. 485-487. For an indication of why Rawls can't use indignation to forge the link between love and the sense of justice, see p. 44 above.

love, even when it is assumed that the sentiment arises in the context of social relations. Indeed, once we set guilt apart from love by distinguishing it from remorse and in this way see how to separate emotions and sentiments the understanding of which presupposes as a context some social order from the natural sentiments the understanding of which presupposes no such context, we should not have any inclination to follow Rawls in connecting the former internally with the latter. These points then clearly apply to authority guilt as well as to the moral emotions strictly so called.

The problem becomes more perspicuous once we press further. Rawls supposes that crucial to the child's development at the first stage is the transition from an egocentric outlook to a parent-centered one. To account for this transition, Rawls cites the child's coming to love its parents, and he formulates a psychological law to explain this development. He assumes as background the institution of the family and, hence, that the child is subject to the legitimate authority of its parents. Accordingly, he takes as part of a parent-centered outlook recognition and acceptance of parental authority, where there was no such recognition in the egocentric outlook that preceded it. Consequently, we can infer that Rawls regards the psychological law as also explaining this change in the child's outlook. This change corresponds then to his thesis that with the onset of love for one's parents comes the liability to feelings of authority guilt. The correspondence, however, doesn't amount to confirmation. Just as we found his thesis questionable, so we should be prepared to question his claim to having explained how a child comes to recognize and accept parental authority.

Much of Rawls's description of this stage is, to be sure, unexceptionable. We can agree that a child's developing love for its parents from a prior condition of egocentricity means that it acquires motives and emotional dispositions of a new kind. It now identifies with its parents and thus takes their well-being as a final end. In other words, its concern to please and to avoid displeasing them, which, we might suppose, previously derived from desires to receive their affection and to avoid the unpleasant consequences of their displeasure, is no longer an exclusively instrumental interest. It ceases, that is, to be merely derivative of egoistic interests and becomes instead basic. So too there occurs a corresponding expansion in the range of emotions to which the child is liable. In particular, besides fear and anxiety, it is now disposed to feel sorrow when its acts bring parental displeasure; and it may even be liable to remorse when it acts from hostile impulses toward one of its parents and imagines that parent's suffering serious injury or death as a consequence.[21]

21. Melanie Klein emphasizes such experiences in her account of moral development during early childhood. See her *Love, Guilt and Reparation*, pp. 262-289. The opposition between

Furthermore, we can agree that the child, being subject to its parents' authority, will be moved to obey their dictates and rules. It has, to begin with, obvious self-interested reasons to obey, inasmuch as it understands these dictates and rules as backed by threats of some unpleasantness should it disobey. In addition, once the child comes to love its parents, its basic desires to please and to avoid displeasing them will prompt obedience, given that it takes obedience as a way to express love. But we should disagree at the point at which Rawls takes ready compliance with parental dictates and rules to imply recognition and acceptance of parental authority.

The motives out of which the child obeys its parents that we have described indicate only that parental dictates and rules have for the child instrumental significance. Neither motive indicates that the child regards them as invested with any authority. Without such regard, a parental dictate or rule signifies merely a conditional threat or a kind of request compliance with which expresses love. It doesn't represent an authoritative restraint on or barrier to conduct. Put differently, the child obeys out of love or fear but not out of respect.

Not surprisingly, then, we can invoke the distinction we drew between the motivational state underlying remorse and the one underlying guilt to further our criticism. It here confirms our earlier point that a gap exists in Rawls's account. To explain how the child comes to love its parents is not yet to explain how it comes to respect them. The former establishes that the child identifies with its parents but not that it accepts their authority, and acceptance of authority is the facet of moral development Rawls means to explain in giving his account of the first stage. It warrants our saying that the child has acquired a morality of authority, that it has come to view the world as including a social order in which it is a subject and over which its parents preside. Missing from Rawls's account, then, is an explanation of how the child, growing up in circumstances in which its parents have and exercise authority over it, develops allegiance to them as the possessors of that authority.

Now we can direct similar criticism at Rawls's account of the second stage, for that account proceeds under the same questionable assumption, namely, that the growth of natural sentiments toward others in the context of a social order is the key to explaining moral development concurrent with that growth. According to Rawls, the key to explaining moral development at the second stage is one's becoming friends with others in the context of joint par-

Klein and Freud on this subject, particularly the absence in her account of the introjection of parental authority, which is central to Freud's, reflects within psychoanalytic theory the dispute between optimists and pessimists that we have here been considering. For Freud's view see, 1930, XXI, pp. 127-130.

ticipation in an association, just as at the first the key was one's coming to love one's parents in the context defined by the institution of the family. Accordingly, the arguments advanced over the last few pages in criticism of his account of the first stage apply, with minor changes, to his account of the second. Inspection of his text bears this out.[22]

We shall need, however, to advance somewhat different arguments in criticizing Rawls's account of the third stage. Since at this stage one acquires a moral sentiment, the sense of justice, we won't need to question whether that sentiment gives rise to feelings of guilt. Rather we should question whether he has adequately explained the acquisition of this sentiment. This, so to speak, reverses the procedure we followed in criticizing his accounts of the earlier stages. There we allowed that Rawls had explained the acquisition of certain natural sentiments. That is, we waived consideration of the psychological laws he formulated and cited in giving these explanations. For at issue was whether these *natural sentiments*, when acquired in the context of a social order, gave rise to feelings of guilt (more exactly, feelings of authority and association guilt). Here, because his accounts of all three stages are parallel and are meant to parallel each other, the issue is whether he has explained how one acquires a *moral sentiment*, which we allow is the source of feelings of guilt. Accordingly, we will focus on the psychological law he formulates and cites in giving this explanation.

Rawls regards this law as explaining how a person at the later phases of the second stage acquires a sense of justice. Such a person, Rawls supposes, understands and complies with the principles of right and justice even before he acquires this sense. Moreover, he has become friends with many individuals through joint participation in associations that these principles regulate, and, following Rawls's account of the second stage, we understand his compliance with moral principles to spring from the natural sentiments these friendships entail. To explain his developing a sense of justice Rawls then offers the following:

Eventually one achieves a mastery of these principles and understands the values they secure and the way in which they are to everyone's advantage. Now this leads to acceptance of these principles by a third psychological law. This law states that once attitudes of love and trust, friendly feelings and mutual confidence, have been generated in accordance with the two preceding psychological laws, then the recognition that we and those for whom we care are the beneficiaries of an established and enduring just institution tends to engender in us the corresponding sense of justice. We develop a desire to apply and to act upon principles of justice once we realize how social arrange-

22. See Rawls, pp. 467–472, esp. pp. 470–471.

ments answering to them have promoted our good and that of those with whom we are affiliated.[23]

Rawls assumes that we will accept this psychological law in view of the other two laws he has formulated and, moreover, in view of his developmental account regarded as a whole. For he means to convey an understanding of moral development as a progression through several stages to the acquisition of a sense of justice, with the same pattern of explanation holding for the advance that occurs at each stage. Each advance entails one's acquiring a morality that is more complex than any morality one acquired at an earlier stage, and hence the explanation of each (and the psychological law it involves) differs from those of the others in reflecting, as a background condition, a social order the complexity of which corresponds to the complexity of the morality one acquires. Thus, Rawls's understanding of moral development is that through repeated operations of the same mechanism one progresses from an egocentric outlook to outlooks defined by moralities of increasing complexity. Consequentiy, if we find the first two explanations satisfactory, we should be likewise disposed toward the third and so toward the psychological law that is its major premiss. By the same token, having found that these first two fall short of explaining how one acquires a morality, we should deny that Rawls has presented a pattern of explanation, of which the third is an instance, that yields cogent accounts of advances in moral development. In other words, his developmental account regarded as a whole doesn't give us reason to accept this third explanation or its major premiss.

There is another reason Rawls offers for accepting his three psychological laws and so, in particular, the third. All three, he declares, reflect a deep fact of moral psychology.

While they have a certain resemblance to these learning principles [the principles of association and reinforcement] they assert that the active sentiments of love and friendship, and even the sense of justice, arise from the manifest intention of other persons to act for our good. Because we recognize that they wish us well, we care for their wellbeing in return. Thus we acquire attachments to persons and institutions according to how we perceive our good to be affected by them. The basic idea is one of reciprocity, a tendency to answer in kind.[24]

Now the existence of this tendency needn't be questioned, and we may even allow that the first and second laws reflect it. We have no reason to disagree. The disagreement enters when we come to consider whether its existence supports

23. Ibid., pp. 473-474.
24. Ibid., p. 494.

the third law. If this law is like the other two in reflecting this tendency, then, just as Rawls invokes them to explain how one acquires attachments to others at the first and second stages, so he invokes the third to explain how one acquires a like attachment at the last stage. And clearly the attachment Rawls means to explain is not an attachment to particular individuals or groups but rather to the principles of justice and right and the institutions through which those principles are realized. In other words, he intends for us to understand the sense of justice as an attachment to these principles and institutions just as we understand the natural sentiments of love and friendship as attachments to particular individuals. The issue then is whether the sense of justice, a moral sentiment, is properly understood as such an attachment. Rawls, we might say, renders the sense as the love of principles of justice, and it is open to question whether such love is a moral sentiment. Does it give rise to moral feelings? Given our earlier points about the natural sentiment of love, we have reason to doubt that it does and thus reason to think that he hasn't explained how one acquires a sense of justice.

That Rawls has explained how one acquires an effective desire to act on principles of justice is not in dispute. The love of those principles undoubtedly yields such a desire. For Rawls, then, this suffices to explain how one acquires a sense of justice.[25] And herein lies the dispute. Not every attachment to moral principles, and so not every desire to act on them, gives rise to moral feeling. On this point our previous observations about the different motives that may prompt a child to obey its parents' dictates and rules are instructive. The child may obey out of respect or out of love. In the former case we allowed that it was liable to feelings of authority guilt should it have disobeyed whereas in the latter we remained unconvinced that this liability obtained. Yet in either case we would say that the child desired to act on the dictates and rules its parents issued. The difference is that, though the child is attached to the parents in either case, only in the former has it come to recognize that they have and exercise authority over it. Accordingly, just as we found a gap in Rawls's account of moral development at this first stage, so we can remark a corresponding gap in his account of moral development at the third. He has explained how one becomes attached at this later stage to moral principles, but this attachment doesn't itself entail any disposition to experience moral feelings. Likewise, he leaves unexplained how one comes to regard the principles of justice as invested with moral authority. Thus, the love of justice the acquisition of which he does explain could be like the love of efficiency or the love of orderliness. One can, after all, become strongly attached to the princi-

---

25. It suffices because Rawls defines a sense of justice as a desire to act on principles of justice; see pp. 312 and 505.

ples of efficiency, to the ideal of fully using one's resources, without regarding these principles as imposing authoritative restraints on one's conduct and without becoming liable to feelings of guilt should one fail to observe them. Consequently, in rendering the sense of justice as the love of principles of justice Rawls fails to convey an understanding of it as a moral sentiment given that essential to moral sentiments is the disposition to experience moral feelings. And, in particular, since Rawls holds that the disposition to experience guilt is essential to a sense of justice, he has failed to explain adequately how one acquires that sense. In effect, he has left unexplained how one advances to a morality of principles.

III

What encouragement can the pessimistic side draw from these criticisms of Rawls's developmental account and the conceptual scheme on which it relies? My answer will be brief. Let us look first to the difficulties we have seen in Rawls's developmental account. The general difficulty, which appears at each stage, is Rawls's failure to explain adequately how one acquires a liability to feel guilt, be it guilt proper or one of its precursors, and the source of this failure is his view that guilt originates in love. That this view underlies his account is indicated fairly clearly by the laws he formulates to explain advances in moral development, for they concern either the development of natural sentiments, love and friendship, toward others or, in the case of the third law, the acquisition of a moral sentiment that, as we noted, Rawls implicitly construes as love of the principles of justice and right. And that this view is the source of failure is shown by the gaps Rawls's reliance on it introduces into his explanations, gaps the foregoing criticisms brought out. These gaps represent places where further explanation is wanted and thus openings for a pessimistic view.

The gap in Rawls's explanation of the first stage is especially telling. The first law is formulated to explain how the child comes to love its parents, but, as I argued, its loving its parents does not suffice to account for its liability to feel authority guilt, given that we are to understand this emotion as characteristically felt over disobedience to parental authority. To account for this liability one must explain how the child comes to recognize and respect its parents as having authority over it, and the distinction I drew between motives of love and motives of respect shows clearly that the first law does not cover this step in the child's development. Nor will adding that the parents, having gained their child's love, teach the child moral attitudes yield the desired explanation. For the key question then becomes what does teaching their child moral attitudes involve? If it only involves transmitting to the child new concepts and beliefs, then such teaching doesn't explain how the range of emotions to which the child is liable enlarges, that is, how the child acquires a liability to a new emotion. At best it will only explain how the child becomes liable to experience an emotion already in its emotional range in circumstances that, before it received instruction, would not have evoked that emotion. If, on the other hand, it involves more, if it involves altering the child's emotional disposition so that the child becomes liable to guilt, a new emotion, then it remains forceful to ask how it accomplishes this. In other words, reference to teaching, since it involves more than enlarging the child's store of concepts and beliefs, still leaves us in the dark on how the child comes to respect its parents' authority. Or, to use an idea of Freud's, it leaves us in the dark on how external authority becomes in the child internal.[26]

Pessimists hope to establish their position by addressing this question of how the parents' authority becomes in the child internal – or the eighteenth century version, how human beings, living in a state of nature, become civilized. Keeping to the former, we may say that the parents of a child stand to that child as external authorities when it has yet to appreciate its position as a subject under their rule and therefore has yet to feel any allegiance to them as authorities to whom it owes obedience. As external authorities, they appear to the child as powerful figures who can use their power to secure its obedience, and the prospect of their doing so inspires fear. At this stage, fear is the emotion that they in their role as authorities evoke in the child. Then, as their authority becomes internal, as the child comes to see itself as part of a moral order over which its parents preside, its fear of their power is transformed into respect for their authority. Correspondingly, its fear of punishment – or of whatever evil the child senses will be the consequence of disobedience – becomes a liability to guilt. Accordingly, the child comes to regard disobedience to parental authority as upsetting the moral order of which it sees itself a part, and to regard confession and punishment as ways it can restore the order it upset, as ways it can right the wrong it committed. Guilt, which makes the child ill-disposed toward itself and which moves it to confess its misdemeanors and submit to punishment thus to some extent displaces fear, which makes it ill-disposed toward the objects of fear and moves it to conceal its actions and to avoid or resist punishment. To borrow again from Freud, fear of punishment becomes a need for punishment.[27]

All of this, to be sure, falls short of explaining how one acquires a liability to feel guilt over violations of moral requirements on conduct or how one

---

26. Freud, 1930, XXI, p. 128; see also 1933a, XXII, pp. 61–62.
27. 1930, XXI, pp. 123–124. Freud first introduced the idea of rendering the sense of guilt as a need for punishment in 1924a, XX, p. 166.

comes to respect the authority from which those requirements issue. It does, however, serve to focus attention on fear of external authority and, moreover, on the sort of situation that calls forth such fear as conditions out of which a liability to guilt develops and so reference to which would be an essential part of the desired explanation. Pessimists thus face the task of constructing a full explanation according to which these conditions initiate this first stage of moral development. That is, starting from considerations of the situation of someone whose desires and emotions are unrestrained by any sense of duty or justice but who is blocked or inhibited from acting on them by others more powerful than he, who impose their will on him and whom he therefore fears, pessimists must explain how this individual comes to accept as binding on him moral requirements on conduct and likewise how he comes to respect the authority behind those requirements. And if they successfully explain this stage of moral development, they will then also have explained how the individual acquires a liability to guilt. In constructing an explanation according to this program they thus take the failings of Rawls's account as promising points of departure for their own. In this way those failings give encouragement to the pessimistic side.

We can now see how the earlier criticisms of the conceptual scheme on which Rawls's developmental account relies also give encouragement to the pessimistic side. Guilt, on the pessimists' program sketched above, has no internal connection with the emotional capacities that are native to human beings. Rather, as pessimists see things, one acquires a liability to guilt when some of these emotional capacities are transformed. This is suggested in the observation that at the first stage of moral development the child's fear of parental power is transformed into respect for parental authority, its fear of punishment becomes a need for punishment. The pessimists' view thus finds support in the distinctions between guilt and remorse and between their underlying motives, motives of respect and motives of love, from which the earlier criticisms followed, for these distinctions show guilt and respect to have no conceptual ties to the natural sentiments and other emotional dispositions from which moral sentiments are distinguished. Likewise, given that we understand the sense of justice as the source in a moral personality of the guilt one feels over moral wrongdoing and the respect one has for the laws of a just social order, these distinctions uphold the pessimists' view that the sense of justice is not continuous with love and friendship, that it is not a form of good will toward humanity. In sum, the criticisms presented in Section I accord well with the way pessimists understand civic virtues and moral sensibilities like the sense of justice as sui generis aspects of a moral personality. Of course, the pessimists' position also includes the thesis that those aspects develop in an individual from society's turning to its own advantage asocial and antisocial drives and motives to which that individual is naturally disposed, and plainly those criticisms do not directly support this thesis. But that they are forceful against recent developments on the optimistic side, while squaring entirely with the pessimists' account, is reason enough for pessimists to persevere.

4

Remarks on some difficulties in
Freud's theory of moral development

In 1923 Freud introduced into psychoanalytic theory a threefold division of the mind that produced a bounty of fresh developments as it revived old lines of investigation and sowed seeds for new ones. Previously, Freud had used, in constructing his theory, a topographical model that was based on the seemingly simple opposition between the mind's conscious and unconscious parts. The conscious part he located at and near the surface of the mind, where via sensory stimulation it came into contact with its environment and where deliberation and decision making about how best to adapt to the environment occurred. The unconscious he located in the mind's interior, where inherited drives, which is to say, instincts, had their source and where many thoughts and ideas the awareness of which would produce distress were buried. By 1923, however, this model had proved unsatisfactory, and Freud abandoned it for a structural, one might say bureaucratic, model according to which the mind was divided into three agencies – ego, id, and superego – and the interactions among them were the basis for explanations of the psychological phenomena Freud sought to understand. This change in explanatory model, contrary to what one might expect, did not result from a discovery of new phenomena, nor did it represent a movement to a deeper level of theory through introduction of novel theoretical entities. In making the change, Freud was not so much signaling a break from his previous views as reorganizing them, a reorganization that enabled him to bring to fruition several ideas the germs of which he had cultivated in earlier writings. The yield, as gauged by subsequent work both inside the psychoanalytic movement and out, was vast.

No area of study flourished more on account of this change than that of moral development. Indeed, Freud ensured this result by giving fundamental place in his new model to an agent of conscience, the superego. Thus he as much as announced that he regarded the study of moral development as basic to psychoanalytic theory, though such an announcement only made official a view that had begun to emerge in previous writings. It is the theory of moral development that Freud constructed and revised during the last period of his career that I will be examining in this chapter.

At the beginning of this period, having introduced his new, structural model, Freud set out to rework his theories of neurosis and other forms of mental illness, and he discussed the topic of moral development in the context of this large project. Later, however, after he had turned his attention from questions of clinical theory to questions of social psychology, he treated the topic as important in itself. Specifically, in the last two chapters of *Civilization and Its Discontents*, the question of how human beings became moral creatures – how man acquired a conscience – defined his inquiry, and he presented an extended discussion of it, giving as the answer his account of how the superego, here viewed exclusively as the agent of conscience and a source of man's liability to a sense of guilt, was formed. One would thus do well to study these chapters closely in examining Freud's theory of moral development.

Accordingly, I propose to take them as the primary text for our examination. I will present it in two parts. In the first I will reconstruct Freud's theory. This will involve distinguishing the phenomena Freud intended his theory to explain, formulating its main hypotheses, and describing how they work together to provide the explanation he sought. The reconstruction, as I indicated, will be based primarily on Freud's exposition in *Civilization and Its Discontents*. This exposition, however, is incomplete, and I shall at some point have to consult other works to fill out the account. Moreover, once it has been filled out, we shall see that it departs from his account of moral development in these other works.[1] This will not only call into question my choice of a primary text but will also make evident that there is no unproblematic interpretation of Freud's theory. The lesson I draw from this is that one must recognize that Freud offered two significantly different accounts of moral development. One fits more closely into his general theory of how one develops a personality; the other, on which my reconstruction is primarily based, gives a more cogent explanation of how one acquires a conscience.

In the second part I will consider the conceptual scheme that underlies Freud's theory as he presented it in *Civilization and Its Discontents*. I will begin by considering Freud's assumptions about the relations that exist among the concepts of superego, conscience, and a sense of guilt. These, we shall see, convict Freud of conceptual confusion and raise doubts about the coherence of his conceptual scheme. I will argue, however, that Freud fell into this confusion because of an unwarranted inference he made about the sense of guilt. Consequently, once this error is exposed, one can render his conceptual scheme coherent. My conclusion, then, will be that Freud's theory, despite the confusion he introduced into it, has an internally secure conceptual basis.

Freud aimed, in presenting his theory, at establishing the thesis that civilized society, acting through its agents, made the individual a moral being, a

---

1. Freud, 1921, XVIII, pp. 105–110; 1923, XIX, pp. 28–39; 1933a; XXII, pp. 61–65. See also Freud, 1924a, XIX, pp. 166–168; 1924b, XIX, pp. 176–177 ; 1928, XXI, pp. 185–186.)

creature of conscience, by turning to its advantage antisocial drives that were part of an individual human being's native endowment.[2] I aim in this chapter at showing that one can, by examining Freud's writings on moral development and working through difficulties internal to them, find in them and in *Civilization and Its Discontents*, in particular, a viable theory in support of that thesis.

I

The foregoing should make clear that in speaking of Freud's theory of moral development I mean his theory of how an individual, growing up in civilized society, acquires a conscience. This, of course, is only a fragment of Freud's general theory of personality, but one can, I think, take it as an object of study without being drawn into a study of the general theory itself. I should also make clear that the fragment with which I'm concerned excludes Freud's views about the origins of conscience in prehistoric man. Freud, as is well known, liked to tie together developmental theories of the individual and of the species, but I aim only at reconstructing his theory of moral development in the individual. What he says about the corresponding development in the species will concern us only in so far as it bears on this reconstruction. Finally, I should point out that the phrase 'Freud's theory of moral development' is a misnomer. Freud did not offer a theory of the development of a conscience beyond its inception. His is a theory of the origins of conscience and not of its full development, and I mean no more than this in calling it a theory of moral development.[3]

It will be useful, for the purposes of exegesis, to distinguish several features of a conscience that Freud's theory addresses. First, one who has a conscience has thereby a moral sense, and this implies, among other things, that one is sensitive to the purview of moral standards and requirements and is disposed to

---

2. See 1930, XXI, pp. 123-124.
3. I should also note that I leave unexplored Freud's views on that part of an individual's moral personality he reintroduced the term 'ego-ideal', after its complete displacement by 'superego', to denote. Thus, in his *New Introductory Lectures on Psychoanalysis* (XXII, pp. 59-66), Freud described the superego as having multiple functions: one was to serve as a conscience; another was to uphold the ego ideal. And his discussion of the sense of inferiority, which immediately follows this differentiation of the superego's functions, suggests, by way of contrast with the sense of guilt, complexities in an individual's moral personality that separation of conscience from personal ideals helps to illuminate. See Franz Alexander, "Remarks about the Relation of Inferiority feelings to Guilt Feelings," *International Journal of Psycho-Analysis* 19 (1938): 41-49, and Gerhart Piers and Milton Singer, *Shame and Guilt: A Psychoanalytic and a Cultural Study* (Springfield, IL: Charles C. Thomas, 1953).

conform one's conduct to them. It also implies that one is liable to certain feelings, which we take to be characteristically moral feelings, and in this regard we will, following Freud, focus exclusively on feelings of guilt. Second, a conscience is a distinct agency of the mind. Characteristically, it makes itself heard when it opposes some wish or desire of its possessor or some action he has performed, and sometimes its opposition is so strong as to make it seem beyond its possessor's control. Thus, we conceive of a conscience as set over and against its possessor and even speak of it as having authority over him. Third, one's conscience, in exercising this authority, can be harsh and unrelenting in its reproaches. Self-punishment is its work, and the suffering this produces is sometimes great and, what is even more striking, disproportionately severe in relation to the transgression or misdemeanor in response to which it is produced. These, then, are the main features of a conscience to which Freud attended in constructing his theory. How one acquires a conscience, understood as a moral sense and as a distinct agency in the mind, and what explains the severity of a conscience are questions he intended his theory to answer.

In answering the first question, Freud dismissed the possibility that a moral sense was innate in human beings. He held, instead, that an individual acquired it in the normal course of developing a personality. The account he gave in *Civilization and Its Discontents* goes as follows. The individual, when very young, forms a strong emotional attachment to those persons, typically his parents, who exercise moral authority over him and on whom he depends for protection and nourishment. The protection and nourishment they provide signify their love for him, and he obeys the orders they give and the rules they impose out of fear of losing that love, which is to say, fear of the dangers such loss implies, including, to his mind, the punishment they threaten to inflict should he disobey. One could then attribute to him a sensitivity to the purview of the moral standards and requirements his parents articulate and lay down and a disposition to conform his conduct to them. But because these only manifest his fear of loss of love, they do not imply that he has acquired a genuine moral sense. He acquires such a sense through the formation of a superego. Only upon its formation can we speak of his having a conscience. Thus, in reference to anxiety the child would feel at this early stage were he to disobey parental authority, Freud wrote,

This state of mind is called a 'bad conscience'; but actually it does not deserve this name, for at this stage the sense of guilt is clearly only a fear of loss of love. . . .

A great change takes place only when the authority is internalized through the establishment of a superego. The phenomena of conscience then reach a higher stage. Actually, it is not until now that we should speak of conscience or a sense of guilt.[4]

4.   1930, XXI, pp. 124-125.

To explain how the superego in regard to its being an agent of conscience is formed, Freud considered further the circumstances of early childhood. To repeat, the child, when young, is subject to his parents' authority and completely dependent on them for protection and nourishment. In these circumstances, he forms a strong emotional attachment to them, which is to say, he comes to love them. At the same time, however, the child experiences desires and impulses that, if acted on, would lead him to disobey his parents. Hence, obedience to parental authority requires that these desires and impulses be thwarted. As Freud put it, the child, in obeying parental authority from fear of loss of love, renounces the satisfaction of instinctual urges. Moreover, as Freud went on to argue, these circumstances are unstable. Having to frustrate his desires and impulses angers the child, and this anger is felt towards his parents, who in their capacity as authorities are responsible for the frustration. Yet he cannot vent this anger for fear of losing their love. Consequently, the aggressive impulses implicit in his anger must themselves be thwarted, and this in turn increases his frustration and so his anger. The circumstances of the young child thus eventuate in his unrelieved hostility towards his parents as the moral authorities who prevent him from satisfying his desires as well as in his love for them as the benefactors who protect him from danger and provide him with nourishment. And because of the instability of these circumstances his hostility grows in force, if not feeling, and so the ambivalence becomes increasingly difficult for him to live with. It resolves itself, finally, by the child's identifying with his parents. Unable to escape from or overcome these authorities while retaining their love, he incorporates them, as it were, into himself. Thus, a superego is formed as external authority becomes in the child internal. To quote Freud,

A considerable amount of aggressiveness must be developed in the child against the authority which prevents him from having his first, but none the less his most important, satisfactions, whatever the kind of instinctual deprivation that is demanded may be; but he is obliged to renounce the satisfaction of this revengeful aggressiveness. He finds his way out of this economically difficult situation with the help of familiar mechanisms. By means of identification he takes the unattackable authority into himself. The authority now turns into his super-ego and enters into possession of all the aggressiveness which a child would have liked to exercise against it.[5]

Admittedly, even if familiar, this process by which one, on the basis of having identified with another, incorporates him into oneself is obscure. Freud himself, in a later discussion, allowed as much.[6] At a minimum, then, we shall want to know what the general circumstances are that initiate it. Is identifica-

5. Ibid., p. 129.
6. 1933a, XXII, pp. 62-63.

tion alone sufficient? In addition, there is a separate question about how the process explains, as Freud clearly believed it did, the second feature of a conscience we distinguished. How does it explain the formation of an agency of the mind that is distinct from the ego? After all, incorporating another into oneself needn't entail the formation of such an agency, and it won't if molding one's character after another in the way, say, an apprentice takes on the personality of the master under whom he studies counts as such incorporation. Hence, even if Freud had, by invoking this process, satisfactorily explained the first feature of a conscience, he might still owe us an explanation of the second. We need, then, to elaborate Freud's theory on these points, and to do this we must go beyond its exposition in the primary text.

In the works in which Freud discussed identification more extensively, he defined it as an emotional attachment to someone that is characterized by one's wanting to be that person.[7] He distinguished this from erotic love, which he defined as an emotional attachment to someone that is characterized by one's wanting to possess that person.[8] A strong attachment of the former kind, Freud held, produces a change in one's personality as one develops traits that match certain personality traits the other has. Some attachments of this kind, however, are too weak to produce any change in one's personality.[9] Thus, one might in such a case imitate the behavior of the person with whom one identified without having one's personality altered, as youngsters, when participating in some sport, often imitate the style of their favorite professional player. This case suggests that the process by which one incorporates another into oneself - introjects him, to use Freud's term - does not necessarily occur whenever one identifies with someone. And, moreover, this would appear to be Freud's view.[10] On the other hand, there can be little doubt that Freud regarded every change in personality that resulted from an identification as occurring through this process.[11]

These changes typically occur, Freud hypothesized, when one can no longer maintain erotic love for another because, say, one's beloved has left one or because external pressures, taboos or other social barriers, for example, force one to give up that love.[12] For some people such loss of love is too great an emotional hardship to bear, and they react by preserving, as it were, within

7. 1921, XVIII, p. 106; cf. 1933a, XXII, p. 63.
8. 1921, XVIII, pp. 105–106 and 1933a, XXII, p. 63.
9. I am reading Freud as having taken identification to be an emotional attachment that is distinct from and precedes the process of incorporating another into oneself. Sometimes, though, he does not distinguish between the two. See 1933a, XXII, p. 63.
10. 1921, XVIII, pp. 106–108.
11. 1923, XIX, pp. 28–29 and 1933a, XXII, p. 91.
12. 1917, XIV, pp. 248–249; 1921, XVIII, pp. 108; 1923, XIX, pp. 29–30; and 1933a XXII, p. 91.

themselves something of that love, somewhat as a parent who suddenly loses a child he dearly loved may react by preserving intact the child's bedroom. We might characterize these reactions as defenses against blows that upset one's emotional equilibrium, but we should note a difference between them. The parent's reaction, as I've described it, is conscious, whereas the reactions Freud sought to understand are unconscious. Thus, on Freud's hypothesis, an individual unconsciously defends himself against the blow a loss of love causes by identifying himself so strongly with the person he loved that he introjects the latter into himself. In this way he keeps some part of his beloved's character within himself. And one consequence of this is that the love he had for that person is displaced onto himself. A strong erotic interest in another becomes a strong interest in oneself, much, one might suppose, as the time and energy the parent in the above example once invested in his child becomes invested in the child's room. Such actions, in either case, ease the emotional strain that loss of love creates.

Freud, however, did not hold that every time an erotic attachment was dissolved the lover identified with and then introjected his beloved. In particular, he observed that when a young child forms an erotic attachment to one of his parents and consequently comes to regard the other as a rival, he will, when the time comes to give up that attachment, frequently identify (or identify more strongly) with and then introject the latter parent rather than the former.[13] This too is a way of defending against the blow the loss of love causes, for it preserves something of that love through an identification with the successful rival.

The observation, to be sure, points up how incomplete Freud's understanding of the process was: why a child, in the situation described above, identified with one of his parents and not the other (or more strongly with one than the other) is a question to which Freud could not give a general answer. But though this question went unanswered, our earlier question, what the general circumstances are that produce, owing to identification and introjection, a change in personality, did get answered. Such change occurs in circumstances in which one is attached to someone, either by erotic love or identification, and comes under severe emotional stress in relation to that attachment. Freud's general hypothesis, then, was that one found a way out of these stressful circumstances by identifying (or identifying more strongly) with that person or a third party. By becoming another, so to speak, one made bearable a situation one could not face as oneself.

With one exception, Freud offered this hypothesis to explain modifications of the ego. Thus, past emotional attachments form, to a large extent, the char-

13.   1923, XIX, p. 32.

acter of an individual's ego, and the psychoanalyst studies the ego, as a geologist studies a fossil, to learn the history of an individual's personal relations. The one exception is the formation of the superego, for this involves more than a change in the ego's character. Rather, as Freud saw it, the superego forms when a part of the ego splits off from the remainder.[14] This occurs, he argued, through the same process as explains modifications of the ego, but owing to special circumstances more than a modification results. These special circumstances include an unusually strong emotional attachment and an unusually weak ego. They are, paradigmatically, the circumstances of early childhood.

The young child's emotional attachment to his parents, who are typically the forebears of his superego, is made especially strong by his great and continued dependency on them for protection and nourishment. At the same time, his ego, having as yet no settled character and being free of the complexity it will have when he matures, is especially weak. That is, it is, at best, minimally able to resist the influences of others.[15] Consequently, when emotional stress, owing to the young child's ambivalence towards his parents, develops in his relations to them and, in accordance with Freud's hypothesis, is resolved through his identifying with and then introjecting them, the effect of his ego is much greater and longer lasting than those in later instances. To quote Freud, "[I]t is entirely in accordance with the emotional importance of this first instance of such a transformation that a special place in the ego should be found for its outcome."[16]

Yet this does not adequately explain how an agency that is independent of the ego is formed. For it remains forceful to ask why these special circumstances cause a part of the ego to become separate from the remainder. Why don't they simply bring about the predominance in one's personality of traits one's parents appeared to have when one was a young child? In the latter event, we need only suppose that changes in the ego's character result and not that an agency distinct from the ego is formed. The problem can be put succinctly. While we would agree that the effects of these circumstances should be great and long-lasting, the formation of a superego is only one of at least two possible outcomes to which these attributes apply.

Freud, as far as I can determine, never addressed this problem, and one could reasonably assume that he failed to notice it. Nonetheless, it does not seriously threaten his theory, for its solution is implicit in his understanding of the phenomenon to be explained. To Freud the superego was, above all, an

---

14. 1921, XVIII, pp. 109–110 and 1933a, XXII, pp. 58–60.
15. 1923, XIX, pp. 29–31.
16. 1933a, XXII, p. 64.

agency of the mind that made itself known by its excessively harsh treatment of the ego. This brings us round to the third feature of a conscience, and the suggestion is that Freud's explanation of the third feature contains an explanation of the second. To explain the superego's harsh treatment of the ego is to explain its independence.

Let us return to the discussion in *Civilization and Its Discontents*. The question about the severity of conscience, why it tends to be great and disproportionately so, is at its center. Freud there considered two hypotheses that offered alternative explanations of this feature. First, one's conscience treats one severely because those persons under whose authority one lived when a young child and on whom, owing to the process we've been considering, one's conscience is modeled treated one severely in their exercise of that authority. In other words, the severity of one's conscience is a continuation of the severe treatment one received at the hands of those who exercised authority over one during one's childhood. Second, one's conscience treats one severely because it draws its power from the aggressive impulses one stifles in conforming one's conduct to the requirements of morality. In other words, one's conscience takes up these aggressive impulses, which would, if uninhibited, lead one to act violently or hostilely toward others, and turns them back onto one in the form of self-criticism and ill feeling. Reproaches of conscience and the bite of conscience are thus forms of aggression that, though originally directed outward toward others, are, through the workings of conscience, turned inward and aimed at oneself.

Freud, though he thought that both of these hypotheses contained some truth, regarded neither as wholly satisfactory.[17] The first, he noted, fails in view of the fact that many people whose parents raised them leniently nevertheless develop consciences as severe as one would expect to find in people who received a strict upbringing. Freud granted that a strict upbringing added to the severity of one's conscience or, at least, reinforced it, but, citing the fact mentioned above, he argued that such strictness could only partially explain that severity. Hence the first hypothesis cannot provide the fundamental explanation Freud sought. The second hypothesis also fails, for while it explains how the severity of a conscience is maintained and increased, it does not explain how it originates. This is because the second hypothesis presupposes that one already possesses a conscience, which works to suppress aggressive drives so that one does not act hostilely or violently toward others. Conse-

17. Note that in this and the next paragraph I am not following the exact order of ideas in Freud's exposition. Rather I've rearranged them in order to bring out more clearly the argument for adopting as the main hypothesis of the theory a different one from the two under consideration. See 1930, XXI, pp. 127–130.

quently, if one assumes, as Freud did, that a conscience is by nature reproach-ful and punitive in its relation to its possessor and that these forms of ill-treat-ment are indicators of hostility and so aggression, one will have to invoke a different hypothesis from the second to explain how a conscience at its incep-tion is liable to ill-treat its possessor in these ways. Thus, because these two hy-potheses, taken singly or together, did not yield a satisfactory theory, Freud introduced a third.

As we have seen from a previous quotation, Freud realized that the young child's ambivalent relations to his parents created a store of unrelieved hostili-ty towards them. This stored up hostility Freud then recognized as the source of the aggressive force with which a conscience is originally invested. Accord-ingly, he formulated the hypothesis that the large store of hostility towards one's parents that developed during early childhood became, through the process of identification with and introjection of them, displaced onto one-self, and in this way a conscience was formed.[18] This hypothesis thus makes good the deficiency of the second and indeed, the second, in providing an ex-planation of how the aggressive character of a conscience is maintained and increased, nicely complements it. Together the two constitute a substantial elaboration of Nietzsche's conjecture about the origin in man of bad con-science.[19]

18.   Ernest Jones attributes to Freud the view that the original severity of a conscience is partly explained by the child's fantasies about his parents. Richard Wollheim makes the same attri-bution in writing that Freud accepted Melanie Klein's account according to which the hos-tility that builds up in the child toward his parents is first projected on to them in the child's fantasies, and then the parents, now imagined as severe authorities, are introjected in the formation of the child's superego. Its original severity thus corresponds to the severity the child imagines his parents as exhibiting in their treatment of him. See Ernest Jones, *The Life and Work of Sigmund Freud* (New York: Basic Books, 1957), v. 3, pp. 285–286 and Richard Wollheim, *Sigmund Freud* (New York: Viking, 1971), pp. 225–226.

   On this view, Freud did not depart as greatly from the first hypothesis as I have suggest-ed. I am unable, however, to find clear textual evidence in *Civilization and Its Discontents*, the work in which Freud acknowledges the importance of Klein's contributions, to support at-tributing the view to Freud. Indeed, Freud seems to have denied it when he wrote, "But the essential difference is that the original severity of the super ego does not – or does not so much – represent the severity which one has experienced from it [the external authority], or which one attributes to it; it represents rather one's own aggressiveness towards it" (1930, XXI, pp. 129–130). The word Strachey here translates as 'attributes', *zumutet*, may be open to alternative renderings that would lessen the conflict between the passage and the view Jones and Wollheim attribute to Freud. Cf. Riviere's translation of *Civilization and Its Discontents*.

19.   Friedrich Nietzsche, "'Guilt,' 'Bad Conscience,' and the Like" in *On the Genealogy of Morals*, W. Kaufman and R. J. Hollingdale, trans. (New York: Vintage, 1969), pp. 84–85. For a possi-ble connection between Nietzsche's and Freud's view on the origin of conscience see Ernest Jones, pp. 283–284.

This third hypothesis is then the main hypothesis of Freud's theory. When stated completely, so that it fully describes the ambivalent and unstable relations a young child develops to his parents, the hypothesis yields answers to the major questions Freud intended his theory to address. It sets out the circumstances that bring about the formation of a conscience, accounts for the original content of the moral requirements that the conscience enforces, and explains the strictness with which it initially enforces them. Moreover, as I have suggested, the hypothesis, given that it explains that strictness, also explains the independence of a conscience, since the strictness implies an opposition between a conscience and its possessor.

At this point, having reconstructed Freud's theory of moral development on the basis of his account in *Civilization and Its Discontents*, we must ask how well this account squares with accounts he gave in other works. Indeed, a question about the propriety of our proceeding as we have will be in order, for even someone with only a passing acquaintance with this area of Freud's thought will have noticed that the most distinctive idea in Freud's theory is missing from our reconstruction, namely, that an Oedipus complex, as Freud called it, characterizes the young child's ambivalent relations to his parents. Thus, one has reason to question our use of *Civilization and Its Discontents* as the basis for reconstructing Freud's theory because in every other work of Freud's in which he discussed how a child develops a superego the Oedipus complex is central to the explanation he gave of that development. In these other works, the explanation clearly reflects the idea he frequently expressed that the superego was heir to the Oedipus complex.[20] This, however, is not true of the work on which we've concentrated. It appears, then, that as a result our reconstruction is deficient.

What is more, this apparent deficiency cannot be removed simply by giving a more complete description of the young child's relations to his parents. For our reconstruction does not just leave the Oedipus complex out of the description of the circumstances of early childhood but in fact makes its inclusion inessential to Freud's theory. As we have described those circumstances, the ambivalent relations which the child develops to his parents and out of which, because of the emotional strain they create, a superego is formed arise from the child's dependency on them for protection and nourishment and his subjection to their authority. He loves them as his benefactors, but he is hostile to them because they, in exercising their authority, prevent him from gratifying all his appetites and urges. Plainly, then, on this description, which follows Freud's account in *Civilization and Its Discontents*, the triangular relation-

20.   1923, XIX, p. 36; 1924a, XIX, p. 167; 1933a, XXII, p. 79, and 1940 XXIII, p. 205.

ship between the child and his two parents that constitutes the Oedipus complex is inessential to explaining the child's ambivalence. We should expect such ambivalence to develop even though the child were raised by a single parent or by several adults. This means that the account we've followed departs radically from what I'll call Freud's standard account, the account on which the Oedipus complex is essential to explaining the child's ambivalent relations to his parents. Consequently, the apparent deficiency in our reconstruction may not be a deficiency at all. It may instead represent a major change in Freud's theory.

The difficulty, of course, with maintaining that Freud made such a change in his theory is that Freud himself gave no indication that he intended to do so. To the contrary, it would appear that he did not regard the account he was giving in *Civilization and Its Discontents* as offering a new explanation of how the child developed ambivalent relations to his parents, especially in view of what he wrote in his next large-scale work, his *New Introductory Lectures on Psychoanalysis*. There, in essays intended to summarize the developments in psychoanalytic theory during the preceding fifteen years, Freud presented the standard account and without any suggestion that he had given a different account not long before. Hence, if he did make the change in his theory our reconstruction represents, he did so unwittingly.

The best argument for holding that he did make this change comes from comparing the two accounts, the standard account and what I'll call Freud's Nietzschean account. To make the comparison, we'll need a brief sketch of the former. Its simplest form will suffice.[21] It begins in the same way as the latter. The individual, when very young, forms strong emotional attachments to his parents. Initially, these are identificatory ties. Later, however, though still early in his childhood, he develops an erotic attachment to one of his parents, while continuing to identify with the other. He then comes sometime afterwards to regard the latter as a rival for the love of the former, a rival who stands in the way of his realizing completely that love. This creates in him hostility toward the rival, and thus ambivalence develops in his relations to that parent. As the child's erotic desires to have the first parent all to himself continue to be frustrated, his hostility toward the second grows and gives birth to a wish to be rid of him. Here, as on the Nietzschean account, Freud depicted the young child's relations to his parents as unstable, owing to the child's coming under increasing emotional stress. On this account, though, the child finds relief by giving up his erotic attachment to the first parent and identifying with that parent or, in the more usual case, intensifying his identification with the second. And in either case the identification gives rise to in-

21. 1923, XIX, 31-32.

trojection. The child incorporates a parent into himself as his ideal. Hence, a superego is formed as the Oedipus complex is dissolved.

This account differs from the Nietzschean account in several respects. First, while both proceed under the general hypothesis, which I formulated above, that introjection following upon identification occurs in circumstances of emotional stress that arises from some erotic or identificatory attachment one has to another, the standard account makes use of the more specific hypothesis that one identifies with and then introjects another when from force of circumstances one has to give up a strong, erotic attachment one has to that person or some third party. This more specific hypothesis has a central place in Freud's theories of personality development and certain forms of neurosis, and therefore the standard account contributes more than the Nietzschean to the unity of psychoanalytic theory. Second, the standard account, in explaining the superego as "the heir to the Oedipus complex," links its formation to repression of sexual drives, whereas the Nietzschean, in keeping with Nietzsche's conjecture, is solely concerned with repression of aggressive drives.[22] This difference is due in part to Freud's having presented the former but not the latter as an account of how the child acquired a sexual identity as well as a conscience. Third, on the standard account, the hostility the child develops toward one of his parents results from his regarding that parent as a rival for the love of the other, whereas on the Nietzschean, the child's hostility towards one or both parents results from his being subject to their authority. Consequently, each account offers a different understanding of the ambivalence that is the source of the emotional stress that brings on the process by which a superego is formed.

This third difference is especially noteworthy. Because each account offers a different understanding of the young child's ambivalence towards his parents, each explains differently how the process by which a superego is formed works itself out. This makes clear the reason for regarding Freud's Nietzschean account as a major change in his theory, for it makes clear that the two accounts cannot be made to coalesce. Specifically, then, according to the standard account, the child identifies with one or the other parent in that parent's role as love-object or rival. The process then works itself out through the child's introjecting that parent and thus setting up as the nucleus of his superego the corresponding parental ideal – masculine or feminine depending on which parent is introjected. This introjection then determines the child's sexu-

---

22. Freud (1930, XXI, 129) at first puts forth the view that conscience results solely from suppression of aggressive drives only as a working hypothesis; but later (p. 130 and especially pp. 138-139) he makes clear that he means to make it part of his theory. For discussion of this difference between the standard and the Nietzschean accounts see T. Reik, *Myth and Guilt: The Crime and Punishment of Mankind* (New York: George Braziller, 1958).

al identity. At the same time, that his newly formed superego is invested with moral authority, is an agent of conscience, is explained only by a fortuity of social circumstance. On the standard account, the person the child introjects has authority over him per accidens. By contrast, according to the Nietzschean account, the child identifies with one or both parents in their role as authorities who govern his life. It is authorities per se with whom the child identifies. The process then works itself out through the child's introjecting these authorities and thus setting up an internal authority as a nucleus of his superego. Hence, the Nietzschean account goes directly to explaining how the superego is invested with authority, and thus how a child acquires a conscience. The standard account, by contrast, explains these facts only indirectly.

Freud, in *Civilization and Its Discontents* and in no other work in which he attempted to explain the formation of a superego, concentrated in this attempt exclusively on explaining how a conscience is acquired, that is, how the superego *in its function as the agent of conscience* is formed. As he there put it, he sought to understand how external authority became, in the child, internal.[23] In other works he attempted to explain how the superego, understood as a theoretical construct with multiple functions, was formed.[24] I'm suggesting, then, that in narrowing his focus he explained without realizing it the child's ambivalent relations to his parents in a way that made reference to the Oedipus complex inessential. The result was a more satisfactory ontogenetic account of the origin in man of a conscience, though, to be sure, it would be an unsatisfactory account of the formation of a superego in regard to its other functions.

II

We meet new difficulties when we turn to Freud's explanation of the origin in man of a liability to a sense of guilt. This remark, I admit, may strike some as odd, for it is reasonable to assume that Freud regarded the origin in man of a liability to a sense of guilt and the origin in man of a conscience as one and the same development. One would arrive at this assumption, reasonably enough, by taking as canonical the definition of the sense of guilt Freud gave when he introduced the superego into psychoanalytic theory, a definition he continued to use in subsequent works. Thus, Freud defined the sense of guilt theoretically as tension between the ego and the superego,[25] and it follows di-

23. 1930, XXI, pp. 124-125.
24. See above fn. 3. Freud sometimes mentioned self-observation as a distinct function of the superego. See 1933a, XXII, p. 66 and 1940 XXIII, p. 205; but cf. 1930, XXI, p. 136.
25. 1921, XVIII, p. 131; 1923, XIX, pp. 50-51; 1924a, XIX, pp. 166-167; 1930, XXI, p. 123; and 1933a, XXII, p. 61.

rectly from this definition that one becomes liable to a sense of guilt only when one acquires a superego, which means only when one acquires a conscience.

Yet new difficulties appear nevertheless. Freud's immediate concern when he introduced the superego was to explain the moral development individuals born into civilized society undergo in early childhood. He had, of course, written about man's moral development in previous works. In particular, a decade before he had presented an explanation of the moral development the species underwent in its prehistory, an explanation in which the experience of a sense of guilt figured importantly.[26] At that time, however, his understanding of the sense of guilt was not especially theoretical and thus would not necessarily be compatible with the theoretical definition he later gave. In fact, as it turned out, the two were incompatible, and their incompatibility not only made the status of his theoretical definition uncertain but also brought forth the difficulties to which I've alluded. For Freud continued to affirm this earlier, phylogenetic explanation at the same time as he was expounding the later, ontogenetic one.[27] He steadfastly regarded the two as parallel constructions, though the incompatibility between the conceptions of the sense of guilt they entailed put them in conflict with each other.

A brief sketch of the phylogenetic explanation should make clear this conflict. Freud, in constructing this explanation, proceeded first by affirming Darwin's hypothesis that human beings in their prehistory lived together in small hordes in each of which a terrible and violent adult male ruled over the rest, which consisted of several adult females and their offspring – this violent ruler, the father of these offspring, having driven off every adult male, which is to say, every challenger to his monopoly on sexual relations with the horde's females.[28] Freud then supposed that the offspring, particularly the males, grew up loving and admiring this ruler as their father and protector but also hating and fearing him as their enemy and oppressor. Their ambivalence toward him thus paralleled the ambivalence young children growing up in civilized society have toward their parents. But unlike the latter, these young males, having reached adulthood and been expelled from the horde, acted on their shared wish to be rid of their father. They banded together, returned, and slew him. In the aftermath, Freud reasoned, their love for him resurged, and they suffered remorse. Freud saw in their remorse consciousness of guilt and concluded that it moved them to expiation, which took the form of their setting their father up, in the guise of a totem, as a deity and their instituting among them-

26. 1913, XIII, pp. 141-143.
27. 1923, XIX, p. 37; 1924a, XIX, pp. 167-168; and 1930, XXI, pp. 131-133.
28. 1913, XIII, p. 141; see also 1913, XIII, p. 125.

selves prohibitions on killing and incest. These expiatory acts, Freud held, marked the beginnings of religion and morality among human beings. In other words, Freud drew from this thought experiment the hypothesis that this train of events recurred in sufficiently many primal hordes to constitute a phylogenetic explanation of the origin in man of religious belief and acceptance of moral restrictions on conduct.

Now the conflict between this explanation and the later, ontogenetic one arises out of the different ways Freud brought the sense of guilt into these explanations. On the former, the sense of guilt, more exactly, a particular experience of it, is among the events and processes that explain how human beings as a species came to accept moral restrictions on their conduct. On the latter, by contrast, the events and processes that explain how a human being, born into civilized society, comes to accept moral restrictions on his conduct also explain how he comes to be liable to a sense of guilt, for above all they explain the formation in him of a superego, of which both acceptance of moral restrictions on conduct and a liability to a sense of guilt are aspects. Plainly, then, Freud had used in these explanations different and, in fact, incompatible conceptions of the sense of guilt, and the result was that he couldn't advance his theoretical definition and at the same time maintain his early, phylogenetic explanation without making his views viciously circular.

Freud brought this difficulty sharply into the open in Chapters 7 and 8 of *Civilization and Its Discontents*. He began his discussion in Chapter 7 by stating his theoretical definition, "The tension between the harsh super-ego and the ego that is subject to it, is called by us the sense of guilt,"[29] and three paragraphs later, in a passage I quoted earlier, he asserted what we already noted was a consequence of this definition. He wrote,

A great change takes place only when the authority is internalized through the establishment of a super-ego. The phenomena of conscience then reach a higher stage. Actually, it is not until now that we should speak of conscience or a sense of guilt.[30]

It is true that in the paragraph preceding this passage, Freud, perhaps mindful of the difficulty his review of his phylogenetic explanation would reveal, referred to a sense of guilt a child experienced before acquiring a superego, but at the same time he indicated that what he was referring to was only fear that the authorities on whom the child depended would withdraw their love, fear prompted by the thought that they might discover that he, the child, had disobeyed them. And the subsequent passage just quoted suggests that Freud did not mean his readers to regard this as, *strictly speaking*, a sense of guilt. Lat-

29.   1930, XXI, p. 123.
30.   Ibid., p. 125.

er in the discussion, then, after having developed what I've called the Niet-zschean account, Freud turned to his phylogenetic explanation for further il-lumination, and in the course of reflecting on it and, particularly, on the ex-perience of remorse at its crux, he brought out explicitly how it conflicted with the ontogenetic explanation he had just completed. Indeed, by presenting it as an explanation of how the species acquired a superego, he made the con-flict between the two direct and the difficulty this entailed unmistakable.

Freud's own proposal for resolving this difficulty involved his acknowledg-ing as applicable to different experiences the two conceptions of a sense of guilt he had been using all along. This proposal is most clearly stated in Chap-ter 8 where he summarized his understanding of how the concepts of super-ego, conscience, and a sense of guilt, among others, are related. The summary begins with statements that accord with the points he made at the beginning of his discussion in Chapter 7.

The super-ego is an agency which has been inferred by us, and conscience is a function which we ascribe, among other functions, to that agency. This function consists in keeping a watch over the actions and intentions of the ego and judging them, in exer-cising a censorship. The sense of guilt, the harshness of the super-ego, is thus the same thing as the severity of the conscience. It is the perception which the ego has of being watched over in this way, the assessment of the tension between its own strivings and the demands of the super-ego.[31]

But then it continues:

We ought not to speak of a conscience until the super-ego is demonstrably present. As to a sense of guilt, we must admit that it is in existence before the super-ego, and there-fore before conscience, too. At that time it is the immediate expression of fear of the external authority, a recognition of the tension between the ego and that authority.[32]

Of course, one could interpret Freud as proposing here no more than a ver-bal resolution to his difficulty. Accordingly, he was simply going back on his earlier restriction on applying the term 'sense of guilt' to experiences of fear and anxiety to which conscienceless children are liable when they disobey their parents, and was not at the same time conceiving these experiences any differently from before. As he initially described them in Chapter 7, they did not manifest genuine moral sensibilities. Thus, Freud wrote:

[A]t this stage the sense of guilt is clearly only a fear of loss of love, 'social' anxiety. In small children it can never be anything else, but in many adults. too. it has only changed to the extent that the place of the father or the two parents is taken by the larger human community. Consequently, such people habitually allow themselves to

31. Ibid., p. 136.
32. Ibid.

do any bad thing which promises them enjoyment, so long as they are sure that the authority will not know anything about it or cannot blame them for it; they are afraid only of being found out.[33]

On this interpretation, then, Freud's proposal introduced no substantive change in his conceptual scheme. It merely extended the range of the term, 'sense of guilt', to include certain experiences of fear and anxiety that didn't, despite their being classified as experiences of a sense of guilt, mark their subjects as moral beings, creatures who possessed genuine moral sensibilities.

But this interpretation leaves out the very experience reflection on which led Freud to propose his resolution, namely, the experience of remorse at the crux of his phylogenetic explanation. Freud expressly took this experience, and not those of fear and anxiety that small children have when threatened with loss of love, as exemplifying a sense of guilt had before the acquisition of a conscience, and he clearly regarded it as manifesting moral sensibilities. It implied consciousness of guilt and moved its subjects to expiation. Hence, we must conclude that Freud in proposing this resolution meant to be introducing a substantive change in his conceptual scheme. He meant to be allowing that the ambivalence characterizing the relations of children to their parents created in those children genuine moral sensibilities even before it led to their acquiring a conscience.

Curiously, at least one critic has interpreted Freud as working the other side of the street on this issue.[34] That is, he reads Freud as never ascribing genuine moral sensibilities to human beings. He bases this reading on Freud's characterization of the sense of guilt as a kind of anxiety, for he takes this characterization to imply that Freud conceived of the sense as essentially indicating a concern with personal security rather than moral rectitude. And without question Freud encouraged such an interpretation when, in giving his proposed resolution, he likened the sense of guilt to, and denominated as one of its types, a certain fear of external authority when he spoke of "two strata of the sense of guilt - one coming from fear of the external authority, the other from fear of the internal authority".[35] With regard to either stratum, Freud had in mind anxiety brought on by demands, threats, and other forms of pressure that came from an authority to whom one was subject; and the emphasis he gave to the parallel between anxiety caused by the pressures of an internal authority and anxiety caused by pressures of an external authority easily leads one to assume that the former was for Freud no more indicative of moral sensibilities than the latter.

33. Ibid., p. 125.
34. David Jones, "Freud's Theory of Moral Conscience," *Philosophy* 41 (1966): 34-57.
35. 1930, XXI, p. 137.

At this point one might begin to suspect that Freud's conceptual scheme is too unsettled to support the explanatory hypotheses he advanced. Indeed, given the last observation, one might dismiss the scheme, and with it Freud's theory, as incoherent. For one thing is certain: the remorse the brothers in Freud's phylogenetic explanation suffer over having killed their father cannot be characterized as fear of external authority. One might wonder whether remorse generally was well-characterized as fear or anxiety, but, be this as it may, anxiety produced by awareness of an external threat does not characterize the remorse suffered in this case. For the external authority, the father, being dead, poses no threat to his sons. They, of course, might be haunted by fantasies of his coming back to life and revenging himself on them, and consequently suffer anxiety over this imagined threat. But such anxiety would be independent of their remorse, for the remorse, on Freud's account, results from the resurgence in them of love for their father, and such fantasies would not be the product of love. Hence, to remove this incoherence from his scheme, Freud would have either to give up characterizing the sense of guilt as a kind of anxiety or to give up the example.

Of these two options the former entails much greater revision of Freud's theory. Freud took 'anxiety' to be a generic term for uneasy and distressful feelings that accompanied severe shock to one's emotional equilibrium or signaled a danger or threat to one's well-being,[36] much as Spinoza took 'pain' to be a generic term for an emotion that accompanied a lessening in one's powers of bodily activity and constituted a corresponding lessening in one's powers of thought.[37] Freud had long distinguished between two kinds of anxiety, which came to be called real and neurotic, according as the shock that was felt or the threat that was signaled had its cause in the external world or in the unconscious. This distinction then underwent change when Freud replaced the topographical model with the structural one. Accordingly, he redefined neurotic anxiety by replacing reference to the unconscious with reference to the id, and he introduced as a distinct kind of anxiety - moral anxiety (*Gewissenangst*, frequently translated as 'fear of conscience') - which he defined analogously by reference to the superego. The general idea, then, was that anxiety was an affective response to pressures that either put one under emotional stress, or, where overwhelming, shocked or severely upset one's emotional

36. 1933a, XXII, pp. 93-95.
37. Spinoza, *Ethics*, bk. 3. I have described Freud's understanding of anxiety in a way intended to allow for both anxiety that occurs as part of what Freud (1926, XX, pp. 166-167; 1933a, XXII, pp. 93-95) called a traumatic situation or traumatic moment and anxiety that signals to its subject what Freud (1926, XX, pp. 134-135; 1933a, XXII, p. 85) called a danger situation. Only the latter corresponds to the kind of anxiety Freud thought characterized the sense of guilt.

equilibrium. And different kinds of anxiety were then defined according to the different sources of pressure to which anxiety was a typical response. Thus, given the structural model and the understanding of anxiety as an experience of the ego, Freud defined three fundamental kinds – real, neurotic, and moral, according as the pressure to which anxiety was a response had its source in the external world, the id, or the superego.[38]

Now Freud usually characterized the sense of guilt as moral anxiety. The demands and reproaches of the superego, the demands and reproaches of conscience, create a tension between it and the ego, the response to which is anxiety, and such anxiety, when coupled with the appropriate thought, the thought that one has transgressed or in some way failed to comply with the demands of conscience, constitutes a sense of guilt. How Freud understood the coupling of this thought to anxiety, and, more generally, how he understood the relation the ideational component of an emotional experience bore to its affective component, is admittedly unclear. Indeed, it is as unclear as the fundamental conceptual issue about the relation of thought to emotion is difficult. But these interpretive questions and the corresponding conceptual issues needn't concern us here. For of more pressing concern is the question of how on this account of anxiety Freud conceived of the sense of guilt that precedes the acquisition of a conscience.

Clearly, the anxiety that characterizes this sense is real rather than moral.[39] It occurs in response to the demands and reproaches of an external authority and also in response to any actual punishment or threat of punishment that authority might inflict or make. And we can recognize in this fact the grounds Freud originally had for restricting the term 'sense of guilt' to experiences of moral anxiety. For he saw that the way one deals with real anxiety differs significantly from the way one deals with moral anxiety. In particular, because real anxiety is a response to pressures perceived as having their source outside of oneself, one can deal with it by trying to shield oneself from those outside pressures. By contrast, one cannot hide from one's conscience. Hence, disobedience to external authority need not generate real anxiety if one successfully conceals one's disobedience from that authority. Moreover, lest one think that no wrongdoer is ever so confident of having successfully concealed his wrongdoing that he is immune from feeling some anxiety over the possibility of discovery and the consequences that would then ensue, we can understand the difference in another way. On this alternative, real anxiety is felt in view of

---

38. 1933a, XXII, p. 85; see also 1923, XIX, p. 57.
39. "Parental influence governs the child by offering proofs of love and by threatening punishments which are signs to the child of loss of love and are bound to be feared on their own account. This realistic anxiety is the precursor of later moral anxiety" (1933a, XX, p. 62).

the possibility that one's disobedience will be discovered and, whether discovered or not, in view of the unpleasant consequence it portends, whereas moral anxiety is felt in view of the disobedience itself, that is, regardless of consequences. And this accords with Freud's own understanding. He writes,

A great change takes place only when the authority is internalized through the establishment of a superego. . . . At this point, too, the fear of being found out comes to an end; the distinction, moreover, between doing something bad and wishing to do it disappears entirely, since nothing can be hidden from the super-ego, not even thoughts.[40]

Furthermore, we can sharpen the difference between moral anxiety and the real anxiety a conscienceless person is liable to experience in response to the demands and threats of an external authority by bringing in Freud's idea that the sense of guilt manifests a need for punishment.[41] The most representative instances of moral anxiety, experiences of bad conscience, exemplify nicely this notion of a need for punishment. For one who suffers bad conscience typically seeks and finds relief in punishment. The bare recognition that one has failed to comply with the demands of conscience, that one has transgressed the moral law in the name of which one's conscience speaks, sets one's conscience against one, and one then suffers inner turmoil that is stirred by the harsh and biting reproaches one's conscience delivers. Further suffering, it seems, is what one's conscience requires as requital for one's transgression, and consequently one is moved to submit to punishment or to engage in some other form of penance or reparative action as the way to quiet one's conscience and recover some peace of mind. This familiar train of experiences suggests quite clearly Freud's notion of a need for punishment. The person afflicted with bad conscience needs punishment to remove the division within him that occurs when his conscience turns against him. He needs it to make healthy or whole the moral personality that has fragmented on account of his having disregarded or challenged the authority of his conscience.[42]

By contrast, the train of experiences we would describe in characterizing the real anxiety the conscienceless person is liable to experience in response to the pressures of external authority does not at all suggest Freud's notion of a need for punishment. Its theme, rather, is fear: fear of external authority, which is to say, fear of the punishment that authority has promised for disobedience. Thus, the conscienceless person, having disobeyed the authority to whom he is subject, regards the punishment promised for such disobedience as a danger to be avoided by concealing his act, or where concealment is impossible, to be

40. 1930, XXI, p. 125.
41. 1924a, XIX, p. 166 and 1930, XXI, p. 123.
42. See my "On the Right to Be Punished Some Doubts," *Ethics* 94 (1984): 191-211. [Chapter 2 in this volume.]

lessened by placating that authority. Unlike the person afflicted with bad conscience, he is not drawn to punishment as a remedy for what ails him. Having no conscience, he suffers no division within himself and likewise experiences no felt need for punishment.

Now this last point makes it plain that, as long as Freud characterized the sense of guilt as a kind of anxiety, he could not correctly maintain both that a sense of guilt manifested a need for punishment and that someone who had not yet acquired a conscience could nonetheless experience a sense of guilt. For the experiences of real anxiety that would, on the latter thesis, count exclusively as the experiences of a sense of guilt to which someone who lacked a conscience could be liable do not, as we have seen, suggest the notion of a need for punishment. We would not on their account ascribe to their conscienceless subjects such a need. To be sure, Freud would not have recognized this inconsistency in his conceptual scheme. But this is because he mistakenly equated these experiences of real anxiety with the experiences of remorse he believed showed that a sense of guilt could be had by someone who lacked a conscience. He saw in the latter, being genuine experiences of remorse, manifestation of a need for punishment and as a consequence assumed straightaway that the former also manifested such a need. But, as I've argued, these experiences of remorse cannot be construed as experiences of real anxiety, and therefore, if the sense of guilt is to be understood both as a kind of anxiety and as a manifestation of a need for punishment, the thesis that someone who had not yet acquired a conscience could nonetheless experience a sense of guilt must be jettisoned.

Still, we shouldn't jettison the thesis without first considering the experiences of remorse that led Freud to affirm it. To be sure, if one follows the rule of least revision in rendering Freud's conceptual scheme coherent, then, as I indicated earlier, one must strike from Freud's theory the conclusion he drew that these experiences exemplify a sense of guilt had by conscienceless people. This, of course, is not to say that the conclusion is false or unwarranted. Indeed, if warranted and true, it stands as a serious threat to Freud's theory when the theory's conceptual scheme has been rendered coherent in accordance with the rule of least revision. And the more serious the threat one takes the conclusion to be, the more inclined one will be to opt for a different way to render the conceptual scheme coherent. Happily, though, we can understand these experiences of remorse in ways that show them not to have the import Freud thought they had. The conclusion he drew was not warranted and so does not threaten what I'll call the favored rendering of his conceptual scheme.

Let us, to begin with, grant that Freud's thought experiment does issue in an example of remorse, that Freud did not err in holding that the several father-killers he imagined in the circumstances of a primal horde of human be-ings ruled by a terrible patriarch would, owing to the love they had for their victim, feel bad about their act and that this feeling is aptly called remorse. How then did the feeling arise? How did these killers come to feel remorse over their deed? One answer appeals to the killers' identification with their victim, which, we should note, is a large component of their love. Because they identified strongly with their victim, their terrifying father, they were dis-posed to put themselves in his place, to regard their act from his point of view. Hence, they were disposed to adopt hostile attitudes toward that act that matched the attitude their father would have adopted and to feel on its ac-count an emotion that reflected the emotion with which he would have react-ed (and perhaps did react) when threatened by violence from those who chal-lenged his rule. Thus, according to this answer, to understand their response one does well to compare it to a response children in our culture learn when they receive their first lessons in moral thinking. A young child ill-treats a playmate, and we then instruct him to think about how he would like it if someone treated him in the same way. Thus we invite the child to put himself in the place of his ill-treated playmate, to take up the same attitude toward his act that we suppose the latter has toward it and to feel on its account an emo-tion that reflects the emotion we suppose the latter feels. And we readily as-sume that the child will follow our suggestion, because we presuppose that he identifies with his playmate. Accordingly, when he does follow our suggestion, we should say that it served as a spur to moral reflection and experience that are grounded in identification. Now on this first explanation, of how the sons in Freud's thought experiment come to feel remorse over killing their father, we should understand the moral reflection they go through as similar to the reflection the child learns to undertake. But unlike the child, no instructor in-vites them to engage in moral reflection. Rather, such reflection and the emo-tional experience it arouses occur spontaneously, solely on the strength of their identification with their victim.

Consequently, when Freud writes,

This remorse was the result of the primordial ambivalence of feeling towards the fa-ther. His sons hated him, but they loved him, too. After their hatred had been satisfied by their act of aggression, their love came to the fore in their remorse for the deed.[43]

we should understand the resurgence of love he refers to as a strengthening of identification that underpins the sons' first remembering or imagining their father's reaction to a violent attack on his life by someone challenging his rule and then, so to speak, putting themselves in the place of this remembered or

---

43. 1930, XXI, p. 132.

imagined father, taking on his hostility toward their act and the anger and rage provoked in him. Thus his hostility and anger become in them self-condemnation and remorse, which is to say that their remorse is to be conceived on the model of anger directed against oneself. But it should now be clear that, on this explanation, the remorse the sons feel follows, and is a consequence of, certain acts of memory and imagination by which an external authority becomes internal. And, therefore, while we might agree that their remorse would count as a sense of guilt experienced before they had acquired a conscience as a fixed part of their moral personality, we should not agree that it would count as a sense of guilt experienced without reference to any internal authority. To the contrary, the beginnings of conscience, the introjection of external authority, here precede and explain remorse. Hence, we cannot say about such remorse *in the sense Freud intended* that it exemplifies a sense of guilt one can experience before acquiring a conscience. And the weak sense in which we can say this doesn't threaten the favored rendering of Freud's conceptual scheme.

One can, of course, defend Freud by arguing that we must assume from the way he worked out his thought experiment and from the conclusions he drew from it that he understood the remorse he attributed to the sons as preceding and initiating the process by which an external authority became in them internal and not, as the above explanation implies, as a byproduct of that process. In other words, the defender of Freud will argue, Freud understood the sons' remorse as arising directly out of the love they had for their father and not as a consequence of any acts of memory and imagination their identification with their father brought forth. The remorse they suffer is thus like the remorse Tolstoy describes Vronsky suffering in the aftermath of Anna Karenina's suicide.[44] For we recognize in Vronsky's remorse his abiding love for Anna as well as his judgment that he bears responsibility for her deterioration and demise.

Clearly, if this is the right reading of Freud, then the conception of remorse implicit in his thought experiment is that of an emotion to which one becomes liable when one develops love for another. In particular, on this conception, love for another makes one liable to feel remorse in the event that one brings about the death of one's beloved. The enmity one would naturally feel toward anyone who attacked someone one loved occurs as remorse and is felt toward oneself when one sees oneself as the attacker. In other words, on this conception, we are to understand remorse as reflecting ill-will and hostility toward oneself that arise naturally, in the same way that one would natural-

---

44. Leo Tolstoy, *Anna Karenina*, David Magorshak, trans. (New York: New American Library, 1961), pp. 772.

ly bear ill-will and behave hostilely toward another had he been responsible for the death of someone one loved. This conception is thus like the previous one in that it represents an understanding of remorse on the model of anger directed against oneself. But more important is the way in which it differs from the other.

On the previous conception, we explained remorse by reference to the anger its subjects imagined an external authority with whom they identified to have felt upon being attacked and to the disposition they had, in virtue of their identification with that authority, to put themselves in his place and so to adopt attitudes and feel emotions that matched and reflected ones he would have adopted and felt. By contrast, on the present conception, we explained remorse by appeal to an analogy with anger that arises directly out of love. That is, we explained it without reference to the hostile and angry responses of an external authority, nor, incidentally, did we refer to punitive responses or threats of punishment that an external authority typically makes. Indeed, on this conception, as the example of Vronsky's remorse makes clear, no reference to external authority is necessary to explain an experience of remorse. Hence, the love the sons in Freud's thought experiment had for their father and their recognition that they were responsible for his death would be the only facts one would need to cite to explain their remorse. And, in particular, one would not need to mention any recognition they had that they had disobeyed or attacked an authority to whose rule they were subject. The upshot of this is that remorse is, on this conception, an emotion distinct from a sense of guilt, for whatever else Freud meant by a sense of guilt, he meant an emotion or affect one experienced in recognizing that one had disobeyed or challenged an authority, either external or internal, to whose rule one was subject, the disobedience or challenge being in thought if not in deed. Consequently, the remorse Freud attributed to the sons does not exemplify a sense of guilt and so a fortiori does not exemplify a sense of guilt experienced before one acquires a conscience.[45]

Either conception, therefore, provides a way of understanding the sons' remorse that is consistent with the favored rendering of Freud's conceptual scheme. In other words, the results of his thought experiment do not, contrary to what Freud assumed, force one to the conclusion that a person might be liable to a sense of guilt before he acquired a conscience. In addition, each conception offers an account of the error Freud made in drawing this conclusion. Thus, according to the first conception, the error lay in his confusing cause and effect. That is, Freud failed to see that in attributing remorse to the

---

45. See my "Love, Guilt, and the Sense of Justice," *Inquiry* 25 (1982): 391–416. [Chapter 3 in this volume.]

sons he presupposed the very thing he meant to explain, their introjection of an external authority. On the other hand, according to the second conception, the conception one would, seemingly, have to invoke in defending Freud against the charge of confusing cause and effect, the error lay in Freud's assumption that an attribution of remorse was at once an attribution of a sense of guilt. That is, Freud failed to see that the emotion he inferred the sons would feel over the patricide they committed, while aptly called remorse, did not qualify on his understanding as a sense of guilt. Now given that one can persuasively defend Freud against the charge of confusing cause and effect, I'm inclined to think that this second account is the more telling. But regardless of where one locates the source of Freud's error, the main point is that the conclusion Freud drew from his thought experiment was unwarranted.

This point is especially important because it shows that the difficulties into which this conclusion led Freud are not endemic to his conceptual scheme. They disappear once one corrects the error we have rooted out from his discussion. And correcting this error, I've argued, means affirming the favored rendering of that conceptual scheme. The correction thus provides coherent foundations to the explanatory hypotheses that constitute Freud's theory of moral development. Moreover, it means, in particular, affirming, as true in virtue of the conceptual relation a sense of guilt bears to conscience, that a person becomes liable to a sense of guilt when and only when he acquires a conscience. The correction thus makes unequivocal Freud's claim to having explained by his account of how a superego is formed man's character as a moral being.

At the same time, the correction doesn't resolve all of the problems we've encountered in the course of our inquiry. There still remains unanswered the objection that this claim Freud made was spurious because he misconceived a sense of guilt as a kind of anxiety. It is no answer, our objector will argue, to point out that Freud distinguished several fundamental kinds of anxiety, including specifically moral anxiety, to which, given the favored rendering of his conceptual scheme, he can be taken to have restricted a sense of guilt. Anxiety, the objector continues, is no more a moral feeling when labeled 'moral' than when labeled 'real' or 'neurotic'. It is in the relevant cases to be understood as a distressful or uneasy feeling that intimates to its subject a danger or threat to his well-being. It is, in other words, an egoistic feeling, not a moral one. Its subject is properly the ego, which is the seat of all anxiety; and the ego's virtually automatic response to anxiety is to master it as best it can, to rid itself as best it can of distressful feeling, for the only end that guides the ego in this situation is to return to a calm and pleasurable state. The above comparison of Freud to Spinoza was thus more revealing than was perhaps realized. And once one realizes that Freud, like Spinoza, advanced an egoistic psychology, one will realize too that Freud's conception of a sense of guilt as a kind of anxiety entails that its subject lacks the moral perspective necessary for him to be experiencing genuinely moral feelings. One must, therefore, conclude that Freud failed to explain how human beings acquired truly moral sensibilities, that is, that he failed to explain man's character as a moral being.

Put in this way, the objection is plainly important and seemingly irrefutable. Indeed, I have no hope of refuting it here. Yet I do not think that we must concede that our inquiry has been more an autopsy than a piece of reconstructive surgery. The moral philosopher's charge against Freud of psychological egoism cannot so easily be made to stick. And even if one could make it stick, it might not be as damning of, or damaging to, Freud's theory of moral development, his theory of the origin in man of a conscience, as our objector thinks. Having accomplished our stated goal of finding in Freud's exposition a coherent conceptual scheme on which to base his theory, I should like to conclude by sketching two rather different answers to this objection, either of which leaves open the possibility that Freud's is a viable theory.

First, the objection rests on a crucial assumption, which we can question. The assumption is that for the purpose of ascribing emotions to someone that person and his ego are identical. Thus, in particular, if a person can be said to be experiencing a specific emotion, then his ego too can be said to be experiencing that same emotion. Now, of course, we could not hope to question this assumption or its corollary if Freud's conception of the ego were on all fours with Descartes'. For the Cartesian ego is identical with the mind, and on Descartes' psychology to ascribe an emotion to some man or woman, men and women being each a union of mind and body, is to ascribe that same emotion to the man's or the woman's mind while allowing in some cases, though not all, that the emotion is manifested in the behavior of his or her body.[46] But Freud's conception is definitely not the same as that of Descartes. For one thing, unlike the Cartesian ego, the ego as Freud conceived of it is not identical to the mind; rather, on his structural model, it is one of the mind's constituents. For another, it is a theoretical agent, and hence one can only acquire knowledge of its character and behavior through comprehension and application of Freud's theory. By contrast, the ego, as Descartes conceived of it, is not a theoretical agent; one acquires knowledge of its character and behavior, not through application of theory, but directly through self-observation. These differences broach the possibility of disparity, on Freud's conception, between the range of emotions one ascribes to a person and the range one ascribes to his ego. That is, they make it worth considering whether, on Freud's conception, one might ascribe a specific emotion to a person while ascribing a

46. Descartes, *The Passions of the Soul*, pt. 1.

different emotion to his ego, whether, in particular, one might ascribe a sense of guilt to that person while ascribing moral anxiety, regarded as a different feeling, to his ego.

The idea is that one might interpret Freud's theory as explaining a sense of guilt and the behavior it prompts by reference to moral anxiety and its theoretical context while regarding the two feelings as different. This explanation is admittedly paradoxical in that a moral feeling is being explained by reference to a seemingly amoral one. But the paradox is benign. It entails no contradiction. There is no more contradiction here than in the physicist's description of a stationary and motionless landmark, a Rock of Gibraltar, as constituted, according to atomic theory, of particles that are continuously in motion. The general principle in either case is that the properties and behavior ascribed to theoretical entities on the theory to which they are integral needn't be coincidentally shared or exhibited by the pretheoretical entities the character or behavior of which the theory is advanced to explain. Accordingly, as applied to Freud's theory, the principle allows that the ego can be thoroughly egoistic in the moral philosopher's sense while the human emotions and behavior the theory is advanced to explain are not. The point then is that to make good the charge against Freud's theory of psychological egoism, one must show that the principle does not apply in this way or does not apply at all. And this our objector has not done.

Second and independent of the first answer, we should question whether the distinction the objector draws between moral feelings and egoistic ones is as sharp as he takes it to be. In particular, we should ask, "If one regards the sense of guilt as a moral feeling, must one then dismiss the possibility of its ever being egoistic?" The objector clearly thinks that one must, but I suspect that he does so because of the logic he builds into his categories, the moral and the egoistic. For him it is true a priori. Yet attention to experience might result in second thoughts. Consider the person whose conscience forbids him from any involvement with evil and demands that he dissociate himself from the evildoing of others. At the same time his conscience is silent about and so does not require his seeking ways to remedy that evil or to put a stop to the evildoing. Thoreau spoke for such people when he wrote in his essay on civil disobedience:

It is not a man's duty, as a matter of course, to devote himself to the eradication of any, even the most enormous wrong; he may still properly have other concerns to engage him; but it is his duty, at least, to wash his hands of it, and if he gives it no thought longer, not to give it practically his support.[47]

47. Henry David Thoreau, "On the Duty of Civil Disobedience," *The Writings of Henry David Thoreau* (New York and Boston: Houghton Mifflin, 1906), v. 4, p. 365.

Of such people we may be inclined to say that they have an exaggerated concern for maintaining their own moral rectitude or securing their own blamelessness and insufficient concern for the suffering or hardship of others, which suffering or hardship is the evil to which their consciences forbid them from contributing. Moreover, whether or not we are inclined to make this criticism of them, we can agree that what would prompt the criticism is the egoistic quality of the moral outlook they have. So too we can recognize this egoistic quality in the qualms of conscience these people experience when they verge on becoming involved with evil in a way their consciences forbid. Their qualms are moral feelings, to be sure, but they are egoistic as well.

Consider too those people who, having acted wrongfully, show more concern for the guilt they have incurred than for any pain or injury they may have caused others to suffer. I have in mind here people who truly feel guilt over their wrongful conduct but show it in a way that manifests little sorrow over the suffering they have caused. Uneasy with themselves because they have done wrong and incurred guilt, they focus narrowly on cleansing their consciences, that is, on the specific expiatory acts required for the wrongs to be righted and the guilt to be removed. They offer apologies and reparations. They ask forgiveness and give assurances of good behavior in the future. But the solicitous manner in which they perform these acts inclines one to say that they do them more from a felt need to be purged of guilt than from appreciation of the hurt feelings they have caused or the damage they have done. Their feelings of guilt are genuinely moral feelings, but they are egoistic as well.

Contrary, then, to our objector's position, these qualms of conscience and feelings of guilt, although moral feelings, have nonetheless an egoistic character and, indeed, would be appropriately described as exemplifying anxiety: anxiety over potential complicity with evil and over actual incurrence of guilt. The contention that Freud misconceived the sense of guilt as a kind of anxiety is therefore questionable, as is the conclusion that he had failed to understand properly our moral sensibilities. On these issues, Freud, guided as he was by close study of the emotional lives of human beings, may have seen more deeply into man's character as a moral being than the moral philosopher, guided as he is by the categories and ideals that are central to his discipline.

93

5

Freud's later theory of civilization: Changes and implications

Freud in the last phase of his work gave increasing attention to questions about civilization, about its roots in and effects on human psychology. He was particularly interested in whether civilization on the whole helped or hindered human beings in their search for happiness, and he dealt with this question in two well-known books, *The Future of an Illusion* and *Civilization and Its Discontents*, the first of which he wrote in 1927 and the second in 1930. This essay is a study of differences between the views that he expressed in these two books. The differences indicate a shift in his outlook, and the essay represents an attempt to understand the reasons behind this shift.

I

The Future of an Illusion ends in optimism. Briefly, Freud's hopeful conclusion was this: Just as healthy individuals overcome their childish ways as they mature, as reason comes to play a greater role in the governance of their lives, so too healthy societies should overcome their primitive practices as they mature as science comes to play a greater role in the governance of their lives. Three years later, when he wrote *Civilization and Its Discontents*, Freud's optimism had dimmed. He ended the work on a somber note. No one, Freud observed, in this age of great technological advances can be confident that the struggle between life-giving and life-destroying forces that shapes civilization will not have a ruinous outcome. No doubt the rise of the Nazis and the Fascists during the intervening years partly explains this shift in his outlook. But his further reflections on the nature of civilization help to explain it as well. By the time he concluded *Civilization and Its Discontents*, Freud had come to see problems in the development of civilization for which the ascendancy of science was not an obvious remedy.

The primitive practice on which *The Future of an Illusion* concentrates is that of religion. Freud saw religion as demanding and extracting from mankind unnecessary sacrifices of happiness and doing so in the service of irrational beliefs. Thus his optimism in foreseeing its decline and eventual replacement by less cruel and more rational practices. Freud based this optimism on an

94

analogy he discerned between religion and obsessional neurosis.[1] In his view the degree of detail to which the analogy held, both in regard to origins and in regard to symptoms, warranted ascribing to civilization the same process by which individuals overcame the common obsessional neuroses of childhood. Essentially this process is one of gradually abandoning wishful and fanciful beliefs that were formed at an early age under the pressures of powerful feelings and drives that had not yet been tamed and channeled, and it occurs through the development of reason. That development brings increasingly intelligent reflections on the nature of things and an increasing confidence in those reflections, and as a result the system of irrational beliefs that immature minds naturally create and cling to gives way to a sounder view of the world. Thus the obsessions that are its products also lose their sway. Correspondingly, then, when social practices depend for their vitality on a system of beliefs that is similarly irrational and that similarly originates in immature thought, the development of science, which is to say the development of institutionalized reason, should have an analogous effect. The practices should decline as the system of beliefs they depend on gives way to sounder theories about the world. Religion, for Freud, was such a practice, and the diminishment in its influence was therefore a welcome sign.

Freud of course recognized that religion extended into areas of thought that were beyond the scope of science, and he acknowledged the historical importance of its teachings and doctrines in these areas. But he was unimpressed with defenses of religion that invoked these facts. In particular, he was unimpressed with the defense that invoked the importance of religion's teachings and doctrines in ethics, its traditional role in providing foundations for morality. Religion's defenders readily interpret this fact as a necessary truth, whereas Freud interpreted it as merely a historical one. Consequently, he rejected the underlying premiss of their defense, that godlessness meant amorality, and he dismissed as unfounded the common fear on which they liked to seize, that if God passed from the lives of men, nothing would be forbidden; all hell would break loose. Morality, Freud believed, could have other foundations than God's will, and accordingly he thought there was a possibility that human beings could be taught to accept morality's prohibitions and requirements without first investing them with religious significance.[2]

To be sure, Freud did not think this possibility existed at every stage of civilization. He did, however, think it existed at an advanced stage. And again he saw in the analogy between religion and obsessional neurosis reason to be optimistic. The very process by which the growth of science leads to the decline

1. 1927, XXI, pp. 42-44.
2. Ibid., pp. 40-41.

of religion should also expand the role of reason in the regulation of human relations. Rational acceptance of the prohibitions and requirements necessary for civilization's existence, acceptance based on a realistic assessment of human beings and their place in nature, should then replace acceptance based on illusions about such matters, illusions that have long served to allay certain deep-seated fears that have persisted since early childhood. At its most optimistic *The Future of an Illusion* contemplates a time when morality's prohibitions and requirements are not only divested of their religious significance but also subject to pruning and revision in the service of human happiness. At that time, Freud wrote, human beings will to a large extent he reconciled to civilization.[3]

How different his attitude in *Civilization and Its Discontents*! Yet one cannot say that Freud had been blindly optimistic in the earlier work and only later opened his eyes. For in its last chapter he expressed an awareness that his hopes for greater human happiness might themselves be founded on illusions about reason. In particular, he conceded that he might be overestimating the power of reason to master the emotional forces that gave religion a character analogous to obsessional neurosis. Perhaps, then, the doubt implicit in this concession grew in his mind and eventually brought about this change in his attitude. While he did not in *Civilization and Its Discontents* return to the analogy and its implications, he did take up questions about morality and the emotional forces that make it such a powerful factor in the inner life of human beings. And as he pondered these questions, he came increasingly to see morality, regardless of its foundations, as an irremediable source of human unhappiness. His view, by the end, leaves little room for hope that human beings, guided by reason, could remake morality into an instrument of their happiness and thereby become largely reconciled to civilization.

The first clear indication in *Civilization and Its Discontents* of Freud's doubts about the possibility of such a reconciliation occurs near the beginning of Chapter 3. Having traced human unhappiness to three sources, the degenerative character of our bodies, the merciless forces of nature, and human relations, Freud remarked:

As regards the third source, the social source of suffering, our attitude is a different one. We do not admit it at all; we cannot see why the regulations made by ourselves should not, on the contrary, be a protection and a benefit for every one of us. And yet, when we consider how unsuccessful we have been in precisely this field of prevention of suffering, a suspicion dawns on us that here, too, a piece of unconquerable nature may lie behind - this time a piece of our own psychical constitution.[4]

3. Ibid., p. 44.
4. 1930, XXI, p. 86.

This suspicion immediately gives birth to a new thought, which becomes the essay's major theme:

When we start considering this possibility, we come upon a contention which is so astonishing that we must dwell upon it. This contention holds that what we call our civilization is largely responsible for our misery, and that we should be much happier if we gave it up and returned to primitive conditions.[5]

From here through Chapter 4 Freud proceeded systematically to develop this theme. Then, in Chapter 5, he began to close in on the suspicion from which it issued.

The argument of Chapter 5 signals a definite break from the view that informs his earlier optimism. The propensity of men to aggress against each other, man's appetite for brutality and cruelty, which did not figure in the argument of *The Future of an Illusion*, makes its appearance in this chapter and is reckoned by Freud to be a threat to civilization of such magnitude that, to subdue it, society has to place seemingly excessive and unreasonable demands on its members. In other words, for civilized society to control human aggression, some of the demands of its morality must seemingly exceed, in the restraint and sacrifice they require, demands that one could reasonably hope human beings would accept and meet out of mature reflection on what was in their self-interest or in the interests they had in common. Freud put the point this way:

In consequence of this primary mutual hostility of human beings, civilized society is perpetually threatened with disintegration. The interest of work in common would not hold it together; instinctual passions are stronger than reasonable interests. Civilization has to use its utmost efforts in order to set limits to man's aggressive instincts and to hold the manifestations of them in check by psychical reaction-formations.[6]

Freud arrived at this conclusion from reflection on the extent to which civilized society fosters attachments of affection - libidinal ties, in his words - among its members. For Freud, all affection is originally sexual, and hence affectionate attachments that are not overtly sexual indicate the influence of an additional factor. In the absence of such a factor, Freud thought, civilized society would consist of people paired off sexually, working together cooperatively out of common interests that the necessities of life create, but otherwise unconnected. That this is manifestly not the case, that within civilized society friendships and affections extend broadly to include outlanders and strangers even, meant that some additional, "disturbing" factor must be at work.[7] And

5. Ibid.
6. Ibid., p. 112.
7. Ibid., pp. 108–109.

Freud concluded that this factor was human aggression: To preserve itself from this destructive force civilization had to foster and sustain widespread affection among human beings, and this task necessarily involved making excessive demands on human goodwill and self-control.

Freud offered as the one telling example the demand to love one's neighbor as oneself. Adopting the viewpoint of someone who had never before heard this demand, Freud argued that it was puzzling, indeed paradoxical. Love, after all, was something special, something to be given only to those worthy of it, something one could not give willy-nilly without greatly diluting its value for those who received it. Moreover, the demand was certainly nothing any sane person, knowing how unloving and selfish human beings could be, would agree to; for the advantages of treating complete strangers with the same love and concern one showed for oneself were small and improbable, while the dangers were just the opposite. In other words, to a rational individual concerned for his own well-being, even one mature enough to realize that to secure it he must work cooperatively with others, this demand would seem unreasonable and extreme. Yet its preeminence and authority in our civilization's morality, Freud maintained (having resumed his own voice and viewpoint), testifies to the importance to civilized society of binding its members together libidinally. Such ties among its members are necessary as a check on their own hostile impulses.

Once Freud concluded that civilization could not, without making demands of this sort, accomplish the vital task of fostering and sustaining affectionate attachments among human beings, his break from the hopeful views he expressed in *The Future of an Illusion* was complete. Those views included at their core the idea that human beings could learn to accept morality's prohibitions and requirements on rational grounds and independently of any religious belief. The grounds that Freud had in mind consisted of considerations of self-interest as they arose in circumstances in which one's survival and happiness depended on one's working cooperatively with others.[8] The circumstances of civilized society are circumstances of just this sort, and the central prohibitions and requirements of its morality, the prohibitions on killing and the use of violence, for instance, and the requirements of honesty and respect for property, constitute, from the perspective of self-interest, eminently reasonable terms of cooperation for someone placed in such circumstances. Thus Freud could contemplate human beings' eventually becoming largely recon-

---

8. See 1927, XXI, pp. 40–41, where Freud described the practical reasons that lead human beings to accept a prohibition on murder and drew from this case the lesson that moral prohibitions and requirements generally could be grounded on such practical considerations, particularly, those of "social necessity."

ciled to civilization: Once they came to a realistic understanding of themselves and their circumstances, they could so reform the morality that regulated their social relations as to exclude all prohibitions and requirements that, from the perspective of self-interest, constituted unreasonable terms of cooperation. The implicit assumption on which this hopeful view rested of course was that excluding such prohibitions and requirements would not gravely damage social cohesion, and this assumption serves to divide the views of *The Future of an Illusion* from those of *Civilization and Its Discontents*. The argument that we canvassed from Chapter 5 of the latter work rejects the assumption. To repeat the argument's conclusions, because of men's propensity to aggress against each other, "the interest of work in common would not hold [civilized society] together; instinctual passions are stronger than reasonable interests."[9]

It is not, we should note, incidental to this argument that it represents the propensity of men to aggress against each other as an instinctual disposition. Freud would not have regarded human aggression as *invariably* resistant to regulation by prohibitions and requirements that, from the perspective of self-interest, constituted reasonable terms of social cooperation if he had considered it as merely a form of conduct that humans engaged in or abstained from according as they thought it served their interests. For the argument to succeed, then, human aggression had to be both a central and an abiding part of human experience – and Freud challenged his readers to deny that it was. In particular, it had to be a phenomenon that would not largely disappear in a juster society or a more hospitable environment. Consequently, it was neither the bare fact of human aggression nor its amount that led Freud to his conclusions. Rather it was the instinctual character of the propensity behind it. Moreover, the more primitive and independent the aggressive instinct that gave the propensity this character, the stronger Freud's argument; and there is no doubt that when Freud advanced this argument, he conceived of the aggressive instinct as virtually primitive and independent of other instincts.[10] Ten years before, in *Beyond the Pleasure Principle*, Freud had revised his theory of the instincts in a way that made a place for an aggressive instinct of this sort, and in the argument we are now considering he filled it.[11]

9. 1930, XXI, p. 112.
10. Ibid., p. 122. The reason for the qualifier "virtually" is given in fn. 11 below.
11. The revision referred to here is Freud's introduction (1920, XVIII, pp. 38-41) of the death instinct into his theory. The death instinct, as the name implies, is destructive in character and originally directed onto oneself. On Freud's theory, however, instincts are readily modified and, in particular, readily take on new objects. Thus, though originally directed onto oneself, the death instinct can be easily turned around and directed outwardly onto others. When this happens, the instinct takes the form of an outwardly destructive or aggressive instinct. Freud initially took sadism to be the singular instance of the transformation of the death in-

Nothing of the revisions Freud made in *Beyond the Pleasure Principle* enters into the argument of *The Future of an Illusion*, however. In particular, Freud did not in the latter work specifically mention aggression as either a source of any of the unreasonable demands civilization placed on human beings or an obstacle to their becoming reconciled to it. This omission suggests that Freud's subsequent break from that work's hopeful views can be at least partly attributed to his coming firmly to accept the aggressive instinct as a virtually primitive and independent one. Indeed, if one were to read *The Future of an Illusion* as reverting to a much earlier stage in Freud's thinking about instincts, the stage at which he divided the primitive ones into two separate classes, those of sex and those of self-preservation, and conceived of aggression as deriving from and dependent on either, then one could cite the revisions he made in *Beyond the Pleasure Principle* to explain his subsequent loss of optimism.

A clear statement of this explanation must start with some general observations about Freud's theory of the instincts. That theory, no matter the stage of its development, presupposes as basic to an understanding of instinctual phenomena a distinction between reflex behavior, behavior that is an immediate response to some external stimulus, and motivated behavior, behavior that results from some inner spring. As Freud drew the distinction, the former is the product of the nervous system, the latter the product of instinct.[12] Accordingly, all human motivation, that is, all human desires and interests, can be traced to primitive instincts. Of course, one may have to pass in reverse through several transformations in tracing a desire or interest back to its original instinct, but that it must originate in some instinct directly follows from a principle that is implicit in the distinction the theory presupposes, the principle that all motivational energy is nothing but instinctual energy.

At the earliest stage of his theory, then, the stage to which I'm suggesting Freud may have reverted in writing *The Future of an Illusion*, all human desires and interests can be traced to the instincts of sex and self-preservation. A useful though admittedly oversimple way of putting this thesis is that human motivation in every instance is at bottom either sexual or self-interested. Now in view of this thesis, the possibility that human beings, once they achieved a

stinct into an aggressive instinct, an instance whose manifest erotic component is explained by the fusion of the sexual instinct with this aggressive instinct. See 1920, XVIII, pp. 53–54; 1923, XIX, pp. 40–41; and 1924a, XIX, pp. 163–164. Finally, in *Civilization and Its Discontents* Freud attributed acts of hostility and destruction that were not distinctly sadistic (i.e., that did not manifest erotic interests) to this transformation of the death instinct into an aggressive instinct. See 1930, XXI, pp. 117–122, where Freud reviewed these and other developments in his theory of the instincts.

12.   1915a, XIV, pp. 118–120.

mature and realistic understanding of themselves and their circumstances, could collectively reform the prohibitions and requirements regulating their social relations so that they constituted reasonable terms of social cooperation should not appear beyond hope. Indeed, this hope is substantially the same as that of classical utilitarians who, taking altruistic and egoistic motives to be the basic categories into which all human motives (or their elements) fell, saw the possibility of enlightened human beings' reforming their political institutions in ways that, while preserving social cohesion, would enable society to promote rather than impede people's interests in happiness. For Freud, of course, at this early stage of his theory altruistic and egoistic motives, when taken as basic, represented the sexual and self-preservative instincts. But making this substitution, one can say that, like classical utilitarians, he saw the possibility of enlightened human beings' rearranging their social relations in ways that, while preserving social cohesion, served their interests in happiness. The rearrangement would come about through their revising morality's prohibitions and requirements, and it would serve their interests in happiness in that it would afford them a decent chance of acquiring and satisfying desires whose satisfaction effectively, even if at several removes, gratified their sexual and self-preservative instincts. Under such arrangements, then, human beings would be largely reconciled to civilization: None of its prohibitions and requirements would compel renunciation of instinct beyond what, from the perspective of enlightened self-interest, would appear reasonable. Thus the hope that Freud expressed in *The Future of an Illusion* would seem to have a foothold in a version of his theory of the instincts that he had by the time of this work jettisoned.

There is still of course the question of aggression. Freud, however, as I mentioned above, conceived of aggression on this early version of his theory as deriving from and dependent on either the instincts of sex or those of self-preservation. Specifically, he conceived of the aggressive instinct as an instinct of mastery that was an ingredient in either of these primitive instincts. As an ingredient in the self-preservative instincts, the aggressive instinct prompts a person to exercise power over his environment when trying to satisfy his survival needs.[13] As an ingredient in the sexual instincts, it prompts a person to conquer objects of his sexual desire when those objects resist his charms.[14] On this version of his theory, therefore, the aggressive instinct, whatever problem

---

13. 1905, VII, pp. 193n.l; 1915a, XIV, pp. 137–139; 1930, XXI, pp. 117.
14. 1905, VII, pp. 157–158. Note that Freud here explained sadism as occurring when "the aggressive component of the sexual instinct . . . has become independent and exaggerated." Thus, in a sense, his later explanation (see fn. 11), which introduces the idea of the fusion of distinct instincts, sexual and aggressive, reverses the explanation at this earliest stage, which uses the idea of one of the instinct's components' breaking away from the others.

it creates for reconciling human beings to civilization, creates no more of a problem than either of the primitive instincts in which it is an ingredient. Consequently, if it is not utopian to think that enlightened human beings can collectively settle on prohibitions and requirements to regulate their social relations that, while preserving social cohesion, afford them a decent chance of gratifying their basic desires for sexual union and personal well-being, then it is not utopian to think that such human beings can learn to moderate the aggressive tendencies inherent in those desires so that those tendencies do not constitute a grave threat to civilized society. And conversely, if one thinks that, because of these aggressive tendencies, there exist grave problems in reconciling human beings to civilization, problems that would not arise in the absence of such tendencies, then one has good reason to abstract the aggressive instinct from other instincts and to conceive of it as primitive and independent of them. Thus the introduction of an aggressive instinct of this sort into a theory that had previously recognized as primitive, independent instincts only those of sex and self-preservation could explain a retreat from hopeful views about human beings' eventually becoming reconciled to civilization. In other words the revisions Freud made in *Beyond the Pleasure Principle*, inasmuch as they implicitly introduced into his theory an aggressive instinct conceived of as virtually primitive and independent, could explain his later retreat from such views. Put simply, the explanation would be that introducing this instinct removed the foothold the views had in the theory, though to apply it to Freud's retreat in *Civilization and Its Discontents* requires backdating, as it were, *The Future of an Illusion*.

II

So far we have followed the main argument of *Civilization and Its Discontents* to the point where Freud concluded that civilized society, in order to preserve itself from the destructiveness of human aggression, had to foster and sustain strong communal ties among its members, and this task necessarily involved making excessive demands on their goodwill and self-control. Freud's conclusion, then, was meant to establish that the set of prohibitions and requirements that regulate social relations in civilization, if social cohesion is to be preserved, had to include some that from the perspective of self-interest, even enlightened self-interest, appeared unreasonable. Morality, in other words, was revealed at this point to be an unavoidable obstacle to reconciling human beings to civilization.

Freud, however, did not stop here. His conclusion at this point was that morality represented an obstacle to reconciling human beings to civilization owing to its content; but he also saw that it represented such an obstacle, indeed a greater obstacle, owing to its mode of regulation. And he recognized too that the obstacle in this case, as in the other, resulted from the ways civilization contained and controlled human aggression. The final two chapters of *Civilization and Its Discontents* extend the argument to these conclusions and thereby bring to completion the development of the work's major theme.

By morality's mode of regulation I have in mind several features of the way morality governs our lives: the authority of its prohibitions and requirements, their stringency, their internalization, and the vigilance of their governance. These features come together in a conscience, which is morality's agent within our personality and the workings of which Freud assigned in his theory to the superego.[15] A short summary should suffice to make clear how these features are reflected in a conscience. Thus, first of all, the authority of conscience reflects the authority of morality, and it gives evidence of this authority in its judicial and punitive activity. To violate a dictate of conscience is to bring down on oneself its reproaches and irritations, which can be severe and unrelenting. Second, the importance of its authority corresponds to the stringency of the prohibitions and requirements it enforces, and traditionally conscience has enjoyed the reputation of having supreme authority over its possessor. Correspondingly, then, the stringency of the prohibitions and requirements it enforces has traditionally been regarded as maximal; all other social norms and personal concerns have to defer to moral prohibitions and requirements on questions of how a person should act. Third, conscience, in being morality's agent within our personality is the product of the internalization of morality's prohibitions and requirements, and the degree of their internalization is indicated by the degree to which conscience, in exacting obedience and punishing disobedience, operates independently of external direction and pressure. Last, that one cannot hide from one's conscience, that in its surveillance of one's thoughts and feelings it is all-seeing, attests to its vigilance and so to the vigilance with which morality governs our lives. To use Freud's simile, conscience is "like a garrison in a captured city," which civilization has installed in our personality to watch over us and to keep us in line.[16]

A rhetorical flourish, of course, is no substitute for argument. The analogy depicts conscience as an antagonistic force in our lives, and our summary of these four characteristic features of conscience suggests much the same picture. But while conscience may have seemed and may still seem like a hostile opponent, a stifler of one's wishes and a producer of anxiety and trouble, escape from which would bring true relief and peace of mind, and while its character may therefore give one reason to think that civilization, by implant-

---

15.   1923, XIX, pp. 35-37; 1930, XXI, pp. 123; 1933a, XXII, p. 66.
16.   1930a, XXI, pp. 123-124.

ing a conscience in each of us, pits its morality against our own happiness, it remains to be shown that the opposition between the two would not dissolve once reason achieved ascendancy in civilized society. Hence, if the workings of conscience are to be proof that morality's mode of regulation is by itself (i.e., apart from morality's content) an unavoidable obstacle to reconciling human beings to civilization, some argument is needed to show that the antagonism dividing a person from his conscience will not yield to reason. The final chapters of *Civilization and Its Discontents*, in which Freud gives an account of how the individual acquires a conscience, provide the argument.

Freud restricted his account to the development of this aspect of personality in early childhood.[17] The account, in its essentials, describes how young children come to have ambivalent attitudes and feelings toward their parents and how this ambivalence grows into an emotionally difficult situation. It then proposes that a conscience forms out of the way the child resolves this situation. Briefly, the condition of young children is that of helplessness and complete dependency on their parents for protection and nourishment. As a result they form strong, loving attachments to their parents. They love them as the very powerful protectors and providers in their young lives, and they see that protection and provision as sure signs of their parents' love for them. They also, of course, see their parents as the supreme authorities in their lives, and they then obey their parents out of fear, fear of the punishment with which parents threaten disobedience, but more important, fear of the loss of parental love that to them such punishment implies. Consequently, by learning to obey parental authority, children acquire a rudimentary ability to tell right from wrong. But they have not yet, at this stage, acquired a conscience; for as long as their motive of obedience is fear of loss of love, they have not yet internalized any of the prohibitions and requirements their parents have placed on them. Hence, unlike someone who possesses a conscience, a young child at this stage may sometimes feel safe misbehaving because he is confident that his misbehavior will go undiscovered. Children, in other words, in not yet possessing a conscience are not yet liable to be troubled by their bad behavior apart from whatever fear they may have of being found out. In not yet possessing a conscience, they are not yet liable to a sense of guilt. On these points Freud wrote directly: "A great change takes place only when the authority is internalized through the establishment of a super-ego. The phenomena of conscience then reach a higher stage. Actually, it is not until now that we

---

17. I am drawing here on a fuller exposition of this account that I have given elsewhere; see my "Remarks on Some Difficulties in Freud's Theory of Moral Development," *International Review of Psycho-Analysis* (1984): 207-225, esp. 208-215. [Chapter 4 in this volume, esp. pp. 67-78.]

should speak of conscience or a sense of guilt."[18] Explaining how this great change takes place, how parental authority becomes internalized authority, becomes then the object of Freud's account.

The key to his explanation is ambivalence. On the one hand, children love their parents as the most important benefactors in their lives. On the other, they develop a large amount of hostility toward them as the authorities who regularly prevent them from satisfying their urges and desires. These circumstances, moreover, are unstable. Obedience to parental authority provokes anger because it frustrates instinctual urges, and the child directs this anger at his parents whom he sees as responsible for the frustration. At the same time, the child cannot act on this anger for fear of losing parental love and so is forced to suppress it. Thus, once again instinctual urges, in this case the urges of an aggressive instinct, must be frustrated in the interest of preserving parental love, and this additional frustration breeds additional anger, and so on. The circumstances of the young child thus eventuate in unrelieved hostility toward parents as well as in manifest love for them. And because of the instability of these circumstances, the child's hostility grows in force, if not feeling, and so the ambivalence becomes increasingly difficult to live with. The child resolves this emotionally difficult situation, finally, by identifying with his parents. Unable to escape from or depose these authorities while preserving their love, the child incorporates them, as it were, into his personality and invests this part of his personality with all the hostility he had been unable to vent. Thus a severe conscience, a harsh superego, is formed as external authority becomes in the child internal. To quote Freud;

A considerable amount of aggressiveness must be developed in the child against the authority which prevents him from having his first, but none the less his most important, satisfactions, whatever the kind of instinctual deprivation that is demanded may be; but he is obliged to renounce the satisfaction of this revengeful aggressiveness. He finds his way out of this economically difficult situation with the help of familiar mechanisms. By means of identification he takes the unattackable authority into himself. The authority now turns into his super-ego and enters into possession of all the aggressiveness which a child would have liked to exercise against it.[19]

The principal idea in this explanation is that conscience owes its initial severity to the large amount of hostility that, at the time of its inception, has developed within the child. This idea, therefore, identifies the aggressive instinct as the original source of the power one implicitly attributes to a conscience in characterizing it as severe. By contrast, the idea's natural alternative, the rival hypothesis that the initial severity of a child's conscience is a contin-

18. 1930, XXI, p. 125.
19. Ibid., p. 129.

uation of severe treatment that the child has received from his parents, the external authorities on whose behavior his conscience is modeled, identifies no specific instinct as the original source of such power. Freud, however, rejected this rival hypothesis because it implies that the more severe a young child's conscience, the stricter his parents; and observation had shown that even children of very lenient parents developed severe consciences. What is more, though Freud did not express this point, the rival hypothesis does not fit the phenomena as Freud understood them. The idea that the severity of conscience is merely a continuation of the severe treatment one received from one's parents is incongruous with the view that a radical change in one's emotional and motivational capacities takes place with the acquisition of a conscience.

On the hypothesis Freud proposed, then, conscience draws its initial power from the store of hostility that has built up as a result of the young child's having repeatedly suppressed his aggressive impulses, and it thus works to redirect that hostility from its original, outward object, the child's parents, onto a new, inward object, the child himself. This redirection of the hostility establishes conscience as an antagonistic force in one's life, and the antagonism is typically exhibited in "bad" conscience or a sense of guilt. Freud then further proposed that the same process explained how conscience continued to be an antagonistic force in one's life after the initial store of hostility had been exhausted. After all, with the acquisition of a conscience, one is regularly forced to renounce the satisfaction of urges and desires in order to meet its demands, and many of these urges and desires derive wholly or in part from one's aggressive instinct. Thus conscience renews itself by tapping the power of the aggressive impulses one suppresses in placating it. It takes aggression that is directed outward onto objects in the world and, using its energy for its demands, reproaches, and irritations, turns that aggression back onto its possessor. As Freud summarily put it, "conscience arises through the suppression of an aggressive impulse, and ... it is subsequently reinforced by fresh suppressions of the same kind."[20]

The real work of conscience therefore, as Freud represented it in *Civilization and Its Discontents*, is to block and deflect its possessor's aggressive instinct so that it does not realize its destructive aim. Civilization, Freud maintained, implants a conscience in each of us to do this work. We are thus invited to see conscience as a device by which civilization ingeniously turns to its advantage antisocial drives that are part of every human being's native endowment and that, if allowed to realize their aims, would create an environment too hostile

20. Ibid., p. 130.

for civilized life to go forward. Indeed, in Freud's view, implanting this device in each of us is the most important method that civilization uses to disarm the aggressive forces in all of us that threaten to destroy it.[21]

Freud's view, it should now be clear, constitutes an argument for the notion that the workings of a conscience cannot be brought fully within the control of its possessor's reason. And while the argument is only implicit in the text, one can easily reconstruct its last stages. Thus, to begin with, the thesis about the real work of conscience puts into question the ideal of a mature conscience working in the service of its possessor's happiness. A conscience that did not trouble one with reminders and urgings more often or insistently than was reasonably necessary, that did not make unwarranted accusations, that did not censor mere thoughts and wishes, and that did not criticize or condemn more harshly than one's conduct deserved might not, if typica! of most people, succeed in doing its real work. For it might not use up enough of the energy of our aggressive drives to preserve civilization from the hostility and brutality of which human beings are capable and which gravely threaten its cohesion. Furthermore, because conscience draws its power directly from the impulses of the aggressive instinct, the level of its activity is to a significant degree a function of the amount of aggression that it has suppressed, and so to a corresponding degree is independent of rational regulation. Reason, in other words, because it cannot come between conscience and the source of its power, has only a limited influence on its severity.[22]

Nor is this last point a purely theoretical conclusion. Freud, as we saw, found evidence for his account in the observation that even children of very lenient parents develop severe consciences. In addition, he was struck by the common observation that the more virtuous a person is, the harsher his conscience treats him.[23] This paradox, as he called it, openly invites a psychoanalytic explanation, and he used it to stake his hypothesis that the instinctual impulses whose suppression conscience compels supply it with new power for compelling subsequent suppressions. Both observations, then, guided Freud's thinking as he worked out his account. The first implies that the severity of a conscience can exceed whatever model of reasonable and fair-minded authority a child's parents present, and the second implies that its severity, contrary to reason, is not proportional to one's actual guilt. Each therefore gives evi-

21. Ibid., p. 123.
22. Freud made this point even more clearly in *The Ego and the Id*. Thus he wrote, "Although [the superego] is accessible to all later influences, it nevertheless preserves throughout life the character given to it by its derivation from the father-complex - namely the capacity to stand apart from the ego and to master it" (1923, XIX, p. 48; see also 1923, XIX, pp. 55-59).
23. 1930, XXI, pp. 125-126. See also 1923, XIX, p. 54.

dence of reason's limited influence on the severity of conscience, and it remained for Freud to determine, using the resources of his theory, the instinctual factor at work and its method of operation.

Near the close of his discussion of conscience in *Civilization and Its Discontents* Freud declared that his intention had been "to represent the sense of guilt as the most important problem in the development of civilization and to show that the price we pay for our advance in civilization is a loss of happiness through the heightening of our sense of guilt."[24] Our sense of guilt, on Freud's conception of it, expresses the antagonism that divides us from our conscience; and because conscience uses the power of the aggressive instinct to do its work, this antagonism, he had argued, is inherent in its workings. Morality therefore, owing to its mode of regulation in advanced civilization, that is, once its authority becomes internalized, far from being something human beings could remake into an instrument of their happiness, becomes an intransigent source of human unhappiness. For Freud this argument, even more than the argument of Chapter 5, confirmed the suspicion he entertained early on in his inquiry. The aggressive instinct is that "piece of unconquerable nature" - that "piece of our own psychical constitution" - that defeats every effort we make to regulate our social relations in a way that furthers our happiness. At this point Freud's shift away from the optimistic conclusions he reached in *The Future of an Illusion* is most pronounced.

III

Freud's shift away from these conclusions raises questions that he did not himself address. Above all, it raises a question about how much of the optimism he expressed in *The Future of an Illusion* the argument of *Civilization and Its Discontents* implicitly retracts. It retracts, as we have seen, the optimistic conclusion about human beings' eventually becoming reconciled to civilization. But the question is whether it also retracts the optimistic conclusion about human beings' eventually overcoming their illusions about themselves and their place in the world. Specifically, does it retract the conclusion about human beings' eventually abandoning their religious beliefs? Freud based these conclusions, it is worth recalling, partly on the idea that morality could have other foundations than God's will and that human beings could learn to accept its prohibitions and requirements in light of them. And since he thought these alternative foundations created the possibility of revising morality in the service of human happiness and thereby reconciling human beings to civilization, the argument of *Civilization and Its Discontents* in cast-

24. Ibid., p. 134.

ing doubt on this possibility indirectly challenges its underlying idea that these foundations are a real alternative to religious doctrines (i.e., that the notion of humans learning to accept moral prohibitions and requirements in light of the former rather than the latter is a real possibility). Hence, the other conclusions Freud based on this idea are also brought into question. Whether the argument implicitly retracts them, however, is something still to be settled.

That it retracts the general conclusion about human beings' eventually overcoming their illusions about themselves and their place in the world seems fairly clear. Unhappiness and the wish for escape that naturally accompanies it give rise to a need for illusion when the unhappiness is deep and the prospect of escape is nil; and *Civilization and Its Discontents* in its conclusion places human beings in just such a condition. Of course, it is possible, at least abstractly, that with the advance of science and reason in civilized society people could collectively learn to resist the pressures of this need, but optimism on this score could not be firmly based on such speculation. Bearing in mind, then, the corrosive effects of cynicism on the human spirit, we may conclude that the argument of *Civilization and Its Discontents* implies the continued importance of illusion to keeping up the authority of morality. That the argument has this implication, however, does not mean that it implies the continued importance of religious beliefs to keeping up morality's authority. There may be, after all, other beliefs that can serve this purpose. Consequently, whether the argument retracts the specific conclusion about human beings' eventually abandoning their religious beliefs remains an open question.

The argument, let us note, does not directly conflict with the main grounds on which Freud drew this conclusion, the analogy between religion and obsessional neurosis conjoined with his understanding of how individuals who suffered from such neurosis overcame it. Rather, it implies the continued existence of a motive for religious beliefs that, according to the optimistic views of *The Future of an Illusion*, was destined to disappear. And while the continued existence of this motive clearly makes Freud's inference from analogy more uncertain, it does not eliminate the basis for his conclusion. The conclusion, then, is not retracted by the argument.

At the same time, its basis would be rather shaky if religious beliefs were the only ones that could plausibly satisfy this motive. That is, if the need for illusion that the unhappiness arising from the possession of a conscience created could plausibly be satisfied only by religious beliefs - specifically, the belief in an almighty god in whose commands moral prohibitions and requirements originated and obedience to whom offered hope of protection and relief from suffering, then the staying power of religion might well prove great enough to withstand the skepticism of science even as science and reason expanded their influence. In other words, Freud's conclusion about the eventual decline of religion, a conclusion he reaffirmed in later works,[25] would be much less threatened by the argument of *Civilization and Its Discontents* if secular beliefs that established the underpinnings of morality's authority and promised rewards for complying with its prohibitions and requirements could replace in the minds of human beings the religious beliefs that served these purposes.

Furthermore, one can find in the ethical and political writings of certain modern philosophers ideas that, if they could gain widespread acceptance, presumably in some popularized form, would be suitable secular replacements for these religious beliefs. I am thinking, in particular, of ideas that have emerged with the rise of democratic institutions in the West. These ideas, whose classical elaboration occurs in works by Rousseau and Kant, constitute an egalitarian creed.[26] On this creed, each fully rational human being, in virtue of his or her rational powers, is capable in principle of joining together with other similarly rational human beings to form a democratic republic in which all participate as equal, lawmaking citizens. What is more, the creed holds that each of us is in fact joined together with others under the common rule of morality, and the moral community we thus form is a realization of this notional democratic republic. Accordingly, morality's prohibitions and requirements are prohibitions and requirements we impose on ourselves. They originate in laws that we, as the legislators of this community, make and adopt. Correspondingly, then, morality's authority derives from our own legislative authority. That is, it derives from the community's sovereignty over its members, a sovereignty in which each of us, as an equal member of its legislature, partakes. Compliance with morality's prohibitions and requirements is therefore, in effect, obedience to laws that one gives to oneself. So in living a moral life – fully complying with morality's prohibitions and requirements out of recognition of their authority – one achieves a kind of freedom, which Rousseau called moral freedom and Kant called autonomy. It is freedom that comes from being subject to no alien authority, from being ruled by no other laws than laws of one's own making. And the inner satisfaction that such freedom brings more than compensates for the loss in gratification of instinctual urges and desires that obedience to moral law entails.[27] Or so the creed promises.

To be sure, these ideas do not correspond nearly as closely to the circum-

25. E.g., 1933a, XXII, p. 168.
26. Specifically, Rousseau's *The Social Contract* and Kant's *Groundwork of the Metaphysic of Morals* and *Critique of Practical Reason*.
27. See Rousseau, *The Social Contract and Discourses*, trans. G. D. H. Cole (New York: E. P. Dutton, 1950), pp. 18–19 and Kant, *Critique of Practical Reason*, trans. L. W. Beck (Indianapolis: Bobbs-Merrill, 1956), pp. 121–123.

stances of the young child as the religious beliefs they would replace, and therefore they do not answer nearly as directly as those religious beliefs the fears that human beings carry forward from these circumstances into adulthood. God, after all, is a much closer analogue of the parents of our early childhood than the supreme legislature of a democratic republic, and the protection and relief from suffering that God bestows come much closer to the benefits of parental love than moral freedom and the inner satisfaction it brings. Nevertheless, these ideas, because they could establish the underpinnings of morality's authority and promise substantial reward for obeying its laws, could be true descendants of the young child's beliefs about parental authority and parental beneficence and so the analogues of those beliefs within the egalitarian creed. Consequently, despite their greater distance from the circumstances of early childhood, they could still come to replace religious beliefs as the latter, under the pressure of an expanding scientific culture, became increasingly difficult to accept.[28] This conclusion, it should be clear, is not meant to be a prediction. The point is merely to show that it represents, within the framework of Freud's theory, a real possibility and as such keeps Freud's optimism about the eventual decline of religion from being undermined by his argument in *Civilization and Its Discontents*. The irony of this, though, is that Kant's ethics, which Freud liked to cite for its seeming expression of traditional religious morality,[29] is in fact no friend of such morality and actually rescues Freud's conclusion about religion's downfall from the implications of his own later argument.

IV

This essay has examined the shift in Freud's outlook that the difference between his reflections in *The Future of an Illusion* on the development of civilization and his reflections in *Civilization and Its Discontents* on the same subject

28. One might also see their replacing religious beliefs as a further development in the internalization by human beings of morality's prohibitions and requirements. Accordingly, the replacement of God's legislation with self-legislation, of the idea that moral laws originate in God's authority with the idea that they originate in one's own authority, would result from one's identifying with one's conscience. And while identification in this case would be with an internal figure rather than an external one, it would nonetheless seem, in view of the great tension that possession of a conscience creates, amenable to psychoanalytic explanation as (once again) identification with the aggressor. Moreover, it corresponds to Freud's belief that the growth of intellect and the increasing internalization of morality are characteristic of the advance of civilization. See 1933b, XXII, pp. 214-215.

29. 1933a, XXII, pp. 61 and 163. This view of Kant's ethics is also implicit in Freud's observation that the Categorical Imperative is the heir to the Oedipus Complex; 1923, XIX, p. 35 and 1924a, XIX, p. 167.

THE SOURCES OF MORAL AGENCY

reveals. Settled changes in Freud's theory help to explain this shift, but the shift was not itself a settled change. Indeed, in his next major work, his *New Introductory Lectures on Psychoanalysis*, Freud appears to have shifted back toward the outlook he expressed in *The Future of an Illusion*. Thus, in its last lecture, which summarizes the argument of *The Future of an Illusion*, he wrote:

Our best hope for the future is that intellect - the scientific spirit, reason - may in the process of time establish a dictatorship in the mental life of man. The nature of reason is a guarantee that afterwards it will not fail to give man's emotional impulses and what is determined by them the position they deserve.[30]

No new theoretical reflections, however, accompany this apparent restatement of his earlier hope. In particular, nothing is said to modify his account of the aggressive instinct's effects on morality's content and mode of regulation or to suggest how, despite these effects, morality could have foundations that enabled it to be an instrument of human happiness. Freud, it would appear, did not himself fully appreciate the implications of his argument in *Civilization and Its Discontents*.

30.   1933a, XXII, p. 171; cf. 1933b, XXII, p. 213.

6

Freud, naturalism, and modern moral philosophy

"The moral law," Kant wrote in his most searching analysis of morality and its origin in practical reason, "... [provides] a fact absolutely inexplicable from any data of the world of sense or from the whole compass of the theoretical use of reason, and this fact points to a pure intelligible world."[1] The fact to which Kant here refers is the fact of motivational force that is inherent in the consciousness of the moral law. On Kant's analysis, its great import lies in the impossibility of tracing this force to the operations of any natural appetite or passion, for this impossibility, Kant held, shows that the force wholly originates in the operations of reason. Accordingly, he dubbed the fact "a fact of reason."

Reason in this case, because it works to determine the will rather than enlarge the understanding, operates as a practical rather than a theoretical faculty, and because these operations of practical reason are disconnected from those of natural appetite and passion, they occur spontaneously, undetermined by the forces of nature. It follows then, Kant concluded, that when we act morally, that is, when we act from recognition of what the moral law requires and for no other reason, we act freely. It follows too that we act autonomously, for the law that we recognize as requiring this action and that thereby determines our will is the law of our own reason and not that of some external agency. As creatures possessing natural appetites and passions, we belong to the sensuous world, the world in which stimulation of the senses whets our appetites, stirs our passions, and so gears us for action. As creatures possessing reason, we belong to the intelligible world, the world in which the legislative processes of our reason alone determine our choices and decisions. In the former world, we live as integral parts of a system of nature. In the latter, we live as independent members of the Kingdom of Ends. These metaphysical doctrines, which should put us in mind of similar doctrines expounded by Plato and Augustine, identify Kant with the dominant spiritualist tradition of Western philosophy and Christian thought, an identification that later parts of his second *Critique* confirm.

Much of the opposition in contemporary philosophy to this tradition of

---

1. *Critique of Practical Reason*, L. W. Beck, trans. (Indianapolis: Bobbs-Merrill, Co., 1956), p. 44.

Christian spiritualism draws its strength from the rise of modern science. That movement consists largely in the progress of the natural sciences toward realizing the ideal of bringing all parts and processes of nature within the scope of scientific theory, and its success, as measured by the enormous range and complexity of natural phenomena that these sciences now explain, has greatly enhanced the credibility of this ideal. Its being a credible ideal, however, does not alone defeat spiritualist doctrines, like Kant's, that place some part or process of nature beyond the reach of scientific explanation, for two equally credible thoughts can nonetheless contradict each other. Naturalism, the belief in the sufficiency of scientific theory for explaining all that belongs to nature, though it has, owing to the success of the natural sciences, become the leading view in contemporary philosophy, has not on the basis of that success alone subverted spiritualist doctrines. To subvert these doctrines requires cogent, scientific explanation of the very part or process of nature that the doctrines deny is wholly explicable within the natural sciences. To subvert Kant's and similar doctrines about the human spirit requires, that is, cogent, scientific explanation of the motivational force that moral thought and judgment typically have, explanation according to which this force is understood as a wholly natural phenomenon. Without such explanation, the opposition of naturalism to these doctrines and the spiritualist tradition they reflect would amount to little more than flat denial of the metaphysics they affirm. It would amount, in other words, to little more than contradiction.

No theory has established a stronger claim to having developed cogent, scientific explanations of moral motivation than psychoanalysis. Indeed, for much of this century psychoanalysis, along with Darwin's theory, has enjoyed a reputation of having clinched the case against Christian spiritualism. To be sure, it has also had plenty of detractors both inside and outside the natural sciences. Its methods and the theoretical harvest they have yielded remain controversial. Its founder and his followers and heirs continue to attract obloquy. Yet despite these objections and attacks, its acceptance in intellectual and academic circles has been sufficiently broad and enduring to secure its claim of having pushed the program of the natural sciences as deeply into areas of moral and social psychology as any rival theory of our mental life. Consequently, for naturalism, psychoanalytic explanations represent as powerful an argument as any against doctrines that except human beings, qua moral agents, from full incorporation into nature.[2]

---

2. One recent development of this argument, which attempts to show how well psychoanalytic explanations can account for the special authority Kant attributed to moral principles, has been undertaken by Samuel Scheffler. See his *Human Morality* (New York: Oxford University Press, 1991), pp. 73–97.

How powerful an argument they represent is the subject of this essay. In taking up this question, I will focus on Freud's theory in particular. Although there have been many developments and innovations in psychoanalysis since Freud, his theory still remains the standard for any general study of psychoanalytic explanation. It still serves as the authoritative statement of the essential ideas of psychoanalysis, the ideas on which its distinctive explanations of human conduct and the conscious thoughts and feelings it manifests draw. These explanations hold that such conduct, thought, and feeling are the work of the subject's unconscious mind, the thoughts and wishes it contains, and the inherited drives from which they derive their psychic force. They are what distinguish psychoanalysis from previous theories of the mind and warrant Freud's claim to having significantly advanced our understanding of human psychology. One might, then, in raising the question of how powerful an argument for naturalism these explanations represent, treat it as a question about this claim. I do not, however, intend to treated it in this way.

Rather I want to grant that Freud's theory represents a significant advance in psychology, particularly an advance over the earlier theories in the field that explained human conduct, thought, and feeling as entirely the products of natural forces. For the question that interests me is whether Freud's theory, considered as an advance over earlier naturalistic theories of psychology, successfully answers the powerful objections that Kant and other defenders of doctrines opposed to such naturalism raised and that none of these earlier theories seems able to answer satisfactorily. This question provides the more telling test of how powerful an argument against those doctrines his explanations represent. It is more telling because the power of his theory to defeat those doctrines is more appropriately gauged by the success of the answers it can give to powerful objections whose premises are all consistent with if not directly supportive of the doctrines than by the significance of whatever advance it has made over earlier naturalistic theories of the mind. Indeed, while it would be easy to conclude from the differences between these earlier theories and Freud's that his, unlike its predecessors, answers these objections successfully, I will argue, to the contrary, that it does not. The doctrines of the spiritualist tradition that oppose our seeing all human thought and conduct as natural phenomena, however far out of favor in contemporary philosophy they may have fallen, remain, I will argue, undefeated by this most influential representative of the natural sciences.

I

Let us call these doctrines 'doctrines of human exceptionalism'. Kant's fact of reason is one example. Others, variants of which find expression in Kant's philosophy, are intuitionist doctrines about the supersensibility of value, Christian doctrines about the divine character of conscience, and libertarian doctrines of free will. All of these doctrines share the idea that something about the moral powers of human beings, our intellect, our sensibilities, our will, sets us apart from beasts. The difference the idea supposes between us and the beasts is this. Beasts belong completely to the natural world. They are creatures whose thoughts and behavior are entirely products of natural forces. While human beings have an animal nature in common with beasts and thus much of their thought and behavior is similarly a product of natural forces, they also, unlike beasts, possess a moral personality in virtue of which their thoughts and behavior have a moral quality and as a result of which not all of those thoughts and behavior are attributable to natural forces. Human beings, therefore, do not belong completely to the natural world. No one has expressed this idea of the profound difference between man and beast more powerfully than Rousseau.

> This passage from the state of nature to the civil state produces quite a remarkable change in man, for it substitutes justice for instinct in his behavior and gives his actions a moral quality they previously lacked. Only then, when the voice of duty replaces physical impulse and right replaces appetite, does man, who had hitherto taken only himself into account, find himself forced to act upon other principles and to consult his reason before listening to his inclinations. Although in this state he deprives himself of several of the advantages belonging to him in the state of nature, he regains such great ones. His faculties are exercised and developed, his ideas are broadened, his feelings are ennobled, his entire soul is elevated to such a height that, if the abuse of this new condition did not often lower his status to beneath the level he left, he ought constantly to bless the happy moment that pulled him away from it forever and which transformed him from a stupid, limited animal into an intelligent being and a man.[3]

Freud, as I have already indicated, was not the first major thinker to depart from these traditional doctrines of human exceptionalism. He was not the first to treat the moral thought and behavior of human beings as wholly natural phenomena. Unquestionably, some ancient Greek deserves the honor: Epicurus, perhaps, or Aristotle, or someone even earlier. In any case, Hobbes and Spinoza, in the seventeenth century, and Hume, in the eighteenth, presented theories of human psychology on which all human thought and behavior, and so a fortiori all moral thought and behavior were explicable by principles of nature. Their theories differed importantly from Freud's, though, in that they represented mental phenomena, which is to say,

---

3. *The Social Contract*, Donald Cress, trans. (Indianapolis: Hackett Publishing Company, 1987), bk. I, ch. viii.

thoughts, feelings, desires, imaginings, and the like, as states of a single, undivided subject. Hobbes took this subject to be the whole person instead of the mind or soul of a person, for his materialism made him skeptical of talk of minds and souls. Spinoza, by contrast, took it to be a human mind, but for him the human mind was the same thing, under a different aspect, as the human body, so special division of the human mind made no sense on his system. And Hume too took the subject of mental phenomena to be a mind, but for Hume the mind was just a convenient fiction, something we invent to unify the disparate images and feelings succeeding one another in what James later famously called the stream of thought. Consequently, none of these great thinkers had a conception of the mind as a divisible realm of thought. None entertained the hypothesis, at the heart of Freud's theory, that the mind was divided into separate regions or domains, tensions between which produced various thoughts and behavior including the thoughts and behavior that spring from the moral powers of human beings.

Indeed, until Freud, the conception of the mind as divided into separate domains belonged principally to rationalist theories of moral psychology that represented reason as pitted against appetite and passion. Such theories went hand in glove with the traditional doctrines of human exceptionalism, which is of course not to say that every believer in such doctrines subscribed to one or another of these theories or that every subscriber to the latter believed the former. Still, because reason has, since the Greeks, been regarded as an essential human trait that distinguishes humans from other animals, representing it as possessing ideas and power that do not come from nature and thus as a counterforce to appetite and passion has been a common theoretical strategy among those who do believe these doctrines. Kant's moral psychology is the preeminent example of modern philosophy. But a slew of other rationalist theories, beginning with Plato's ethics, exemplify the strategy as well.

This strategy, it is important to note, amounts to more than distinguishing reason from appetite and passion. In particular, it amounts to more than taking them to be distinct mental faculties. Hume, after all, included such distinctions in his theory, but the distinction he made between reason and passion, for instance, merely followed his fundamental distinction between ideas and impressions, thoughts and feelings, and did not entail the sort of opposition that suggests a conception of the mind as divided into separate domains. Specifically, it did not entail that reason and passion ever opposed each other as forces. By contrast, the rationalist distinction entailed such opposition because rationalists attributed to reason the power to influence its possessor's will. Thus on rationalist theories of moral psychology conflicts between reason and passion consisted in the opposition of motivational forces, each striving to determine the will. Moreover, these theories further divided reason from passion by holding that ideas and principles peculiar to the former were essential to its operations but inessential to the latter's. Passion, according to these theories, could be excited and prolonged solely by sensory experience or its mnemonic residue, whereas reason required ideas and principles peculiar to its domain, even when it operated on materials furnished by the senses, memory, or imagination.

Many of these ideas and principles were, to be sure, ideas and principles of logic. But not all were. Rationalist theories also included in the domain of reason the fundamental ideas and principles of morality. Indeed, their inclusion was essential to the theories' account of reason's power to influence the will. For that influence had to be transmitted through practical thought, and these ideas and principles were the materials of practical thought that effected the transmission. Thus, the theories typically counted among the ideas and principles peculiar to reason ideas of goodness and perfection, whose presentation before the mind could pull the will in the direction of their realization, and principles of right and wrong, the recognition of whose authority could restrain one's impulses to pursue pleasure, power, sexual union, and other objects of appetite and passion. It was then sufficient for completing the strategy of using these theories as groundwork for doctrines of human exceptionalism to deny that human minds came into possession of these moral ideas and principles through the workings of nature. This denial implied that reason operated independently of natural causes when it influenced the will and, therefore, that the moral thought and behavior attributable to these operations lay beyond the reach of natural science.

Clearly, what makes rationalist theories of moral psychology well suited for grounding doctrines of human exceptionalism is their division of the mind into two or more distinct domains of activity at least one of which is the domain of reason. Moreover, the division's suitability for grounding these doctrines matches the suitability of a conception of the mind as undivided for developing theories that oppose these doctrines. It should be no surprise, then, that traditionally the disputes between the doctrines' exponents and opponents turned on questions about the structure of the human mind.[4] Thus the conflicts of feeling and motive that rationalists took as evidence of the mind's having distinct domains were for thinkers such as Spinoza and Hume no dif-

---

4. An important exception to this is Descartes, who both insisted on the essential unity of the mind and subscribed to doctrines of human exceptionalism. This position required that he exclude all mental phenomena from the natural world and correspondingly deny that beasts had minds. To simplify our discussion, I ignore this Cartesian position. Its thesis about the mindlessness of beasts long ago doomed it to the graveyard of dead philosophical views.

ferent from any other instance of mixed emotions or competing impulses. That is, while these latter thinkers recognized experiences of being both drawn toward and repelled by the same object, they denied that such experiences ever amounted to more than the simultaneous arousal of desire and aversion in view of the prospective pleasure and pain associated with the object. Likewise, while they recognized experiences of being torn between two objects of interest, they denied that such experiences ever amounted to more than the simultaneous arousal of competing desires in view of the prospective pleasure that the consummation of either would bring. In other words, they saw in none of these experiences evidence of a motivational force that could not be reconciled with the mechanisms by which the prospects of pleasure and pain influenced the will or with comparably reactive mechanisms by which primitive urges and emotions exercised a similar influence. Unconvinced that such a force existed, these thinkers saw nothing to warrant a conception of the mind as divided.

Against their views, rationalists could and did appeal to the common experience of exerting oneself contrary to the attractions of some prospective pleasure or the repulsions of some prospective pain.[5] Thus they argued that the awareness of a power within oneself to resist these influences, an awareness, they maintained, that anyone of sound mind had, was evidence of a motivational force that was not reducible to a desire for pleasure or an aversion to pain. Nor was it reducible to any similarly reactive mechanism, such as a survival instinct, a maternal instinct, or a herd instinct. For this power of which anyone of sound mind was aware, so their argument continued, was the power to set oneself on a course of action in conformity to ideas of good ends or principles of right action that, as ideas and principles of reason, were not reducible to ideas of pleasure and pain or expressions of instinctual demands. Consequently, no matter what the reactive mechanism one supposed, it would still be such that, upon experiencing the impulse to action it produced, one could exert this power in an effort to restrain oneself from acting on that impulse. Hence, to the extent that abandoning belief in one's having such a power was difficult, the rationalists' argument for conceiving of the mind as divided was persuasive. And given that, in their traditional debate with anti-rationalists such as Hume, the latters' conception of the mind as undivided was identified with naturalism, a persuasive argument for a conception of the mind as divided translated into a persuasive argument against naturalism. It translated, in other words, into a persuasive argument for a doctrine of human exceptionalism.

5. See, e.g., Thomas Reid, *Essays on the Active Powers of the Human Mind*, essay IV, ch. vi; and Kant, *Critique of Practical Reason*, p. 30.

II

Freud's theory changed the significance of this debate. Once the theory took hold, conceiving of the mind as divided no longer signaled belief in human powers that went beyond the natural world. Because Freud's conception of the mind was at once different from the rationalists' conception and part of a naturalistic program in psychology, it broke the traditional connection between the question of the mind's structure and the question of its place in the natural world. Whereas the rationalists' conception, in the way it represented the mind as divided, corresponded to a distinction between what was unique to human beings and what was common to both them and beasts, Freud's, in its representation of the mind as divided into a conscious and an unconscious domain, did not. Neither being conscious nor being unconscious was to be understood as solely a property of human minds. A beast's mind too could have both a conscious and unconscious domain. A dog too could be conscious of its surroundings when awake and have dreams when asleep. Freud's conception, in other words, unlike the rationalists', offered no hook on which to hang a doctrine of human exceptionalism.

To the contrary, in Freud's view, all mental states and activity, whether those of human minds or the minds of other animals, belonged to the natural world. All were appropriate objects of study by natural science. His distinction between the mind's conscious states and activity and its unconscious ones was, then, as he presented it, a major contribution to that study. Yet owing to complications and changes in what he wrote about the mind's different domains, how this distinction and so his division of the mind are to be understood is, in fact, a problematic question, a question with multiple answers. As a result, determining with what success Freud explained mental states and activity as natural phenomena, determining, that is, the cogency of his theory as an argument against doctrines of human exceptionalism, requires sorting through the different answers the question has.

The problem arises because Freud, as he readily acknowledged, used the term 'unconscious' ambiguously.[6] On the one hand, he used the term as a synonym for latent. An unconscious thought in this sense was a thought that existed but was not, as we say, present to the mind. Accordingly, the subject had the thought and might even have been influenced by it but was nonetheless unaware of it. On the other hand, he used the term as a synonym for repressed. An unconscious thought in this sense was a thought that was kept latent by a force that opposed its becoming present to the mind. Such opposition, moreover, was necessary because the thought expressed a basic drive – it

6. See, e.g., 1923, XIX, pp. 13-15.

represented an instinct, as Freud put it – and being invested with the force of that drive, would not have remained latent unless its force were blocked. In other words, an unconscious thought, on this second use, unlike the first, was the site of conflict between two inner forces: the instinctual force that powered the thought and a counterforce, the repressing force, that kept the subject unaware of this powerful thought. On the first use, then, which Freud called the descriptive use, being conscious and being unconscious were contradictory properties in the sense that, if a thought was conscious, then it was not unconscious, and conversely. By contrast, on the second use, which Freud called the dynamic use, being conscious and being unconscious were not contradictory properties in this sense. For on this dynamic use the term 'unconscious' did not apply to latent thoughts that were unrepressed. Freud called such thoughts 'preconscious' instead, and in introducing this term he affirmed an implicit ambiguity in his use of the term 'conscious' that corresponded to the ambiguity in his use of the term 'unconscious'. Clearly, then, whether one takes these two terms in their descriptive sense or in their dynamic sense will effect how one conceives of the two domains into which he divided the mind.

Specifically, if one takes the terms in their descriptive sense, one will conceive of the domains as mere containers of mental states or areas of mental activity, whereas, if one takes the terms in their dynamic sense, one will conceive of the domains as parts of a whole each of which is in tension with the other. The question, of course, once these two conceptions are distinguished, is how well-suited each is to a naturalistic program in psychology. Are the reasons for seeing Freud's way of dividing the mind as unsupportive of doctrines of human exceptionalism as sound if one applies the second conception in understanding that division as they are if one applies the first? That they are sound on the first conception is clear since a conception of the domains as containers or areas applies to both the minds of beasts and those of humans. At the same time, this conception, because it follows from taking the terms in their descriptive sense, has no explanatory power. Hence, only the second conception grounds the characteristic explanations of psychoanalysis. Only the second yields explanations of thoughts and behavior as the products of inner conflict.

On this second conception, however, the soundness of the reasons for seeing Freud's way of dividing the mind as unsupportive of doctrines of human exceptionalism is unclear since it depends on the nature of the forces in virtue of which the two domains, on this conception, are in tension with each other. Specifically, the more sophisticated the agency of repression, the harder it will be to suppose that this force operates in the minds of beasts as well as in human minds and thus the easier it will be to find in Freud's way of dividing the mind support for a doctrine of human exceptionalism. To be sure, even if repression were unique to human beings, this would hardly mean that psycho-analysis was committed to some doctrine of human exceptionalism. Nonetheless, as long as its account of repression left open the possibility that its motivational force did not qualify as a natural force, one could not say that the conception of the mind as divided that psychoanalytic explanations required was well-suited to a naturalistic program in psychology.

At first glance, this may appear to be an idle worry. Looking at Freud's mature account of repression, one could easily conclude that the operation consisted of mechanisms that were not peculiar to the human mind.[7] Thus, on this account, repression is initially a reaction to anxiety. The anxiety alerts the subject to a preconscious or barely conscious thought that is invested with instinctual force and that threatens much greater distress should the subject become fully aware of it and thus compelled to acknowledge it. Repressing the thought is the subject's means to relieving this anxiety and avoiding the much greater distress it signaled. Accordingly, whatever attention the thought had initially received from the subject is withdrawn; its traces forgotten; and the thought is then blocked from again becoming conscious or nearly conscious. In this way the subject gains an immunity from the anxiety and the danger it signaled, though renewed exertions of repressive force are necessary to retain the immunity. And of course the gain may have costs in the illnesses and disturbances that psychoanalysis, using this account of repression, famously explained. But these need not concern us here. What is worth noting instead is that, on this account, repression is a reaction to anxiety on a par with someone's reacting to anxiety that signals great and imminent danger in his surroundings. There is a difference of course, since the latter reaction could produce flight to a place of safety, a means of escape that is unavailable to the subject of the former. But this difference is due to a difference in the circumstances of the danger – an anxiety-provoking thought, after all, cannot exist independently of its subject while a burning building, say, can – and therefore does not make repression any more peculiar a reaction to anxiety than flight. In either case the core mechanism is a common phenomenon of animal life.[8]

7. Using Freud's mature account is, admittedly, anachronistic. By the time Freud offered it, he had abandoned the second conception in favor of the threefold conception that represented the mind as divided into ego, id, and superego. I use the mature account nonetheless because the exposition is much easier and more comprehensible. To present the earlier account, on which anxiety was a consequence rather than an initiator of repression, requires expounding Freud's views about transformations and distributions of libidinal energy, and this would make the exposition unnecessarily complicated. Nothing in the difference between these two accounts, as will be seen below, affects my argument.

8. See Freud's remarks on the "automatism of the pleasure-pain principle" in 1933a, XXII, pp. 89-90.

The conclusion follows, however, only if recognition of the danger the anxiety signals and the manner of its removal do not entail any peculiarly human endowment. The analogy, that is, between anxiety that signals danger in one's surroundings and anxiety that signals a dangerous thought argues for understanding the motivation and operations of repression as no different from those of flight or other animal reactions to perceived dangers only if recognizing the dangerousness of the thought and gaining immunity from it through repudiation and amnesia do not entail ideas or principles peculiar to the human mind. For if they did, the worry over whether the motivational force of repression was a wholly natural force would remain. To determine, then, whether they do, we must discover what it is about a repressed thought that, on Freud's account, explains why it would cause great distress in the person who had it if he were to become fully aware of it and compelled to acknowledge it. And to find the answer, we shall have to look beyond its being invested with instinctual force, for Freud did not think every preconscious or barely conscious thought that is invested with such force caused anxiety sufficient to trigger repression. To find the answer, we must look instead at the thought's content. There we shall discover what makes the thought seem so dangerous.

Freud himself indicated as much by characterizing exertions of repressive force as a kind of censorship one exercised as a way of keeping oneself ignorant of hateful and frightening wishes that one harbored.[9] These wishes were thoughts of what would gratify the instinct with whose force they were invested, and the instincts Freud had in mind were powerfully erotic and destructive instincts that, given the normal familial context of infancy and early childhood, bound the child to its parents. Thus, the corresponding wishes were typically sexual and lethal wishes whose complete gratification, were it really possible, would be the stuff of tragedy. Incest and parricide were Freud's most important examples. What makes the wishes seem so dangerous to the subject, then, is the nature of the acts that would gratify them. Fulfilling these wishes means transgressing barriers erected to preserve relations with the most important figures in the subject's life, personages on whom he depends for protection and nourishment. Hence, repudiating and expelling the wishes and vigilantly blocking their return becomes necessary to ward off the extreme threat to his welfare and life they represent. Here it is plain how the content of the wishes makes them seem so dangerous. What is more, the recognition of danger and the removal of its source that initiates and constitutes repression seemingly contain ideas that are peculiar to the human mind. Surely, to see an act as a transgression and to repudiate the wish to engage in such action imply

9. See e.g., 1916-1917, XVI, pp. 294-296.

a kind of moral understanding of one's universe and sense of what is good and evil in it that is beyond the ken of beasts. Freud's account of repression, once it is fully fleshed out, thus leaves open the possibility that the motivational force of repression, owing to some of its components, did not qualify as a force of nature.

III

To make headway, at this point, we must move past Freud's account of repression and the conception of the mind on which it was originally based. Neither will ultimately answer our question about the cogency of psychoanalytic explanations as arguments against doctrines of human exceptionalism. To find answers we must consider yet another conception of the mind as divided that Freud developed. This conception corresponded to a sense in which he used the terms 'conscious' and 'unconscious' that differed from the descriptive and the dynamic senses we have already considered. On this third use, which Freud marked by the abbreviations Cs. and Ucs., the terms stood for distinct systems of thought and activity within the mind. Cs. named the system of perception and reflection, whose processes were intelligent and, with the acquisition of language, subject to principles of logic.[10] Ucs., by contrast, named the system of thoughts and wishes that gave direct expression to instinctual demands and whose processes reflected the unruly play of instinct and was for that reason completely alien to logic. Repression, which was an activity of the Cs., had a significant role in distinguishing the two systems, but it was not the sole criterion of that distinction. As a result, Ucs. included more than repressed thoughts, though it did not include preconscious ones. This third conception of the mind, then, was equivalent to neither of the other two. By allowing Freud to attribute to the mind unconscious thoughts that, while more than merely latent, had never undergone repression, it gave him more room to explore the work of the instincts outside the theory of repression.

Eventually, though, Freud came to realize the inadequacy of even this conception for explaining all of the unconscious thought and activity, in the descriptive sense of 'unconscious', that he conceived of as more than merely latent. In particular, he realized that this third conception was as ill-equipped as the second to explain how the forces of repression themselves could be unconscious. As a result, he abandoned his use of 'conscious' and 'unconscious'

10.. Freud did not consistently use the same abbreviations for this system. Sometimes he used Cs., other times Pcpt-Cs. Sometimes he distinguished a preconscious system Pcs. from Cs., other times he treated them as one system, using Cs.(Pcs.) to indicate the merger. See, e.g.,1915b, XIV, passim; and 1923, XIX, pp. 13-27.

(and the abbreviations Cs. and Ucs.) as names for the domain from which repression issued and the domain in which repressed thoughts and wishes were found and replaced them with 'ego' and 'id'. This change, moreover, was not just a matter of relabelling. Freud had for some time been working out ideas about the operations of the ego while only loosely identifying it with the system of perceptual and reflective thought that the abbreviation Cs. stood for. Renaming this domain 'the ego' thus enabled him to consolidate these newer ideas with his older ideas about repression and psychosexual development, and this consolidation produced an even richer conception of the way the mind was divided.

For our purposes, the most important result of this consolidation was the addition of an internal agency of morality and value, the super-ego, to this systemic or, as Freud came to call it, structural conception of the mind. The super-ego, Freud explained, develops out of the ego as a result of the processes, occurring in infancy and early childhood, by which the ego acquires personality. And though he sometimes described the super-ego as a "grade in the ego," he mostly treated it as a distinct domain of the mind.[11] Thus, on this structural conception, the mind was divided into three distinct domains, and interactions among these domains, primarily those in which the ego mediated between the other two, became the basis of psychoanalytic explanations.

The addition of an agency of morality and value answered a long-standing complaint against psychoanalysis: that in concentrating on diseases and perversions of the mind, it ignored the higher side of human nature. Freud thought this complaint was unfair, both as a matter of accuracy and as a matter of proper scientific methodology. For one thing, he pointed out, "we have from the beginning attributed the function of instigating repression to the moral and aesthetic trends in the ego."[12] For another, he argued, a science must grow piecemeal according to the evidence it finds and should not be expected to lay out a complete theory all at once.

So long as we had to concern ourselves with the study of what is repressed in mental life, there was no need for us to share in any agitated apprehensions as to the whereabouts of the higher side of man. But now that we have embarked upon the analysis of the ego we can give an answer to all those whose moral sense has been shocked and who have complained that there must surely be a higher nature in man: "Very true," we can say, "and here we have that higher nature, in this ego ideal or super-ego, the repre-

11. 1923, XIX, p. 28.
12. Ibid., p. 25. And also, "Since we have come to assume a special agency in the ego, the super-ego, which represents demands of a restricting and rejecting character, we may say that repression is the work of this super-ego and that it is carried out by itself or by the ego in obedience to its orders," 1933a, XXII, p. 69. Cf. 1926, XX, p. 94.

sentative of our relation to our parents. When we were little children we knew these higher natures, we admired them and feared them; and later we took them into ourselves."[13]

Clearly, this development in Freud's theory brings to a head the question of how cogent psychoanalytic explanations are as arguments against doctrines of human exceptionalism. The addition of the superego promises both to resolve our earlier worry about the nature of repression's motivational force, since it enlarges Freud's account of repression in a way that speaks directly to that worry, and to answer the rationalist objections to naturalist programs in psychology I described above, since it supplies an explanation of the kind of inner conflict on which those objections were based. Whether it fulfills these promises, however, depends on how well the operations of the superego, as Freud characterized them, explain the moral agency of human beings and on whether that explanation is sufficient to show that such agency is entirely the product of natural forces.

For the most part, Freud characterized the superego's operations as supervisory, restrictive, and punitive. The model was that of a harsh and biting conscience, which operated as a moral guide and disciplinarian, instructing its possessor on matters of right and wrong, opposing his wishes and desires when they prompted wrong action, and plaguing him with criticism and blame if he ignored that opposition. Indeed, Freud frequently identified possession of a superego with possession of a conscience, though his considered view was that conscience was only one of the superego's principal functions.[14] A second function was that of holding up ideals by which its possessor could measure how admirable his life and personal qualities were. This function lay mostly in the shadows of Freud's writings on the superego, and it was only in one of his last works that he explicitly made the distinction between it and conscience a part of his theory. There he drew the distinction by reintroducing the term ego ideal, a term he had previously used interchangeably with superego, and giving it the narrower meaning of 'idealfunktion'.[15] The distinction then enabled him to discriminate between affects of conscience and affects of self-appraisal, the sense of guilt and the sense of inferiority, in particular, and others, following his lead, have used it to distinguish between the emotions of guilt and shame and to explain how these emotions complement

13. 1923, XIX, p. 36.
14. 1933a, XXII, p. 60.
15. Ibid., pp. 62–66. The distinction had been drawn by Freud as early as his essay on narcissism (1914, XIV, pp. 93–97), but it did not become a settled part of his theory until much later, when he came to see aggression as a primitive drive, distinct from libidinal forces, and was then able to attribute the workings of conscience to the former and those of the ego ideal to the latter.

each other.[16] In these distinctions, both Freud's and his followers', one can see how Freud's theory incorporates into its explanation of moral agency ideas of goodness and perfection as well as principles of right and wrong. Conscience preserves and enforces the latter; the ego ideal maintains the former. Hence, the two kinds of practical judgment to which rationalists ascribed the motivational force of reason in its struggles with appetite and passion each have a place in Freud's account of the superego.

In that account, these two kinds of judgment are differentiated exactly as the two functions to which they correspond are differentiated. The chief differential in either case is the motivational force driving the operations that define those functions. The operations of conscience owe their motivational force to aggressive drives; the operations of the ego ideal owe theirs to sexual drives. And these drives are then traceable, according to Freud, to the basic instincts of destruction (or death) and Eros. Consequently, on Freud's theory, judgments of morality and value have motivational force that is traceable to these basic instincts. How these judgments come to have such force, how a person's conscience and ego ideal become vehicles of these basic instincts, are questions whose answers are found in the way Freud explained the formation in the young child of a superego. The main theses of this explanation are well known. They describe the process by which the child internalizes parental figures as a way of resolving severe emotional conflict in its feelings towards its parents, a conflict that invariably arises out of the normal familial circumstances of early childhood. Thus, to the extent that this explanation covers the essentials of the phenomena and is plausible, Freud explained the moral agency distinctive of human beings.[17]

This explanation, moreover, offers an account of the kind of opposition between distinct domains of the mind that rationalists regarded as opposition between the force of reason and the forces of appetite and passion. Accordingly, such opposition is understood as a conflict between the forces of the superego and the forces of the id. The latter derive from the basic instincts and, in the cases that match what rationalists described as excitations of appetite and passion, are experienced as the impulses and urges of primitive desires and emotions. The former originate in the very same instincts, but because they operate in the superego and power its agency, they can oppose primitive desires and emotions that are invested with the same instinctual force. They are

16. See, e.g., Gerhart Piers and Milton Singer, *Shame and Guilt: A Psychoanalytic and a Cultural Study* (Springfield, IL: Charles C. Thomas, 1953), pt. 1, ch. 3; and Richard Wollheim, *The Thread of Life* (Cambridge, MA: Harvard Univ. Press, 1984), ch. 7.

17. For details of this explanation and a discussion of problems internal to Freud's exposition, see my "Remarks on Some Difficulties in Freud's Theory of Moral Development," *International Review of Psycho-Analysis* 11 (1984): 207-225. [Chapter 4 in this volume.]

then experienced as dictates of conscience or aspirations of the ego ideal. And just as the rationalists characterized the opposition between the force of reason and the force of passion as a struggle for the determination of the will, so Freud characterized the opposition between the forces of the superego and the forces of the id as a struggle for complicity of the ego. In this way, Freud's theory explains the experiences of inner conflict on which rationalists based their objections to earlier naturalistic theories. Insofar as these experiences require divisions within the mind to be satisfactorily explained, Freud's theory represents a significant advance over these earlier theories.

IV

This advance notwithstanding, we cannot yet conclude that Freud succeeded in showing that the moral agency of human beings was entirely a product of natural forces. Indeed, we could not draw this conclusion even if we accepted as unproblematic and well-supported his account of the superego's operations. To be sure, if the spurs of a strict conscience or the aspirations of an ego ideal, which these operations explain, supplied the only motivational force that the judgments of morality and value distinctive of our moral agency ever had, the conclusion would follow from his account of them. But whether these spurs and aspirations exhaust the possibilities is still an open question. Perhaps children, as they grow up and receive a moral education that fits them for adulthood, develop capacities for acting on ideas and principles whose force as motives cannot be attributed to the operations of the superego. Developing such capacities would not, after all, be inconsistent with one's still being subject to the strictures of conscience or the pressures of high ideals; it would not, that is, be inconsistent with one's having a powerful superego. What it would mean, though, is that the operations of the superego were not the only sources of moral motives. Freud's theory excludes this possibility by assuming that moral development subsequent to the formation of a superego involves nothing more than enhancement and modification of this agency's operations. But this assumption is hardly uncontroversial. Freud's explanation, let us grant, is a complete and compelling account of the sources and workings of moral motives in young children. But whether it is a complete and compelling account of the sources and workings of moral motives in human beings, whatever their age or level of maturity, is another matter.

The moral development of a young child consists not only of internalizing parental figures but also of learning from direct instruction what sort of conduct is praiseworthy and what sort won't even be tolerated. In receiving this instruction the child learns the language of right and wrong, good and bad, responsibility and punishment, and so forth as well as the specific norms and values that are communicated through the use of this language. And in learning the language, along with these norms and values, the child learns how to think systematically about right and wrong and how to deliberate to conclusions about what ought to be done. If the acquisition of these cognitive powers brings, as it should, a new understanding of oneself and one's relations with others, perhaps it brings new capacities for motivation as well. Or perhaps the self-understanding we develop in acquiring these cognitive powers requires that we understand what moves us in circumstances in which we act after deliberating to a conclusion about what ought to be done as thoughts whose motive force originates in our own affirmations and exertions.[18]

Freud, it is important to note, ignored this aspect of a child's moral education. Indeed, sometimes, it seems, he wrote as if the cultural transmission of norms and values were entirely a matter of each generation's acquiring the personality traits of previous generations through the unconscious processes of personality development that his theory described.[19] Of course, if judgments of right and wrong, good and bad, had motivational force solely in virtue of their being invested with instinctual force, as Freud believed, then the acquisition of the cognitive powers those judgments imply would affect only how that force was channeled and directed and not how it originated. In this case, it would make sense for someone whose interest was in the germination of moral agency and not in its flowering, who thought that the former and not the latter contained the ultimate explanation of the agency's activity, to ignore the way learning the language of morality and value increased a child's cognitive powers of moral judgment. But the belief that such judgment has motivational force solely in virtue of its being invested with instinctual force is not philosophically innocent. It implies a controversial thesis about the nature of moral judgment, a thesis that contradicts but does not refute rationalist theses about the nature of such judgment. In other words, Freud's explanation of the moral agency distinctive of human beings argues against doctrines of human exceptionalism only by assuming as a premiss a thesis that contradicts propositions about the nature of moral judgment on which rationalists traditionally based those doctrines.

Freud, of course, did not have a philosophical theory of moral judgment. He was not directly engaged in the modern debate about its nature. As a psychologist, however, he held views about voluntary action and human motiva-

---

18. The possibility is contained in P. F. Strawson's distinction between participatory and objective standpoints and can be traced back to Kant's doctrine of the two standpoints, that of nature and that of freedom. See Strawson, "Freedom and Resentment," *Proceedings of the British Academy*, 48 (1962): 1-25; and Kant, *Groundwork of the Metaphysics of Morals*, Paton, trans. (New York: Harper Torchbook, 1964), pp. 124-126.
19. 1933a, XXII, pp. 66-68.

tion that, though they may not have committed him to any recognized, affirmative position in this debate, did implicitly commit him to opposing a range of such positions. He held, in particular, the view that the springs of all voluntary actions were motives whose force originated in biologically basic instincts,[20] and the antirationalist commitment implicit in this view is unmistakable. Among other things, the view includes, as a special case, Freud's belief that the judgments of right and wrong, good and bad, have motivational force solely in virtue of their being invested with instinctual force. Thus it directly opposes the rationalist's thesis that one's understanding of the ideas of goodness and perfection and the principles of right and wrong alone give rise to the motivation to act on judgments of value and morality in which those ideas and principles are applied. Freud held this view about the instinctual origins of the springs of all voluntary action not because he had evidence to support it. Nor did he reach it from reflective considerations on the philosophical questions it raised. Rather the view was a fixed point in his work. He used it as a guide to interpreting the observations he made and to constructing theoretical schemes that greatly increased the explanatory power of those interpretations. As a fixed point, however, its probative value – and thus the probative value of the explanations that proceed from it – is limited.

This limitation is itself instructive. Consider the conflict that arises when one realizes that the demands of one's conscience are excessive. On the one hand, one feels a need to obey these demands yet, on the other, one concludes, having recognized their unreasonableness, even arbitrariness, that one ought to resist them. One's judgment thus opposes the forces of one's superego. On Freud's theory, if this judgment comes from a greater understanding of reality – in this case, inner reality – and of the adjustments one must make to reduce its harshness and achieve some measure of happiness, as presumably it does, its motivational force is the force of the ego's initiative in negotiating peace among the id, superego, and the requirements of reality.[21] The fixed point we have noted in his theory then requires that this force originate in some basic instinct, and Freud, as befits his genius, advanced a remarkably fertile hypothesis that explained the instinctual sources of the ego's initiative in such matters.[22] At the same time, nothing beyond the fixed point argues for applying this hypothesis to the example of a mature individual recognizing the irrationality of a felt need and judging, as a result, that it ought to be resisted. Nothing in the theory beyond its own antirationalist commitments, therefore, argues against a rationalist understanding of the conflict presented in this example.

20. See 1915a, XIV, pp. 118–120.
21. 1933a, XXII, pp. 75–78.
22. Ibid.

Leaving these antirationalist commitments aside, we could instead explain the motivational force of the individual's judgment as the result of her deliberating from certain general values and principles the understanding of which she had acquired in developing her powers of practical reason. Accordingly, we would understand the conflict between the force of the individual's judgment and the force of her overbearing conscience as arguing against the view that the springs of all voluntary actions are motives whose force originates in biologically basic instincts. We would understand it, that is, as Kant and other rationalists understood the conflicts on which they based their objections to naturalistic theories of moral psychology. Thus, to the extent that the explanation is persuasive, it represents a forceful objection to Freud's theory. To the extent that it is persuasive, Freud's theory, like its predecessors, fails to answer satisfactorily the objections of the rationalist school.

We have now reached the conclusion I forecasted at the beginning of the essay. It is a conclusion on which Kant presumably would have smiled. Ironically, though, we have reached it from consideration of an example on which he undoubtedly would have poured scorn. The idea that conscience could be a source of excessive demands would have struck him as preposterous nonsense. Conscience, for Kant, was the same as pure practical reason, or rather it was for him the form such reason took in the human soul. The severity of its strictures, the rigor of its demands, corresponded, in his view, to the exalted authority of reason in the life of a moral agent, and consequently its strictures and demands could never be intelligibly characterized as unreasonable or arbitrary.[23] Quite the contrary, he thought the fact of reason was most evident on just those occasions when conscience insisted on self-sacrifice beyond what we would ordinarily think was reasonable for others to expect of an individual.[24] Thus, the example, if it were to stand, would at the same time as it kept alive

---

23. His exaltation of conscience crests in a well-known passage from the conclusion of his second *Critique*: "Two things fill the mind with ever new and increasing admiration and awe, the oftener and more steadily we reflect on them: the starry heavens above me and the moral law within me. I do not merely conjecture them and seek them as though obscured in darkness or in the transcendent region beyond my horizon: I see them before me, and I associate them directly with the consciousness of my own existence. . . . The former view of a countless multitude of worlds annihilates, as it were, my importance as an animal creature, which must give back to the planet (a mere speck in the universe) the matter from which it came, the matter which is for a little time provided with vital force, we know not how. The latter, on the contrary, infinitely raises my worth as that of an intelligence by my personality, in which the moral law reveals a life independent of all animality and even of the whole world of sense – at least so far as it may be inferred from the purposive destination assigned to my existence by this law, a destination which is not restricted to the conditions and limits of this life but reaches into the infinite." *Critique of Practical Reason*, p. 166. Cf. J. J. Rousseau, *Émile or On Education*, Allan Bloom trans. (New York: Basic Books, 1979), p. 290.

24. *Critique of Practical Reason*, p. 30.

the possibility of Kant's fact of reason suggest that he had mislocated it in the dictates of conscience.

At this point, one might be drawn, in the interest of defending Kant, to the thought that the example itself is a Freudian artifact: we so readily accept it, one might think, because we are still in the grip of Freud's ideas. Yet such a thought would be mistaken. Observations about the excessive stringency and harshness of conscience predate Freud and had found support by the time his work became influential. No less a psychologist than Mark Twain made them a part of his commentaries on the human condition. There is, for instance, his wonderful short story "The Facts Concerning the Recent Carnival of Crime in Connecticut,"[25] in which he tells of the first and last time he confronted his conscience in visible form. It was the first time because, as Twain notes, he had never before asked to see his most pitiless enemy. It was the last because Twain ended the encounter by throttling his conscience to death, whence the Connecticut crime spree mentioned in the story's title. The throttling, moreover, as we are brought to see, was well-deserved. His conscience was the most obnoxious, belittling, sarcastic scold imaginable. Set against Twain's humorous description, Kant's thoroughly rapturous view of conscience should appear suspect. Kant may have been right about the nature of moral judgment and the fact of reason he believed his analysis of it disclosed. But if he was, he was right despite the energy with which conscience enforces such judgments and not, as he seemed to think, in view of it.

---

25. Mark Twain, *Tom Sawyer Abroad, Tom Sawyer, Detective, and Other Stories, Etc., Etc.* (New York: P. F. Collier and Son Co., 1924), pp. 302-325.

7

Reason and motivation

Descartes, near the beginning of the Meditations, raised and then immediately dismissed the possibility that he was mad. He had embarked on an investigation into the power of reason to discover truths that by virtue of their being indubitable could constitute the foundations of scientific knowledge, and since his plan of investigation was to test his own reasoning powers, taking them to be exemplary, he had to assume that he had a rational mind. Thus he dismissed out of hand the possibility of his being mad. Nonetheless, he took it to suggest another: he might be dreaming. For the thoughts one has while dreaming can be as fantastic and incoherent as the thoughts madmen have in their waking lives. What is more, dreaming is consistent with possessing a rational mind. It is a state to which, as far as Descartes could tell, everyone is liable when asleep. That he might be dreaming was therefore a possibility Descartes could not immediately dismiss. It was a proper object of inquiry, and as long as it remained open, he could make no claim sustainable by reason to having knowledge of particular states and events of the physical world.

Although Descartes's investigation concerned the power of theoretical reason, his way of proceeding can serve as an object lesson for those investigating the power of practical reason. The lesson is not, of course, that these investigators should attend to the limits that dreaming might place on the power of practical reason. It is, rather, that they should consider whether the assertions they would make or the conclusions they would draw about practical reason are consistent with various disorders of the mind to which people who are not mad are liable. To be sure, these investigators can safely ignore disorders that involve a defect of reason. But they cannot assume that every disorder of the mind involves such a defect. There are some disorders affliction with which is or appears to be consistent with possession of fully developed and nondefective rational faculties, and therefore to ignore such disorders when investigating the power of practical reason is to run the risk of overgeneralization or of mistaking for a necessary truth about practical reason a proposition the truth of which is contingent upon the absence of disorders of this kind in every rational mind.

133

This lesson applies, above all, to investigations into the power of practical reason to originate action. The thesis that practical reason is endowed with such power has a prominent place in the history of ethics. Rationalist philosophers from Plato to late twentieth century Kantian revivalists have made it a central doctrine in their theory of moral agency. According to this theory, a moral agent is a person in whom reason is capable of ruling both appetite and passion, and more generally of governing the conduct of its possessor's life. Furthermore, on this theory, one achieves moral excellence when one's passions and appetites submit to the rule of reason, when the moving principles of one's conduct are dictates of reason the intelligibility of which does not depend on some antecedent desire. And obversely, one flirts with moral vice when reason fails to rule, when it operates only in the service of desire. Indeed, the theory must represent all moral failings as failures of reason, else it would have to allow that even in a person who had achieved moral excellence reason shared with some other part of the mind the powers of governing its possessor's life. Consequently, the theory becomes problematic once one takes seriously the possibility of personality or emotional disorders affliction with which is consistent with the possession of fully developed and nondefective rational faculties. The idea behind this essay is to take this possibility seriously, to bring it to bear on a current, influential version of the rationalist theory with the aim of finding problems with that version and determining their gravity.

I

As the last remark indicates, the rationalist theory of moral agency has more than one version. In what I call its Platonic version, the theory is grounded on the thesis that motivational states are internally related to judgments of good and evil, right and wrong, worth and depravity, or other values the recognition of which normally guides the conduct of a rational creature. More exactly, the theory, in this version, is grounded on the thesis that one cannot make such a judgment without being moved toward acting appropriately: toward pursuing or protecting what one judges to be good, toward shunning or eradicating what one judges to be evil, toward conforming to what one judges to be right, and so forth. It is grounded, in other words, on the thesis that such judgments are intrinsically motivational.

In another version, which originates in modern philosophy, the theory is grounded on the thesis that motivational states are internally related to certain judgments that reflect a deep understanding of the nature of rational agency or the nature of persons. These judgments need not be judgments of value like those on which the Platonic theory is centered. They may, instead, be judgments about one's own condition or that of some other rational agent, or they may be hypothetical judgments about what the world would be like if every rational agent who faced circumstances similar to one's own acted in a certain way. In either case, the form the internal relation takes must be the same as the form it takes on the Platonic theory. That is, the judgments must be intrinsically motivational. Moreover, explaining their intrinsic motivational force requires spelling out the conception of rational agency or personhood these judgments reflect, for the general idea behind this version of the rationalist theory is that an understanding and acceptance of one's essential nature disposes one to act in ways that express that nature and to forbear acting in ways that would seemingly deny it. The explanation thus requires a metaphysical construction. This is what spelling out the relevant conception of rational agency or personhood amounts to. Accordingly, for convenience sake, let us call this version of the rationalist theory the metaphysical theory.

The most famous theory of this type is of course Kant's. Kant held that certain judgments reflecting an understanding of one's rational agency as essentially free were intrinsically motivational. To act on these judgments was to express one's nature as a free being, more specifically an autonomous one, and no person who understood and accepted that he was an autonomous being could be wholly indifferent to performing acts that seemingly denied his autonomy. The full development of Kant's theory, however, involves a metaphysical construction that is notoriously difficult to comprehend. Since every version of the metaphysical theory derives its significance and cogency from the metaphysical construction at its base, one would make better progress in critically assessing the theory by leaving assessment of Kant's version to the specialists and turning to a more tractable one. This way of proceeding has an obvious drawback, though. The question of whether Kant's version is sounder than more tractable versions must remain open. But then one can only do so much.

The version I propose to consider is due to Thomas Nagel.[1] Nagel develops two distinct but parallel metaphysical constructions, corresponding to each of which is a type of judgment that he maintains is intrinsically motivational. More exactly, Nagel maintains that a judgment of one or the other type is intrinsically motivational when it reflects an understanding of oneself that the relevant metaphysical construction spells out. Thus, in the one case, he holds that to understand oneself as a temporally extended being, a being who exists over an extended period of time, is to take a perspective from which certain

---

1. *The Possibility of Altruism* (Oxford: Clarendon Press, 1970). Hereafter abbreviated *PA*. Nagel revised his theory in later works. See, e.g., *The View from Nowhere* (New York: Oxford, 1986), pp. 164-188. The revision, however, does not affect the argument of this essay, and accordingly I will restrict the discussion of his theory to its presentation in *The Possibility of Altruism*.

judgments about one's future interests and desires are intrinsically motivational. Indeed, according to Nagel, prudence, which, construed narrowly, is the virtue of making adequate provision for satisfying one's future interests and desires, is essentially the disposition to take this perspective and to maintain it in the face of temptation to ignore all but one's present interests and desires. In the other case, Nagel holds that to understand oneself as "merely one person among others equally real"[2] is to take a perspective from which certain judgments one makes about another person's interests and desires are intrinsically motivational. Altruism, Nagel contends, which is the virtue of helping others to satisfy their interests and desires, is essentially the disposition to take this latter perspective and to maintain it in the face of temptation to ignore everyone's interest and desires but one's own.

Nagel develops these two constructions as parts of a general theory of rational motivation. They are the focal points of his exposition, but the theory he intends is more than a theory of prudential and altruistic motivation. Nagel's view, put roughly, is that rational action properly understood is action the motive of which is a judgment one makes from a suitable perspective, a perspective that is defined by a specific conception of oneself alone or in relation to one's world. Prudential and altruistic action are then, for Nagel, two species of rational action whose differentiae are the judgments that constitute those actions' motives, judgments that are made form different perspectives. This is a significantly stronger view than Kant's. For Kant took moral motivation to be the only kind of motivation that the operation of reason could generate. That is, he believed that the human capacity for moral conduct was the only evidence we had of reason's conative power, and he took the contribution of reason in all other cases of rational conduct to be the determination of means to the ends given in the desires and affections that are the basic motives of that conduct. Nagel's view is stronger then because he applies the kind of explanation Kant believed moral conduct required to a much wider range of conduct. Since our question is whether this kind of explanation is ever cogent, that Nagel has given it a wider range of application than Kant is immaterial. The real test is whether it is a cogent explanation of conduct in those cases its application to which Nagel thinks best exemplifies its cogency. These are the cases on which he mainly stakes his version of the metaphysical theory.

II

One way to put our question is this. Does the metaphysical theory's distinctive conceptual apparatus yield cogent explanations of action that substanti-

---

2. *PA*, p. 14.

ate the rationalist's belief in the conative power of reason? Specifically, does Nagel's version of the theory yield such explanations? Of the two that Nagel has worked out in detail, namely, that of prudential action and that of altruistic action, he presents the former as the less disputable. And it surely is. Moreover, the plan of his argument is first to establish, through presenting and defending his explanation of prudential action, that explanations of this kind are cogent, and then to extend them, through presenting and defending his explanation of altruistic action, beyond the realm of wholly self-regarding action. Accordingly, he deliberately works out the latter explanation as a formal analogue of the former. The analogy thus serves to transfer cogency from one explanation to the other. Or, in other words, objections that would seriously threaten his explanation of altruistic action if it were presented by itself are kept at bay by presenting it as the formal analogue of an explanation that seems much less open to objection. All of this implies that a critical inquiry into Nagel's theory that is informed by an interest in finding out whether some version of the metaphysical theory is sound must, to be truly probative, focus first and chiefly on Nagel's explanation of prudential action. This explanation is his theory's capital. From it his explanation of altruistic action is derived as profit.

Nagel's explanation of prudential action proceeds from a small set of uncontroversial assumptions about rational agents. He assumes, first, that a rational agent has some desires; second, that the desires a rational agent will have in the future are not in every case identical or continuous with those he presently has; and third, that a rational agent can know about such cases. This last assumption is pivotal. The bare recognition that in the future one will have a certain desire is, Nagel maintains, a consideration that in itself can be motivational. Moreover, this will be true even if one presently lacks that desire.

Circumstances of the sort Nagel invokes here occur all the time. It is a cold evening and will get colder. I am about to leave my house for the theater. I know that in five hours I will have returned and will be on the other side of the front door wanting to get inside out of the cold. I do not now want to get inside out of the cold. I am inside. I turn on the porch light to facilitate my later reentry. Nagel's view is that my recognizing that I will later want to get quickly back inside my house, along with some bits of knowledge about switches, lights, the advantage of well-lit porches for putting keys in locks at night, and the like, and some elementary reasoning from means to ends suffices to explain my turning on the porch light before leaving my house. In particular, on this view, no reference to a present desire for the satisfaction of this future desire or a present desire for my future happiness is necessary to explain my action. Indeed, no reference to any present desire whose object is

137

some future state of affairs is necessary. One might insist that the explanation include reference to a present desire I have to turn on the porch light, but such a reference, Nagel argues convincingly, would do no more than make explicit that my recognition of a desire I will have in the future, when it is combined with other knowledge and some means-to-ends reasoning, has motivational force that is directed toward producing a specific action. In other words, the desire to turn on the porch light is as much a consequence of those cognitive states and processes as the act itself, though it is a logical consequence while the act is a causal one.[3] Nagel's general thesis, then, is that in explaining prudential action, understood narrowly as action taken to insure or facilitate the satisfaction of a future desire, one need only refer to the agent's cognitive states and processes. No other psychological state or process, specifically no noncognitive one, is among the mutually independent and jointly sufficient conditions of the action.

One can describe the dispute into which Nagel enters as follows. It is a dispute over how to explain prudential action. All parties agree that in the standard case part of the explanation is the agent's recognition of a desire he will have in the future. Some, however, find it difficult and even impossible to see how the agent's recognition of a future desire could be in itself motivational, and this leads them to include in the explanation reference to a present desire the agent has for the satisfaction of this future desire. Including this reference would certainly be a natural way to fill out the explanation if one thought that, for there to be motivation, some desire must complement the agent's recognition of a future desire. It would be a natural way for those committed to the view that all rational motivation factors into a belief and a desire. Nagel, who argues against this way of filling out the explanation, develops the first of his two metaphysical constructions as a more plausible alternative. The difficulty in seeing how the agent's recognition of a future desire can be in itself motivational will, he hopes, disappear once one thinks of the recognition as reflecting the agent's understanding of himself as a temporally extended being. More exactly, Nagel hopes that it will disappear once one contrasts the temporally neutral perspective a person who has this conception of himself takes with the temporally biased perspective taken by a person who lets his present desires and interests distort the view he has of his future. To take the former perspective is to identify with all stages of one's life, and a person who identifies with his future life need only foresee that he will have a certain desire in the future to be moved toward insuring or facilitating its satisfaction. By contrast, to take the latter perspective is to be dis-

3. See *PA*, pp. 29-30.

sociated from one's future life, and in a person who is thus dissociated fore-sight that one will have a certain desire in the future will not be in itself mo-tivational.[4]

Enough of the conceptual apparatus Nagel develops for explaining pruden-tial action has now been outlined to allow us to begin testing his theory. The severest test is generated not by considering any acts of prudence, for the the-ory seems easily to cover all such acts. Rather, it is generated by considering whether a person could ever lack prudential motivation despite his recogniz-ing that he will have in the future a certain desire. According to the theory, such a person must have failed to identify with his future life. That is, he must have failed to take the temporally neutral perspective that corresponds to a conception of oneself as a temporally extended being and so can be de-scribed as dissociated from his future life and, indeed, from his life as a whole. Not every deficiency in prudential motivation, however, obviously en-tails such dissociation, and this is true even if one sets aside deficiencies due to ignorance of future interests and desires. The remaining cases, specifically those in which the agent is not obviously dissociated from his future life, thus represent important test cases for the theory.

A person who is under the influence of strong desires or violent emotions and who, as a result, is unmoved by his knowledge of his future interests and desires is arguably the best example of someone whose deficiency in pruden-tial motivation is explained by dissociation from his future life. For at such times one may be so consumed by one's present circumstances that one's life in the future, even the near future, may seem distant and unreal. But what of the person who is undisturbed by strong desires and violent emotions? Could he be likewise deficient in prudential motivation? If he could, then on Nagel's theory he too must be dissociated from his future life. Yet such dissociation in someone who is not in the grip of some desire or emotion seems beyond belief. The theory, one could then conclude, must implicitly dismiss such an individual as fictitious or the product of an implausible hypothesis, and in fact Nagel explicitly makes this point. He writes,

It is obvious that people are prudentially motivated and do care what will happen to them; someone who remained totally unmoved by the possibility of avertible future harm or accessible future benefits would be regarded as wildly peculiar by anyone no matter what his theory of motivation.[5]

One should be wary, however, of such sweeping dismissals and strong state-ments.

4. See *PA*, pp. 58–62.
5. *PA*, p. 37.

Clearly, Nagel's point is undeniable when taken, as he appears from its context to have intended, to be about someone who, while seriously concerned about how he fares in the present, is completely unconcerned about how he will fare in the future. Such a person would seem to have, as a matter of principle, dissociated himself from his future life. He would seem to have adopted and kept to the principle of living strictly in the present. And "wildly peculiar" is as apt a description of him as any. Such principled indifference to one's future, however, is not the only kind of indifference that can underlie a deficiency in prudential motivation. Specifically, someone may be indifferent to his own future, not because he has adopted and kept to a principle requiring that he disregard his future, but because he has become severely dejected.[6] Severe dejection, moreover, does not obviously entail dissociation of the sort Nagel's theory predicts, and it cannot then be readily dismissed as fictitious or the product of an implausible hypothesis. It is an abnormal condition, to be sure, but it is not wildly peculiar. Hence it poses problems for the theory.

A clearer definition of these problems and some measure of how serious they are require further description of the severely dejected person. One plausible description is this. He is someone who feels so low and dispirited and who is so apathetic and enervated that one would describe him as having lost all interest in and enthusiasm for life. He languishes for days, mostly in bed, sometimes in an armchair, staring blankly into space or at the television before him. He talks to no one or virtually no one, eats little, and sleeps a lot. This person might have fallen into such a state because someone with whom he was much in love had jilted him and had done so in a way that was deeply wounding, or because he was fired at work for cause and subsequently shunned by workers and friends. In the first case we can imagine that his low spirits are accompanied by thoughts of being unloved and unlovable, and in the second they might be accompanied by thoughts of being a failure and an incompetent. In either case such thoughts would reinforce his feeling bad about himself and would sustain his diminished sense of worth. And in either case the possibility of an avertible future harm or an accessible future benefit might well leave him completely unmoved. Similarly, knowing that in the future he will have a certain desire might not move him at all toward insuring or facilitating its satisfaction.

It would be natural to say about such a person that he had ceased to care

6. For the use of such cases in criticizing the thesis on which the Platonic theory of moral agency is grounded, see Michael Stocker "Desiring the Bad: An Essay in Moral Psychology," *Journal of Philosophy* 76 (1979): 738–753.

about himself, and in saying this one would imply that the interest and emotion people normally invest in the ends and goals they pursue in the conduct of their lives had in his case been withdrawn. Accomplishment of those ends, achievement of those goals, whether day-to-day or long-term, now fails to arouse in him any interest or concern. Accordingly, insofar as the ends and goals around which one organizes one's life are the basis for projecting one's life into the future, one might also say about him that he had ceased to identify with his future life. But in saying this one would be referring to a failure of emotional identification rather than a failure of understanding. That is, one would not be saying that he had failed to see his future life as one stage in a single life of which his present life is an earlier stage. So too, one might describe him as being dissociated from his future life and, indeed, from his life as a whole. But again one would not mean by this that he had failed to take and maintain a temporally neutral perspective on his life. Rather one would mean that the pursuits that had given shape and direction to his life had ceased to engage his interest and concern. The overall point is that dissociation of the sort Nagel's theory defines does not enter into the foregoing account of the severely dejected man's indifference to his future life. Severely dejected, a person can stop caring about himself, and as a result his knowing that he will have in the future a certain desire need not move him toward insuring or facilitating its satisfaction. At the same time, so it would seem, he can perfectly well conceive of himself as a temporally extended being and can take and maintain the corresponding temporally neutral perspective. Certainly it would come as a surprise to discover that taking and maintaining this perspective was a general cure for severe dejection.

This explanation of the severely dejected man's deficiency in prudential motivation yields, by contraposition, an explanation of prudential action that is an alternative to Nagel's. For in explaining the deficiency by reference to a failure of affect rather than of understanding, one implies that some emotion or desire is an essential factor in prudential motivation. Specifically, in explaining the deficiency by reference to the severely dejected man's having ceased to care about himself, one implies that in prudential motivation, understood narrowly as a type of rational, self-regarding motivation, the operation of self-love is essential. Introducing self-love as an essential factor in prudential motivation will perhaps call to mind Butler's moral psychology, and accordingly I dub this alternative explanation the Butlerian explanation.[7] It represents, let us note, an alternative that directly opposes Nagel's theory on the question of

7. See Joseph Butler, *Fifteen Sermons Preached at Rolls Chapel* (London: Bell, 1949), sermons I and XI.

whether prudential motivation bears out the rationalist thesis that reason has conative power.[8]

The problems that confront Nagel's theory are then twofold. First, the theory must explain the severely dejected man's deficiency in prudential motivation. Second, its explanation of prudential action must survive the competition it faces from the Butlerian explanation. These problems, moreover, should be seen as rather serious. For the explanation the theory offers of the severely dejected man's deficiency in prudential motivation appears to be inadequate, and this apparent inadequacy makes the theory's explanation of prudential action less attractive than its competitor, since the latter derives from an apparently adequate explanation of the severely dejected man's deficiency. Whether the theory, either as so far outlined or with the addition of more of its conceptual apparatus, has the resources for overcoming these problems is the question that we must now address.

III

It should be clear that the first problem cannot be overcome by pressing the theory's favored way of explaining plausible cases of deficiency in prudential motivation. One would have misunderstood our severely dejected man's condition if one described him as being in the grip of such strong desire or violent emotion that his future appeared to him distant and unreal. To be sure, when severe dejection results, as in the case at hand, from events like being jilted or fired, events that cause injury to one's self-esteem, one may tend for some time to dwell on those events, to go over and over again in one's mind what happened and how things might have gone differently. For some time then one might be said to be consumed by the past, and by hurt pride as well, and consequently it might be said that one's future appears distant and unreal. But severe dejection typically outlasts this period. One continues to feel

8. Butler's discussion of what he called "cool or reasonable self-love" (ibid., passim) in fact lends itself to two opposing positions. On the one hand, one might read him as holding that the principle of self-love is a principle of reason that prescribes one's own happiness as an ultimate end of action. This reading leads to Reid and Sidgwick, both of whom identified self-love with the principle of rational prudence, which they took to be a fundamental principle of practical reason. On the other hand, one might read him as holding that the principle of self-love is a part of human nature that is distinct from the rational powers of human beings and that conscience or the principle of reflection alone governs the contribution of those powers to the choice of ultimate ends. This reading leads to Kant, who excluded self-love or what he called "the principle of happiness" from being a fundamental principle of practical reason. It is this second reading that I am identifying as the Butlerian position. I believe it is more faithful to Butler's views than the first reading – that Kant, on this score, is closer to Butler than either Reid or Sidgwick. Pursuing the point here, however, would be a digression.

low and dispirited long after one has ceased to dwell on the past and the pain of injured self-esteem has dulled. Far from being in the grip of strong desire or violent emotion, one will be in a condition that is notable for the weakness of appetite and lack of affect that characterize it. Hence, if Nagel's theory is to hold that a person in such a condition is, in the relevant sense, dissociated from his future life, it will have to explain the person's deficiency in prudential motivation in a way that differs from its favored way of explaining plausible cases of such deficiency. And the theory, given the outline of it presented to far, offers little hope of yielding such an explanation.

As an alternative attempt to save Nagel's theory from the threat the first problem poses, one might maintain that the severely dejected man is someone whose deficiency in prudential motivation is irrelevant to the theory. It is irrelevant, one might argue, because no one who falls into a state of such severe dejection that considerations of future interests and desires fail to move him qualifies as a rational agent. Or, one might argue, it is irrelevant because such a state of severe dejection is pathological. Neither argument, however, should carry conviction. To see why, let us consider each in turn.

In asserting that the severely dejected man fails to qualify as a rational agent, one would presumably be basing this assertion on the man's aimless and passive existence. One's assumption, then, is that to be a rational agent a person must organize his life around ends and goals of some sort and be pursuing them. Hence, the severely dejected man is said not to qualify as a rational agent because his life, during this unhappy period, contains too little in the way of purposeful conduct to warrant describing him as pursuing ends and goals around which he has organized his life. The assumption at the base of this argument, however, is much stronger than the small set of assumptions about rational agents Nagel makes in working out his explanation of prudential action. Essentially, for the purpose of explaining prudential action, Nagel conceives of a rational agent as a person who can use his reasoning powers to determine how to satisfy desires he both has and recognizes that he has and how to make easier and more certain the satisfaction of desires he recognizes that he will have in the future. Certainly, on this conception, the severely dejected man qualifies as a rational agent. For however aimless and passive his life at this time may be, he is not a zombie. His reasoning powers need not be impaired or so impaired that he cannot use them to determine how to satisfy his desires or to anticipate their occurrence in the future. And he does have some desires, though their motivational force is much less than it would be if his mood were cheerier and his spirits higher. His appetite is weak, but it need not be nonexistent. And fatigue and irritability make him subject to desires to sleep and to be left alone. Granted, the overall absence of purposeful conduct in his life precludes him from satisfying any conception of rational agency that is significantly grander than Nagel's. But then on what grounds could one restrict the application of the theory to persons who satisfy some significantly grander conception?

Moreover and obviously, one would gain nothing by so restricting the theory's scope. The demand that the theory explain the deficiency in prudential motivation common to severe dejection would, if the theory were so restricted, simply reappear as a demand that reasons be given to show that severely dejected persons were being excluded from the class of rational agents because of defects in their powers of practical reason. Substituting a significantly grander conception of rational agency for Nagel's would, in other words, simply be an unsuccessful dodge.

At this point, one might, in trying to save Nagel's theory, be drawn to the argument that the severely dejected man's condition is irrelevant because pathological. For whatever conception of rational agency a theory of rational motivation requires or presents, one might think, no such theory should be expected to explain deficiencies in prudential motivation that are part of some pathological condition. Now there is no point to questioning this argument's premiss that the severely dejected man's condition is pathological. Certainly, such an affectless and enervated condition as the one I described would have been diagnosed at one time or another over the last hundred years as neurasthenia, melancholy, or clinical depression. There is, however, a point to questioning whether its being pathological is by itself a good reason for dismissing it as irrelevant. Pathological states, certain ones anyway, can reveal important elements in healthy and normal conditions of human life, and consequently to disregard them solely because they are pathological is to invite ignorance about what contributes to a healthy, normal human life. Of course, those pathological states that we explain by reference to the presence of some disease-causing agent reveal nothing more about health and normality than that healthy, normal people are not infected by this agent. Polio, which we explain by reference to a virus, reveals nothing more about healthy people than that they do not have this virus. But some pathological states, by contrast, we explain by reference to the absence of a health-promoting agent or a deficiency in a health-promoting substance, and these states, then, do reveal the importance to human health and normality that those agents and substances have. Scurvy, which we explain by reference to a vitamin deficiency, reveals the importance to human health that vitamin C has. Thus, if the severely dejected man's condition is best explained analogously to scurvy rather than to polio, then to ignore it when expounding a theory of prudential motivation is to risk a failure of understanding all that is essential to such motivation. In particular, if the severely dejected man's condition is best explained by reference to a deficiency in self-love, then to ignore it is to risk blinding oneself to the role self-love has in such motivation.

It of course remains open to anyone who wishes to try to save Nagel's theory to argue for the opposing way of explaining the severely dejected man's condition, to argue, that is, for explaining it analogously to polio. But in making this argument one necessarily abandons the argument that severe dejection is irrelevant because pathological. One argues instead that the nature of its pathology makes it irrelevant. Now the most promising argument along this line appeals to the onset of some pathological attitude like self-hatred or self-loathing.[9] Taking this line, one argues that the man's severe dejection is due to the presence of some such attitude rather than to a deficiency in self-love, and accordingly one points to the harsh self-criticism that is common to severe dejection, criticism that expresses anger and hostility that the subject feels toward himself. These feelings register the presence and sway of a pathological attitude like self-hatred. Here, one concludes, is the root cause of the man's wretched state, and once this cause is acknowledged, the first problem vanishes as a threat to Nagel's theory.

This line of argument, however, faces two powerful objections. First, one can object that to take self-hatred as the root cause of the severely dejected man's condition is to mistake something that commonly aggravates severe dejection for its sine qua non. That is, while no one would dispute either the observation that harsh self-criticism expressing anger and hostility felt toward oneself is common to severe dejection or the assertion that this criticism and these feelings support an ascription of self-hatred, one can question the cogency of the subsequent inference that self-hatred explains severe dejection. After all, the two are not well matched. Dejection is a state of low spirits and gloomy mood. One lacks interest in and enthusiasm for the pursuits that in large part define one's life. As one's dejection becomes worse, one's indifference and inertia become more pronounced. It becomes increasingly apt to describe one as having given up. Self-hatred, by contrast, prompts action, specifically, self-destructive action. How a state that essentially motivates action explains a condition a defining feature of which is a general lack of motivation is then a real puzzle. To get around this puzzle one might, as some writers have done, hold that the lack of motivation is due to mental exhaustion that follows an orgy of self-hate. But this attempt only hides the puzzle in confusion. Being tired and emptied of mental energy is not the same as being dispirited. Moreover, the puzzle itself suggests a deeper confusion at work, a

---

9. See, e.g., Richard Wollheim, *The Thread of Life* (Cambridge, MA: Harvard University Press, 1984), pp. 251-252.

confusion between the onset of self-hatred, self-loathing, or the like and a loss of self-esteem or a deflation of one's sense of worth, a loss or deflation that allows such hostile attitudes to take hold. It is a confusion reflected in the failure to distinguish between self-destructive behavior and giving up on oneself. Or to borrow from Edward Bibring's criticism of the classical psychoanalytic theory of depression, one must recognize "the decisive difference between the 'ego killing itself' and the 'ego letting itself die.'"[10]

Second, one can object that no tenable theory of human psychology can give a role to self-hatred while denying the existence of self-love, and the most plausible view of the relation between self-hatred and normal self-love is that the former is an attitude whose presence and strength indicate some diminishment or weakening of the latter. Consequently, given this view, explaining the severely dejected man's condition by reference to the presence of self-hatred does not compete with, but rather supplements, explaining his condition by reference to a deficiency in self-love. In other words, this last proposal for saving Nagel's theory fails to explain the severely dejected man's condition in a way that avoids the implication that self-love is an essential factor in prudential motivation. Thus it fails even to engage the first problem, which is to say that to engage it along this line requires expounding a decidedly less plausible view of the relation between self-hatred and normal self-love than the one expressed above.

These two objections, though they may not foreclose altogether this line of argument, certainly show that hope for its eventual success is rather remote.

IV

Before taking up the second problem, we should consider whether Nagel's theory contains any other ideas that might enable it to handle the first problem. In particular, we should consider whether an important distinction Nagel introduces into his theory, a distinction that I have not yet mentioned, could serve this purpose. Thus, in the course of defining a perspective of temporal neutrality and explaining how judgments made from that perspective can be

10. Edward Bibring, "The Mechanism of Depression" in *Affective Disorders: Psychoanalytic Contribution to Their Study*, Phyllis Greenacre, ed. (New York: International University Press, 1953, pp. 13–48). The classical psychoanalytic explanation is found in Freud, 1917, XIV, pp. 239–258. It is worth noting that the deeper confusion of self-hatred with loss of self-esteem built into the classical explanation is due to views about what drives self-hatred that Freud later changed. Specifically, he came to attribute such hatred to an original aggressive drive that is distinct from the libidinal forces on which the classical explanation depended. Cf. 1921, XVIII, pp. 109–110 and 1930, XXI, p. 129. For an account of the change in his views see my "Freud's Later Theory of Civilization: Changes and Implications," *The Cambridge Companion to Freud*, Jerome Neu, ed. (Cambridge: Cambridge University Press, 1991), pp. 287–308. [Chapter 5 in this volume.]

intrinsically motivational, Nagel distinguishes practical judgments from mere beliefs.[11] On his view, while either practical judgments or mere beliefs can issue from a perspective of temporal neutrality, only the former are intrinsically motivational. Or as he puts it, practical judgments have motivational content; mere beliefs do not.[12]

What Nagel means by a practical judgment's motivational content is not easy to say. Roughly, he means to denote the property that a conclusion of deliberation has when it recommends doing a certain action, a recommendation whose force the deliberator should feel if he appreciates the import of the considerations on which it is based. The common view among philosophers is that such deliberation proceeds under the impetus of the desire whose satisfaction is its object, and the motivational force attributed to the deliberation's conclusion is then traced back to that desire. Nagel's account of prudence, however, neatly overturns this common view, since it makes clear that the desire whose satisfaction is the object of the deliberation, being a future desire, can be neither the source of the impetus under which the deliberation proceeds nor the source of the motivational force attributed to the deliberation's conclusion. Opposing this common view, Nagel takes the conclusion's motivational force to derive from the considerations from which the deliberation proceeds and on which its conclusion is based. His point is that, while these considerations include the recognition of a desire, they do not include any desire itself. Accordingly, Nagel locates the conclusion's motivational force in its content. Because this force, on his view, cannot be traced back to some antecedent desire, it must emerge from the considerations from which the deliberation proceeds and the way they combine to produce its conclusion.[13] It is thus contained in the conclusion, which is to say that the conclusion, as a practical judgment, has motivational content.

This distinction between practical judgment and mere belief appears then to give Nagel's theory a way to handle the first problem. It appears, that is, that the theory can draw on the distinction to explain the severely dejected man's deficiency in prudential motivation consistently with its allowing that the man regards his future from a temporally neutral perspective. The explanation would be that the deficiency is due to the man's failure to make the relevant practical judgment despite his recognizing that he will later have a desire

11. See *PA*, pp. 63-67.
12. *PA*, pp. 64-65 and 109-110.
13. Thus Nagel writes, "An account in terms of the structure of reasons and their relations to their conditions and to each other has the advantage of rendering the motivation of action by those conditions significantly more intelligible than does the mere postulation of intervening desires. It explains the peculiar intelligibility of prudential motivation . . ." (*PA*, p. 31).

whose satisfaction he can now facilitate. This explanation, moreover, is consistent with his recognizing this desire from a temporally neutral perspective, since the recognition of the desire need not be anything more than mere belief. Thus, though he believes he will later have a certain desire and though he has this belief from a temporally neutral perspective, what he believes, being the content of mere belief, is not in his mind a consideration that weighs in favor of his taking action to facilitate the satisfaction of this desire. Consequently, he bases no practical judgment recommending such action on it. Despite the belief, he is unmoved to take such action.

Clearly, though, this deployment of Nagel's distinction between practical judgment and mere belief yields only a redescription and not an explanation of the severely dejected man's deficiency in prudential motivation. For one can still ask what it is about the man's severe dejection that explains why his recognizing that he will later have a certain desire is nothing more than mere belief. Why, that is, doesn't what the man believes count for him as a consideration weighing in favor of his taking prudential action, as presumably it would if his mood were better and his spirits higher? Why, to use Nagel's expression, doesn't it have motivational weight, as presumably it would if he were not so dejected? One answer, of course, is that, being severely dejected, he has no interest in satisfying his future desires, whereas he would have this interest if his mood were better and his spirits higher. This answer fits in well with a Butlerian explanation of the man's deficiency in prudential motivation, since an interest in satisfying one's desires is a consequence of self-love. But for an obvious reason it does not fit in well with any explanation Nagel's theory would give. The answer implies that the source of the motivational weight the man's belief would presumably have if he were not so dejected would be a desire antecedent to that belief, and hence one could not incorporate the answer into Nagel's theory without rendering the theory's special notion of motivational content groundless. Incorporating the answer into the theory would, in other words, eliminate the basis for taking practical judgments as intrinsically motivational. The theory therefore must look for a different answer.

Unfortunately, any other answer seems bound to be equally unfitting, and for the same reason. For it must cite some factor in the severely dejected man's condition to explain why his belief that he will later have a certain desire lacks motivational weight, and it is hard to see how such a factor would not be external to the content of that belief. It is hard to see, then, how this factor could fail to imply that the source of the motivational weight the belief would have if the man were not so dejected would be some antecedent desire. Thus, for Nagel's distinction between practical judgment and mere belief to enable his theory to handle the first problem, the theory must, consistently with its thesis that practical judgments have motivational force in virtue of their having motivational content, be able to explain why the severely dejected man fails to make the relevant practical judgment, and no such explanation seems possible. Adding the distinction to the general sketch of Nagel's theory we have given does not, therefore, seem to help the theory overcome the first problem.

It is time then to take up the second.

V

Failure to find a way for Nagel's theory to overcome the first problem means that one cannot cite the theory's greater simplicity as a reason for favoring its explanation of prudential action over the Butlerian explanation. Measured only by its power to explain cases of prudential action, the theory does at least as well as the Butlerian explanation. Hence, if these cases had exhausted all the phenomena that were relevant to evaluating the two explanations, one would have to conclude that the latter introduced an unnecessary factor, self-love, and thus by Ockham's razor must yield to Nagel's theory. Acknowledging the relevance of severe dejection, however, blocks one from drawing this conclusion. Unresolved, the first problem therefore nullifies what in its absence would be a strong and perhaps decisive reason in favor of Nagel's theory.

The theory's difficulties with the first problem also bring into doubt the viability of its notion of motivational content. Hence, what in the absence of this problem would appear to be a theoretical advance may instead be a theoretical liability. This setback, so to speak, is due to the notion's failure to do the job Nagel meant it to do. His idea, recall, was that by attributing motivational content to practical judgment he could distinguish such judgment from mere belief without locating the difference in some desire that is antecedent to the deliberation that yields the judgment. Yet, as we saw in Section IV, adding the distinction to his theory does not eliminate the problem of explaining the severely dejected man's lack of prudential motivation. It merely redefines it as the problem of explaining why the man's recognition that he will later have a certain desire lacks motivational weight. Though Nagel's notion of motivational content is what he needs to ground his rationalist theory, necessity in this case may actually be the mother of an ill-conceived invention.

What gives the notion of motivational content the appearance of being a theoretical advance is the argument from which Nagel got his inspiration for it. The argument proceeds from reflection on deliberation whose conclusion is a prudential judgment, specifically, the judgment that one ought now to make such and such provision for satisfying a desire one knows one will later have.

149

Because the motivational force of this judgment cannot derive from that future desire, it must derive, so the argument goes, from the considerations on which the deliberation is based and the way they combine to yield its conclusion. The argument, clearly, rests on the assumption that there are only two alternatives, either the motivational force of a practical judgment originates in the desire whose satisfaction is the object of the deliberation that yields the judgment or it originates in the considerations on which the deliberation is based and the way they combine to yield its conclusion.[14] Recognizing that the first alternative cannot explain prudential motivation, Nagel affirms the second and develops it by introducing the notion of motivational content to capture its account of the judgment's motivational force. This development appears then to be an advance in the theory of rational motivation, as long as the assumption that the two alternatives exhaust the field goes unchallenged. Once the Butlerian explanation of prudential motivation is seen as an alternative to Nagel's, however, this assumption becomes questionable.

The question, then, is whether the Butlerian explanation is liable to the same criticism as the one Nagel makes of the first alternative. Is it a genuine alternative to the latter as well as to Nagel's theory? The answer can be found in Bulter's observation about the relation of self-love to what he called our particular desires. Self-love, he observed, entails an interest in satisfying one's particular desires.[15] Accordingly, deliberation whose object is the satisfaction of a particular desire can yield a practical judgment whose motivational force does not originate in that desire but rather in the agent's interest in its satisfaction. Thus, by introducing a higher-order interest, what Butler called a general desire,[16] whose object is the satisfaction of lower-order or particular desires, the Butlerian explanation avoids the difficulty that Nagel's criticism brings out in the first alternative. Unlike that alternative, it can attribute the motivational force of a prudential judgment to one desire, the higher-order interest that self-love entails, while allowing that the object of the deliberation that yields the judgment is the satisfaction of another, the particular desire the agent foresees having. The point is that the interest self-love entails can be the source of the judgment's motivational force without its satisfaction's being the object of any deliberation, for deliberation about how to satisfy a particular desire can occur without one's also deliberating about how to meet one's interest in satisfying one's particular desires. To think otherwise is to miss the import of Butler's seminal distinction between the object of a partic-

---

14. *PA*, pp. 35–43. The first alternative, which Nagel rejects, corresponds to Donald Davidson's account of rational action. See Davidson, *Essays on Actions and Events* (Oxford, Oxford University Press, 1980)
15. *Sermons*, XI, par. 5 (p. 167).
16. Ibid.

ular desire and the satisfaction of attaining that object.[17] It is to make the same mistake as the one Butler, using this distinction, exposed in psychological egoism. While Nagel does not make this mistake, he does err in assuming only one alternative to his theory. His effective criticism of this alternative still leaves the Butlerian explanation as a serious competitor.

Nagel further criticizes the first alternative for allowing any desire, no matter how peculiar, to be such that an agent's foreknowledge of it would give him a reason for taking prudential action.[18] That one will have a certain desire, Nagel points out, is not always a consideration that weighs in favor of taking action to satisfy it. This point implies that the motivational weight of such a consideration cannot come from the force with which the desire operates on the agent, for every desire, when present, operates with some force and would therefore, if motivational weight came from that force, have to be such that its presence created a consideration in favor of taking action to satisfy it. Nagel's point thus opposes the first alternative. At the same time, it is consistent with his own theory, since on his theory a consideration that favors taking certain action has weight independently of the force with which the relevant desire, or indeed any desire, operates. Nagel's attribution of motivational content to practical judgments presupposes as much. So in this respect too Nagel's notion of motivational content may appear to be an advance in the theory of rational motivation.

The point, however, is also consistent with the Butlerian explanation. Self-love, though it entails an interest in the satisfaction of one's particular desires, does not entail an interest in satisfying all of them. To the contrary, it can lead one to discriminate among them, to invest interest in satisfying some and to distance oneself from others. Self-love entails an interest in satisfying one's particular desires because it entails an interest in living a happy life, and needless to say discrimination among one's particular desires is necessary for achieving such happiness. On the Butlerian explanation, then, the fact that one now has or later will have a particular desire, the desire, say, to take a walk, counts for one as a consideration weighing in favor of taking a walk only if one has an interest in satisfying that desire. Absent the interest and regardless of the force with which the desire, if present, operates on one, the fact is not a consideration that weighs with one. The consideration's motivational weight, in other words, does not come from the force with which the desire to take a walk operates. It comes rather from one's interest in satisfying that desire.

It follows that considerations of future desires can have weight, even though the desires, being prospective rather than real, do not yet operate on the agent.

17. Ibid., XI, par. 6 (pp. 167-168).
18. *PA*, pp. 39-41.

Furthermore, the magnitude of their weight corresponds to the strength of the interest one has in satisfying the desires. This point is then immediately extendible to considerations of present desires. The magnitude of their weight likewise corresponds to the strength of the interest one has in satisfying those present desires and not to the strength of the desires themselves. Consequently, rational motivation on the Butlerian explanation, no less than on Nagel's, registers the weight of the considerations in favor of taking certain action rather than the strength of the particular desires whose satisfaction would be the object of that action. Either explanation implies a difference between actions in which the agent is guided by considerations that weigh in favor of his taking such action and actions in which the agent responds to the strength of particular desires that impel him. Either, that is, implies a difference between deliberative and impulsive action, though the one uses the notion of a higher order interest, the other the notion of motivational content, to account for the difference.

So far we have found no reason to favor Nagel's explanation over the Butlerian explanation. Neither its greater simplicity nor the theoretical advances it appears to make argue for its superiority. There still remains the possibility of direct objection to the Butlerian explanation, specifically, to the concept of self-love on which it relies. Yet the only possibility, short of denying that self-love is an intelligible concept, is to deny that it is an explanatory one. Butler himself may have implicitly recognized this possibility when he argued against the idea that self-love and neighbor love were necessarily opposed.[19] His argument, however, presupposes his conception of self-love and therefore fails to eliminate this possibility. He argued that since neighbor love was a particular desire, it did not necessarily oppose self-love, which was a general desire, and by negating his conclusion and inverting his reasoning one can produce an argument against his conception. Its conclusion would be that self-love is not a general desire and, indeed, not any single desire at all. This argument thus represents a serious, direct objection to the Butlerian explanation.

The argument in detail is this. To say that someone acts from self-love is to say no more than that he acts from a desire for some purely personal good or advantage, and any one of a host of particular desires could fit this description: avarice, ambition, the desire for fame, the desire for love, the desire for sensual pleasure, and many others besides. The key point is that the person does not act out of any interest in or concern for the welfare of others, except insofar as he sees benefiting them as a way to secure for himself some personal good or advantage. Self-love is seen most clearly in the psychology of the unbridled egoist, that familiar philosophical foil whose governing trait is that

19. *Sermons*, XI, par. 11 (pp. 172-174).

the ends he pursues, while they include such things as sensual pleasure and the accumulation of wealth and power, exclude altogether bringing happiness to others or saving them from misery and pain. He is someone who could never truthfully say to another, "I did it for your sake." In a sense, then, the import of describing someone as acting out of self-love is negative. The description serves to exclude a range of motives from the explanation of the person's action rather than to specify any single motive that could explain his action. Self-love, therefore, is not an explanatory concept.

This argument, of course, would not represent a serious objection to the Butlerian explanation if it amounted to no more than a quibble about the proper use of the term 'self-love'. To avoid this conclusion, one must take its denial that self-love is an explanatory concept as denying the necessity of attributing a higher-order interest to human beings to explain their pursuit of happiness. For to allow that the attribution was necessary would be to admit a use for 'self-love' on which it expressed an explanatory concept, namely, its use as a name for this higher-order interest. Hence, the principal implication of the thesis that self-love is a negative concept is to deny that human beings possess such an interest. This is hardly a benign implication.

To be sure, the implication might not seem especially worrisome if the Butlerian attribution of self-love merely introduced into human psychology an interest that had certain formal relations to a person's particular desires, relations that the expression 'higher order' captured. But the attribution does more than this. It also introduces an interest that unites those particular desires whose satisfaction is its object. The attribution of self-love is an attribution of an interest in oneself and in the life one is living, and through this interest a person invests interest in those particular desires whose satisfaction, in his view, would contribute to his well-being and enrich his life. Alternatively, to follow Butler, it is an attribution of the desire for happiness, and a person then invests interest in his particular desires according as their satisfaction, in his view, contributes to his happiness.[20] Either description makes clear how, through the work of self-love and the higher-order interests it entails, otherwise unconnected particular desires become united in one personality and how their possessor's life thus acquires definition. The process, no doubt, is gradual and becomes more reflective with greater experience and maturity. Reflection, though, is not essential to it. Particular desires become united through the work of self-love, not as a result of being meaningfully fitted together in view of their objects, but rather as a result of being referred to the same person and located inside that person's life. The question, then, is what could give these desires such unity in the absence of a higher-order interest.

20. Ibid., XI, par. 5 (p. 167).

And that there appears to be no promising answer spells trouble for the thesis that self-love is a negative concept.

The trouble is brought out most clearly in the way success or failure, advancement or disappointment, in the pursuit of some particular end can, as it often does, affect the attitude and confidence a person brings to the pursuit of some other particular but quite unrelated end. The common explanation is that such success heightens self-esteem, such failure diminishes it, and boosts and blows to one's self-esteem tend to color one's entire outlook on one's life and to affect one's self-confidence generally. This explanation, however, presupposes a higher-order desire or interest, for to understand how a boost or a blow to a person's self-esteem can color his outlook on life and affect his self-confidence one must suppose that the person, at the time of the boost or blow, is concerned about what sort of person he is and what kind of life he is living, which is to say, one must suppose that he has invested interest in himself and in his life. Without such a higher-order interest, whose work unites the different desires that prevail in the different areas of a person's life, nothing, it appears, could account for the way the vicissitudes of self-esteem affect mood and initiative throughout all these areas.[21] How, then, one could hold that self-love was a negative concept and not be committed to viewing people as possessing emotionally fragmented personalities is hard to see.

There is still, admittedly, the possibility, as a last-ditch objection, of denying that self-love is an intelligible concept. Presumably, the temptation to make this objection comes from some such thought as that a lover and his beloved are necessarily distinct individuals. That is, it comes from assuming that one can make sense of self-love only by strict analogy with love of another. This assumption, though, is false. As the argument that supports taking self-love as an explanatory concept shows, one can construe the concept as that of a higher-order interest, an interest whose object is the satisfaction of particular desires, and accordingly self-love is not strictly analogous to love of another. Indeed, this point is implicit in Butler's argument against taking self-love as necessarily opposed to neighbor love.

Direct objections to the Butlerian explanation do not, then, provide reasons to favor Nagel's. They fail to show that the concept of self-love on which the explanation relies is unusable, much less incoherent. And since this concept has theoretical advantages comparable to the ones that would otherwise recommend Nagel's notion of motivational content, it follows generally that

21. The connection between self-esteem and self-love and the idea that the vicissitudes in the former correspond to changes in the strength of the latter are Freud's. See Freud, 1914, XIV, pp. 98-100. See also Heniz Kohut, *The Analysis of the Self* (New York: International Universities Press, 1971).

neither these theoretical advantages nor the concept's alleged difficulties argue for Nagel's explanation as against the Butlerian explanation. At the same time, the problem the former has accommodating the phenomena of severe dejection gives strong reason to favor the latter. In the end, it points to the conclusion that the former's shortcomings, in comparison with the latter's strengths, are due to its use of a made-up notion of motivational content where a more complex understanding of the structure of rational motivation is wanted.

VI

I hope that extending my critique to Nagel's explanation of altruistic action will at this point be seen as unnecessary. With the reader's indulgence, I will leave it as an exercise. Despite this bit of unfinished business, the critique shows, I believe, that the claim of Nagel's theory to have vindicated the rationalist theory of moral agency is dubious at best. In addition, though, I hope it also makes a persuasive case for the importance of mental disorders to the study of practical reason.

APPENDIX: NAGEL'S NOTION OF MOTIVATIONAL CONTENT

Nagel's notion of motivational content is, as Sections IV and V above suggest, the most significant theoretical innovation in his theory. If it is viable, then the theory should be able to explain the severely dejected man's lack of prudential motivation consistently with its conception of practical judgment as intrinsically motivational. The argument of Section IV shows that Nagel's distinction between practical judgment and mere belief offers no real hope for realizing this possibility. There are, however, two other possibilities that a full critique of Nagel's theory should consider. This appendix deals with them.

The first is contained in Nagel's distinction between motivational content and motivational efficacy. Nagel introduces this distinction to explain cases of imprudence in which the agent, owing to weakness of will, sloth, panic, or the like, fails to act on a well-founded practical judgment.[22] His idea is that, though this practical judgment has motivational content, the agent in each of these cases fails to act on it because a strong, opposing desire, inclination, or emotion overmatches whatever motivation force it has in virtue of that con-

---

22. *PA*, pp. 65–67. Note, it is implicit in attributing a well-founded practical judgment to the agent that he regards his future from a temporally neutral perspective. Thus these cases do not involve dissociation.

tent.[23] The judgment, in other words, despite its motivational content, is in these circumstances motivationally inefficacious. Accordingly, if the circumstances of the severely dejected were similar to those of the weak-willed, the slothful, and the panic-stricken, the theory could explain the former's deficiency in prudential motivation in the same way.

The question is whether the circumstances are similar. To compare, let us consider those of the weak-willed agent. Here is a typical example. Julie has a term paper due in three days. Getting a good grade on it is important to her. Julie, however, also loves to go to baseball games. Watching baseball is a weakness of hers. As she sits down to work on her paper, a friend calls and invites her to today's game. Julie is torn. She knows she ought to decline her friend's invitation and work on her paper. But she cannot resist. After briefly hemming and hawing, she accepts. A schematic description of this example will help to bring out the relevant circumstances. There are, to begin with, certain facts about Julie's life, about her present and future desires, in particular. She is aware of these facts and takes them in from a temporally neutral perspective. Some of them count for her as considerations weighing in favor of her doing one thing. Others count for her as considerations weighing in favor of her doing another. She cannot, however, do both and must decide between them. Because she sees that, on balance, the first set of considerations outweighs the second, she concludes that she ought to do the action it favors. In drawing this conclusion, she makes up her mind as to what she ought to do. Thus, when she does the other action instead, she exhibits weakness of will.

It should be evident from this schematic description that the weak-willed agent's circumstances are importantly different from the severely dejected man's. Whereas the facts that the weak-willed agent takes in about her present and future desires weigh with her, the facts the severely dejected man takes in about his present and future desires do not weigh with him. That is, for the weak-willed agent, such facts count as considerations that weigh in favor of doing certain actions, whereas for the severely dejected man the fact he takes in about a desire he will later have does not count as a consideration that weighs in favor of doing some action. The former faces conflicting considerations all of which have for her motivational weight. The latter faces a fact about a future desire, which has for him no motivational weight.

This difference then shows that Nagel's theory cannot adapt its explanation

---

23. At one point (ibid.), Nagel writes that a practical judgment can fail to move a person to action even when no desire, inclination, or emotion opposes it. Here Nagel seems actually to disconnect motivational content from motivational force, for the judgment would have to issue in action if it had motivational force and was unopposed. Since Nagel appears to allow for this possibility for no other reason than to make his theory consistent with isolated cases of inaction, it can be safely ignored.

of the weak-willed agent's deficiency in prudential motivation to explain the severely dejected man's deficiency. The weak-willed agent, as we've seen, makes a practical judgment as to what she ought, on balance, to do based on the considerations favoring different actions she weighs, and her deficiency in prudential motivation therefore consists in the insufficiency in the motivational force of this judgment. The severely dejected man, by contrast, makes no practical judgment as to what he ought to do based on such considerations, nor could he since the fact he takes in about a future desire does not weigh with him. Consequently, his deficiency in prudential motivation does not consist in an insufficiency in the motivational force of some practical judgment. Unlike the weak-willed agent, he makes no judgment with motivational content, so his deficiency in prudential motivation cannot be identified with some well-founded but motivationally inefficacious practical judgment. The distinction between motivational content and motivational efficacy does not yield an explanation of this deficiency.

The second possibility of the theory's explaining the deficiency consistently with its conception of practical judgment as intrinsically motivational lies in Nagel's rendering of practical judgment as judgment about what one has reason to do. Nagel uses this rendering to capture what he means by a practical judgment's motivational content.[24] He takes reasons for action to be distinct from but parallel to reasons for belief, and correspondingly, on his theory, practical reason is distinct from but parallel to theoretical reason.[25] In practical reasoning one makes a practical judgment in light of the reasons for action one weighs, just as in theoretical reasoning one forms a belief in light of the reasons for belief one considers. Thus action contrary to what one judges one has most reason to do is attributable to a failure of practical reason, just as disbelief contrary to what one sees one has most reason to believe is attributable to a failure of theoretical reason. Accordingly, Nagel's theory could, consistently with its conception of practical judgment as intrinsically motivational, explain the severely dejected man's deficiency in prudential motivation as a failure of practical reason if the man, in failing to act prudentially, acts contrary to what he judges he has most reason to do.

The idea behind this explanation is again to assimilate the severely dejected man's condition to that of the weak-willed agent. For weak-willed action is a paradigm of action contrary to one's better judgment, which is to say, one's judgment as to what one has most reason to do. The question, then, is whether the previous argument against treating the severely dejected man's condition as on all fours with that of the weak-willed agent applies in this

24. See *PA*, p. 65.
25. *PA*, p. 20-22. See also *PA*, pp. 64-65.

case. If practical judgment is understood, according to Nagel's rendering, as a judgment about what one has reason to do, does the argument still show that the severely dejected man makes no practical judgment and therefore, unlike the weak-willed agent, does not act against such a judgment? The answer depends on whether one interprets the term 'reason for action' subjectively or objectively.

To bring out this difference, consider again the weak-willed agent's deliberations. For her the relevant reasons for action are the facts about present and future desires that she weighs. Some of these facts are reasons for one action. Some are reasons for another. And in taking them in, she sees that she cannot do both and that, on balance, there is more reason to do one than the other. Thus, when she judges accordingly and acts contrarily, she acts irrationally. Plainly, if what 'reason for action' means in this schematic description is a fact that would count for a rational agent as a consideration weighing in favor of his doing a certain action if he took it in and understood its implications, then there is no material difference between Nagel's rendering of the agent's practical judgment and the rendering it has on our earlier schematic description. Hence, on this subjective interpretation, whichever rendering of practical judgment one applies, the severely dejected man makes no such judgment.

By contrast, if what 'reason for action' means is a fact that would count for a rational agent as a consideration weighing in favor of his doing a certain action, provided that he not only took it in and understood its implications but also met some further, objective criterion of reasonableness, a standard of normality, say, or an ideal of wisdom and equanimity, then there is a material difference between the two renderings. On this objective interpretation, whether a fact is a reason for action depends not on the agent's actual frame of mind but on the frame of mind he would have if he had the orientation and temperament of a reasonable person. Hence, the severely dejected man could make judgments about what he had reason to do, for nothing about severe dejection prevents someone from applying an objective criterion of reasonableness to a set of facts he has taken in and whose implications he understands. On the objective interpretation, he could make a practical judgment if practical judgment were rendered as Nagel renders it.

This interpretation, however, is of no use to Nagel's theory. This is because Nagel's theory, like any theory of rational motivation in which the term 'reason for action' is fundamental, conceives of a rational agent as an agent whose conduct is responsive to reasons. Accordingly, different interpretations of the term yield different conceptions of rational agency, and to be of use to Nagel's theory an interpretation must yield a conception that is no stronger than the one implicit in the small set of assumptions about rational agency that Nagel makes in working out his account of prudential action. The objective interpretation, though, by relativizing what qualifies as a reason for action to the motivational capacities of agents who meet some objective criterion of reasonableness incorporates those capacities into the conception of rational agency it yields, and consequently that conception is stronger than Nagel's. In effect, then, an attempt to defend Nagel's theory by adopting the objective interpretation of 'reason for action' is an attempt to exclude the severely dejected man from the class of rational agents, and this attempt fares no better than the one we considered in Section III that explicitly excluded him from that class. Like the earlier one, it too requires a conception of rational agency that is significantly grander than Nagel's.

The attempt represents a rationalist tendency to use the term 'reason for action' and the different meanings it can have as a cover for inflating the power of practical reason. After all, one who lacks the motivational capacities the possession of which would make him responsive to those facts that, on the objective interpretation, count as reasons for action would not ordinarily be thought thereby to have defective powers of *reason*. Indeed, if his lack of these capacities were due to a deficiency of self-love, as the Butlerian explanation implies, then to take the facts to which he was unresponsive as reasons for action would be to make self-love an ingredient of practical reason and thus to inflate the power not only beyond anything Nagel intended but also beyond our ordinary understanding of a power of reason. Clearly, then, even if the objective interpretation were available to the theory, nothing would be gained from the theory's adopting it since the problem severe dejection poses would reappear as the problem of justifying the inflation of practical reason the interpretation brings. And since adopting the subjective interpretation merely reaffirms the earlier conclusion that the severely dejected man does not make a practical judgment relative to the desire he foresees having and makes no provision to satisfy, we can conclude that defining the motivational content of a practical judgment in terms of the agent's reasons for action does not help the theory to explain the man's lack of prudential motivation consistently with its conception of practical judgment as intrinsically motivational.

159

8

Empathy and universalizability

What makes psychopaths, as characterized in modern psychiatry and portrayed in literature and film, such fascinating figures? What is it about their evident lack of morality that transfixes our imagination as it chills our souls? To describe them, as they were once described, as moral imbeciles, does not even begin to convey the peculiarity of their condition. Though amoral, they appear nevertheless to be capable of reasoning, weighing evidence, estimating future consequences, understanding the norms of their society, anticipating the blame and condemnation that result from violation of those norms, and using these cognitive skills to make and carry out their plans. Some have been described as highly intelligent and socially adept, people whose gift for facile, ingratiating conversation can beguile even those already alerted to their pathology. The swiftness of their thought plainly does not fit with the ideas of stupidity and feeblemindedness that the older description carries.

Nor are psychopaths well described as maniacs, pyro-, klepto-, homicidal, or otherwise. They are persistent wrongdoers, to be sure, but they are not or not necessarily driven to commit their misdeeds. No inner compulsion or violent emotion is essential to their disorder. Think of Richard Hickock as depicted in Capote's *In Cold Blood*,[1] or Bruno C. Anthony, brilliantly portrayed by Robert Walker in Hitchcock's *Strangers on a Train*.[2] Each is a smooth and bloodless operator, not someone subject to irresistible impulses, not someone governed by personal demons.

Think too of the contrast Capote sets up between Hickock and his partner in crime, Perry Smith. Smith, who wielded the knife and pulled the trigger in the murders for which he and Hickock were executed, is depicted by Capote as a man with a very weak grip on reality, given to dream and delusion, and also prone to explosive rage. In Capote's reconstruction of the crime, these factors combine to ignite Smith's murderous action, and the savagery of his conduct is made even more extraordinary by the prior concern he shows for the comfort and, indeed, safety of his victims. Both during the commission of the

---

1. Truman Capote, *In Cold Blood* (New York: Random House, 1965).
2. Burbank, CA: Warner Brothers Pictures, 1951, directed by Alfred Hitchcock; screenplay by Raymond Chandler and Czenzi Ormonde.

crime and in the subsequent events leading to execution, Smith exhibits this soft side as well as a capacity for sympathy and connection. These are dispositions wholly absent in Hickock's character. Capote describes him as an exceptionally shallow man, always scheming, filled with petty emotions when his schemes fail, and incapable of deeper feelings either for himself or others. In particular, he feels no compunction about his actions, however wrong or injurious they may be, and exhibits no shame, regret, or remorse over them. The crime is his idea, and he befriends Smith because he sees in Smith's capacity for violence something very useful to forwarding his criminal ambitions. He, on the other hand, is not, despite his bluster, inclined to violence. And unlike Smith, he has no trouble keeping a clear head and a steady mind as he pursues his evil ends.

Of course, you might think there is nothing really peculiar about Hickock's character. He is like any number of common thieves, con artists, and gangsters who lead lives of crime, a vicious man who is interested only in himself and who cares little about others. To call him a psychopath is just to put him in that grab bag category psychiatrists use for any habitual wrongdoer or troublemaker who is not obviously psychotic. Yet this category, despite its overuse by many psychiatrists, can be more tightly constructed so that it applies to a distinct type of personality, a type defined by specific emotional deficits and imaginatively rendered in Capote's description of Hickock.[3] These deficits include the inability to enter into genuine friendships or to form attachments of loyalty and love, and also the lack of a capacity for moral feeling and emotion, the lack of a conscience. If one makes possession of these deficits a defining condition of the category, then the difference between a psychopath and your run-of-the-mill career criminal is clear. In the latter's life, unlike the former's, there are or can be people to whom the criminal is emotionally committed and in relations with whom he is liable to some experience of moral feeling, some stirrings of conscience. Thus even for as hard-bitten and callous an outlaw as the one Humphrey Bogart played in *High Sierra*, a man known to police and prosecutors nationwide as "Mad Dog" Earle, there is an Ida Lupino to whom he is attached by bonds of trust and love and in relations with whom experiences of regret and remorse are possible. By contrast, in the life of a psychopath, on this tighter construction of the category, there can be no Ida Lupinos.

Tightening the category by making these emotional deficits essential to it not only saves the term 'psychopath' from becoming merely a fancy word for habitual wrongdoer but also sharpens the issues of moral responsibility and criminal liability that it raises. For 'psychopath' is not exclusively a term of clinical practice. It is also a term psychiatrists, criminologists, and other legal

3. See Hervey Cleckley, *The Mask of Sanity*, 5th ed. (St. Louis: Mosby, 1976), pp. 337-364.

theorists use to pick out a class of criminals whose crimes result from severe mental disorder but who do not meet the law's standard tests for being insane. Those tests concern the agent's moral knowledge and his capacity for self-control, whether he knows the difference between right and wrong and whether he can conform his conduct to the limits the law imposes, and it is generally conceded that psychopaths, whatever the nature of their disorder, know right from wrong and have the requisite self-control. Consequently, whether they are morally responsible for their crimes is an issue on which opinion divides according as one believes wrongdoing that is the product of severe mental disorder is blameless, no matter how grave the offense, or believes wrongdoing that the agent knows or should have known is wrong and that he could have averted merits blame, no matter how screwy the agent. The psychopath, as a mentally disordered individual, thus puts pressure on our traditional criteria for moral responsibility, the more so the more one can characterize the disorder as something other than a proclivity for wrongdoing.

Admittedly, the pressure it puts on the traditional criteria shrinks to nothing when those exerting it can produce no more compelling evidence of the disorder than the agent's persistent wrongdoing. In this case, the argument for excusing psychopaths from moral responsibility comes to little more than psychiatric ipse dixitism. The argument, however, gains considerable strength when one uses possession of certain emotional deficits to define the disorder. The classification of individuals as psychopaths then becomes less hostage to psychiatric prejudices about morally deviant behavior and more determinable by evidence that can stand apart from such deviance. Accordingly, the evaluation of these individuals as mentally disordered becomes less controversial, perhaps even uncontroversial, and the issue narrows to whether this disorder, when severe, excuses the sufferer from moral responsibility for the wrongs that result from it.

At the same time, those who press this strengthened argument for excusing psychopaths from moral responsibility rely on a characterization of their personality whose coherence is open to question. Psychopaths, they tell us, suffer from an affective disorder rather than a cognitive or volitional one. Jeffrie Murphy writes, for instance, "[U]nlike the psychotic, the psychopath seems to suffer from no obvious cognitive or volitional impairments," and three paragraphs later he continues, "Though psychopaths know, in some sense, what it means to wrong people, to act immorally, this kind of judgment has for them no motivational component at all. . . . [T]hey feel no guilt, regret, shame, or remorse (though they may superficially fake these feelings) when they have engaged in harmful conduct."[4] To be sure, Murphy hedges these remarks in ways

---

4. "Moral Death: A Kantian Essay on Psychopathy," *Ethics* 82 (1972): 284–298, esp. pp. 285–287.

that avoid commitment to an incoherent thesis. He says only that psychopaths *seem* not to suffer from any *obvious* cognitive or volitional impairment and only that there is *some* sense in which they have knowledge of right and wrong but are unmotivated by that knowledge. Still, in talking of moral feeling and motivation as if they were separable from the cognitive and volitional capacities that being a moral agent entails, he suggests a possibility that should not go unchallenged. Insusceptibility to moral feeling and motivation may imply cognitive impairments. And while tightening the category of psychopath by making certain emotional deficits essential to it naturally leads to identifying it as a type of affective disorder, it does not follow from this identification that the condition entails no cognitive disorder. In particular, it does not follow that it entails no deficiency in the faculties of moral judgment.

The question is an old one. It is a question of internalism in one sense of that now protean term. Does a moral judgment, specifically, a judgment of what it is right to do or what one ought to do, imply a motive to moral conduct or a liability to moral feeling? Could moral judgments be truly practical or action-guiding if making them did not have this implication? The question is at the heart of many of the disputes in metaethics that have dominated Anglo-American moral philosophy in this century. Long-running disputes about the concept of a moral judgment, about the meaning of the words 'right' and 'ought' when they are used to express moral judgments, and about the status of the properties, if any, that one predicates of actions when one makes such judgments are in large part due to intractable disagreements on this question. Consequently, if we treat the question from within metaethics, we cannot expect to get very far toward determining whether being a psychopath entails some deficiency in one's faculties of moral judgment. Whether the judgments of right and wrong psychopaths make are genuinely moral judgments, whether they use the words 'right' and 'ought' in a distinctively moral sense, and whether they predicate moral properties of actions when they say that an act is right to do or ought to be done are no easier to determine than the same questions asked about ordinary moral agents on those occasions when they judge that it would be right to do some act but are unmoved to do it and feel no regret or remorse about failing to do it. Naturalists, descriptivists, and realists will give us one set of answers. Emotivists, prescriptivists, and projectivists will give us another. And nothing in the behavior or thought of a psychopath, as distinct from that of an ordinary moral agent, argues for one set as against the other.

We can avoid the impasses of metaethics, however, if we treat the question from within psychology. The psychopath makes judgments about what it is right to do and what a person ought to do, in some sense of 'right' and in some sense of 'ought', yet is insusceptible to moral feeling and moral motivation. Accordingly, rather than ask whether this insusceptibility implies an inability to make moral judgments, we should consider different cognitive operations that can yield judgments about what it is right to do or what one ought to do and ask whether the insusceptibility implies an inability to engage in one or another of these. We can then leave for metaethics the question of whether any of them is essential to making moral judgments. Hence, the question of internalism, as a question asked within psychology, is a question about cognitive involvement in moral feeling and moral motivation. To be more exact, it is a question of whether some cognitive operations that yield judgments of what it is right to do and what one ought to do also yield motives to act in accordance with those judgments and liabilities to feelings of shame, regret, or remorse over failures to heed them.

We have now reached the principal question of our study. It has, as I have formulated it, two parts: one about motives and the other about feelings. They do not, however, require separate answers. Given that a person could not be susceptible to these feelings if he were insusceptible to the motives and conversely, answering either part suffices for answering the other. We can thus simplify the study by limiting it to one of the parts, and since the question of internalism with respect to motives is more tractable, we shall make steadier progress by pursuing it and leaving the question with respect to feelings aside.

The first thing to note, however, in focusing on motives, is the distinction between the internalism of hypothetical imperatives and that of categorical ones.[5] The distinction corresponds to two different ways in which a judgment about what it is right to do or what one ought to do could have motivational force. On the one hand, it could have such force relative to a desire the stimulation of which is independent of the cognitive operation that yields the judgment. This occurs where the operation is means-to-ends reasoning and the end being reasoned about is the object of a desire that is the occasion of the reasoning. On the other hand, the judgment could have motivational force in itself. This would occur if the force originated in the same cognitive operation that yielded the judgment. The first case is that of hypothetical imperatives; the second is that of categorical. Clearly, some cognitive failure would have to explain insusceptibility to the motivational force of the latter, whereas it need not explain insusceptibility to the motivational force of the former since such insusceptibility could be explained, instead, by the absence of the desire rela-

---

5. See Thomas Nagel *The Possibility of Altruism* (Oxford: Clarendon Press, 1970), pp. 7-12. The terms 'internalism of hypothetical imperatives' and 'internalism of categorical imperatives' are mine, not Nagel's, but they correspond to the distinction he draws between the internalism of Hobbes's ethics and the internalism of Kant's. See also my "Sidgwick on Ethical Judgment" in *Essays on Henry Sidgwick*, ed. by Bart Schultz (Cambridge: Cambridge University Press, 1992), pp. 241-258. [Chapter 9 in this volume.]

tive to which the judgment is made. Consequently, only the internalism of categorical imperatives gives a definite answer to our question about psychopathy. This means that, in considering cognitive operations that yield judgments about what it is right to do or what one ought to do of which internalism is true, we shall need to attend to the kind of internalism it is. Ultimately, what we are after in treating the question of internalism from within psychology is whether the internalism of categorical imperatives is true of any of these judgments.

To treat the question of internalism in this way presupposes that a person can possess knowledge of right and wrong in different forms. These forms, let us suppose, correspond to different levels of sophistication or maturity if not incomparably distinct types of thought. At the least sophisticated level is mere knowledge of the conventional moral standards observed in the person's community, knowledge that one normally acquires fairly early in one's upbringing. Later, as one's relations with others become more complex, one comes to understand the reasons for these conventions and to comprehend the ideals that give them meaning. One thus acquires more sophisticated knowledge. Psychopaths presumably, being minimally socialized, at least have knowledge of their community's conventional moral standards. It follows then, given the tighter construction of psychopathy we are now using, that a person could possess such knowledge without being motivated to act on it. To what extent psychopaths possess the more sophisticated knowledge that comes from understanding the reasons for the conventions and the ideals that give them meaning is, however, uncertain. Consequently, whether a person could possess knowledge of right and wrong at increasingly deeper levels of sophistication without limit and still be insusceptible to moral motivation is a different matter. The question of internalism, even if closed at the shallowest levels, is open at deeper ones.[6]

Kant's ethics offers, arguably, the most important modern account of this deeper knowledge of right and wrong. On his account, such knowledge consists of a formal principle that governs the workings of practical reason. The statement of the principle that most clearly displays its formal character is its

---

6. Strictly speaking, the relative depth of the knowledge is irrelevant to whether the question of internalism with respect to it is open. For what keeps the question open is the possibility of there being some form of knowledge of right and wrong that no psychopath could possess, and the possibility of such knowledge does not rest on its level of sophistication as compared with the deepest level of the knowledge attributable to psychopaths. At the same time, making the supposition that any form of knowledge of right and wrong that psychopaths could not possess must be deeper than that which they do possess introduces a scheme that facilitates our treatment of the question of internalism from within psychology, and it is for this reason that I make it.

first formulation in Kant's system. Loosely put, this first formulation is that one act only on those rules that one can understand and endorse as rules for all human beings or, as Kant would say, universal laws. Fundamental moral knowledge then, on this account, is knowledge of a formal criterion of validity, the criterion of universalizability, that one applies to rules of action, including conventional moral standards, but also including personal imperatives, institutional directives, and other more immediate practical principles. Indeed, Kant thought that in every rational action there was at least implicitly some rule the agent followed, and in this way he brought all rational conduct within the scope of his fundamental principle of morality.[7] It will be useful to adopt Kant's view of rational action since doing so will simplify our discussion without affecting the argument. Let us assume, then, as part of this account, that every rational action proceeds from some rule. Accordingly, our deeper judgments of right and wrong in every case consist in applying the criterion of universalizability to this rule.

How one is supposed to apply the criterion, however, is a controversial matter. There is no agreement either on what method of application Kant intended or on what method makes the most sense. Nonetheless, the point of applying the criterion is clear. It is to enforce consistency in practical thought and moral judgment. For if I am required to understand the rule of my action as a universal law and endorse it as such, then I cannot decide to do something that I would object to if it were done by another whose circumstances were relevantly similar to mine. Likewise, I cannot excuse myself or excuse a friend, for that matter, from doing an action I think others ought to do if our circumstances are relevantly similar to theirs. Understanding and endorsing the rule of one's action as a rule for all human beings means applying it, without exception, to anyone whose situation meets the description contained in the rule of the circumstances that trigger its application.

The criterion thus serves as a filter on a person's reasons for action since rules of action specify such reasons. How it filters these reasons is not hard to see. If a person in considering whether to do an action to which he is inclined, double-parking, say, when in a hurry, tests its rule by applying the criterion of universalizability and finds that it fails, he must then, on penalty of being inconsistent, abandon further consideration of acting on that rule. This means he must dismiss as reasons for double-parking those facts about his circumstances that he would have taken as reasons if he had accepted the rule without testing it or had mistakenly thought it had passed. In short, a person who applies the criterion of universalizability in considering whether to double-park

---

7. See *Groundwork of the Metaphysic of Morals*, trans. H. J. Paton (New York: Harper & Row, 1964), p. 80.

will exclude from being a reason for the action any fact that he would reject as a reason for another's double-parking if the latter's circumstances were relevantly similar to his own. He will conclude, then, unless of course he finds a reason that survives the test of universalizability, that he ought not to double-park.

Furthermore, his excluding from being reasons for double-parking facts that fail the test should correspond to his checking the inclination to double-park that initiated his deliberations, for otherwise the test would be idle. An aversion to inconsistency, it would seem, thus combats and, if sufficiently strong, suppresses the inclination to double-park when reasons for the action are invalidated by the test of universalizability. Application of the criterion would appear, then, in this case to yield both the judgment that one ought not to double-park and a motive to abstain from such action. It would appear, in other words, to be a cognitive operation that can at once yield judgments of what one ought to do and motives to act in accordance with those judgments. And if this is indeed so, then it shows that one can draw from Kant's ethics an account of our deeper knowledge of right and wrong that supports taking internalism to be true of that knowledge.

Of course, if a person's aversion to inconsistency is due to a desire to be rational that he acquires in the same way as he acquires the desire to be financially secure, then the motive that applying the criterion of universalizability yields is ultimately external to the cognitive operation. In this event, the account would at most support the internalism of hypothetical imperatives. It would be similar, that is, to an account of our knowledge of annuities that showed how one's calculations of the interest earned from an annuity can at once yield judgments about accrued benefits and motives to purchase annuities that would have those benefits. But if one holds, as Kant did, that an aversion to inconsistency is inherent in reason, that a rational mind spontaneously seeks consistency, then the motive would be internal to the cognitive operation and the account would therefore support taking the internalism of categorical imperatives to be true of our deeper knowledge of right and wrong.

The statement that an aversion to inconsistency is inherent in reason is open to interpretation, however. There is more than one thesis it could express. The least controversial is that the mind abhors contradiction. No doubt this thesis too has its share of opponents. Someone somewhere has surely argued that even the Law of Contradiction is a social construction, part of the knowledge/power regime that oppresses us all. I suspect, though, that the thesis enjoys widespread acceptance among philosophers and psychologists, acceptance that is by no means confined to enthusiasts for computer models of the mind. Be this as it may, the thesis that the mind abhors contradiction is too weak to justify taking the motive that applying the criterion of universalizability yields to be internal to that cognitive operation.

This is because basing a decision to act on reasons that fail the test of universalizability does not entail a contradiction The inconsistency it entails is of a different sort. If I decide to double-park, for instance, because I'm in a hurry, though I realize that I would object to another's double-parking even if he too were in a hurry and faced circumstances that weren't relevantly different from mine, then it's likely that I would manufacture an excuse to ease my conscience. But suppose I didn't. Suppose, instead, I thought to myself, while setting the parking brake and realizing that I would object to another's doing what I was doing, "I may double-park here; after all, I'm in a hurry and who's going to stop me!" In this case – call it the case of the psychopathic thought – I would in effect be drawing conclusions about what I may do and what another ought not to do that could not both be justified. Indeed, my conclusions would be arbitrary, since I would be treating my circumstances as justifying a license to double-park but denying that another's, which are not relevantly different from mine, provide similar justification. But to say that these conclusions are arbitrary is to say that there is a lack of uniformity or regularity in my drawing them, not that there is a contradiction between them. Inconsistency in the sense of lack of uniformity is not the same thing as inconsistency in the sense of contradiction.

Still, there appears to be something illogical about my drawing these conclusions. After all, if I think that I may double-park but that another, whose circumstances are relevantly similar to mine, ought not to, then either I am ignoring facts about my circumstances that, as facts about his, I take as reasons against his double-parking or I am ignoring facts about his circumstances that, as facts about mine, I take as reasons for allowing me to double-park. Yet nothing in my circumstances as compared with his appears to justify this differential treatment of similar facts. The arbitrariness of my drawing these two conclusions qualifies as illogical, it would appear, in virtue of being a violation of the Principle of Sufficient Reason.[8] Perhaps, then, one could interpret the statement about the mind's inherent aversion to inconsistency as the thesis that the mind abhors such arbitrariness as well as contradiction. Obviously, this thesis would warm the heart of any good rationalist. But it would also leave many a voluntarist cold.

The difficulty in taking the Principle of Sufficient Reason as a principle of logic from whose violation every rational mind shrinks, the voluntarist would argue, is that not every rational mind feels compelled to justify decisions and

8. See Don Locke, "The Trivializability of Universalizability," *Philosophical Review* 78 (1968): 25-44.

judgments he or she makes that are to some degree arbitrary. Suppose on Wednesday I decline your offer of cream to put in my coffee, having accepted a similar offer from you the day before. My behavior might seem odd in the absence of any relevant difference between Tuesday's and Wednesday's circumstances, but its oddity might not bother me in the least. To be sure, some people have a low threshold of tolerance for inconstancy in their lives and in the absence of a reason justifying a reversal of decisions would feel uncomfortable about declining Wednesday's offer, having accepted Tuesday's. But there are others who have no qualms about seeing today's decision as independent of yesterday's and thus as needing no justification despite its reversal of yesterday's, and I may be one of them. The important thing is that their greater tolerance of inconstancy does not impugn their rationality. An aversion to the kind of arbitrariness to which violations of the Principle of Sufficient Reason belong is therefore external to the cognitive operation in which the principle acts as a constraint on one's practical decisions and judgments. Or so the voluntarist would argue.

At this point, however, it is necessary to distinguish, at least in the case of the psychopathic thought, between the decision I reach and the judgments I make. For the voluntarist might be right to deny that the Principle of Sufficient Reason must constrain the former and wrong to deny that it must constrain the latter. The difference between the two is that the former is detachable from the reasons on which it is based and the latter are not. The former is detachable in that decisions, resolutions, and other acts of mind that, as we say, commit the will go beyond the reasons one has for such commitment. Those reasons may in effect dictate that the action be done, yet indecision or irresolution may keep one from deciding to do it. Conversely, one may decide to do something on the spur of the moment, as a matter of whim, or as a sheer act of will, which is to say for no reason at all. "I'll do it" is the natural expression of a practical decision, and this assertion is intelligible independently of there being reasons behind it. By contrast, judgments about what one ought or ought not to do are not detachable in this way from the reasons on which they are based. The judgment that one ought to do a certain action implies that one's circumstances require or merit the action, and therefore it implies that certain facts about those circumstances are reasons for doing it. The judgment, in other words, is not an intelligible thought independently of there being reasons behind it. One cannot coherently think, "I ought to do such and such, though there is no reason for my doing it."

Applying these points to the case of the psychopathic thought, then, we can say that, while I might not be constrained by the Principle of Sufficient Reason to decide against double-parking, since the decision goes beyond whatever reasons might dictate that I not double-park, the principle should constrain me to conclude that I ought not to double-park, given that I think that another, whose circumstances are relevantly similar to mine, ought not to. For if his circumstances require that he not double-park and they are relevantly similar to mine, then by the Principle of Sufficient Reason mine must also require that I not double-park, and because the conclusion that follows from my understanding of my circumstances in comparison with his cannot be detached from the reasons on which it is based, I am not free to ignore the principle. Hence, when I conclude to the contrary that I may double-park, I have not merely shown a greater tolerance of inconstancy than a person who feels constrained to apply the same considerations to himself as he applies to others, I have actually shown muddled thinking. The absence of any aversion to the arbitrariness of my permissive judgment, in other words, implies a cognitive failure. The voluntarist, in this case, in denying that the principle constrains judgments about what actions my circumstances require or permit, misapprehends the nature of those judgments.

It would be hasty, though, to infer from this result that internalism is true of our deeper knowledge of right and wrong as it is represented by Kant's initial account of morality's fundamental principle. The problem is that to see one's circumstances as relevantly similar to another's circumstances is already to be sensitive to the practical consequences of the comparison, for one cannot know which similarities are relevant and which differences are irrelevant without knowing what they are relevant and irrelevant to. Consequently, if one is unprepared to regard the interests of others as worthy of the same consideration as one's own and therefore unprepared to accept the practical consequences of such a fair-minded outlook, one may not see as relevant similarities that a person who is so prepared does see as relevant and one may see as relevant differences that that person sees as irrelevant. An unwillingness to suspend or revise the pursuit of one's interests, even where persistence in that pursuit harms others, may thus show itself in one's regarding as irrelevant similarities between one's circumstances and those of another that a more fair-minded person would regard as relevant. It may thus show itself in conflicting practical judgments like those in the case of the psychopathic thought without one's thereby running afoul of the Principle of Sufficient Reason. The principle, in other words, could be a potent constraint on one's practical thought yet never actually constrain that thought in a way that confirms internalism.

The problem, clearly, arises from there being different ways in which people view themselves in relation to others. The egocentric agent, the agent who sees the effect of his actions on other people's lives as much less important than their effect on his own (and conversely), will not regard his circumstances as relevantly similar to other people's when his present him with opportunities for improving his life, advancing his interests, and so on, and theirs present

170

them with the same opportunities for improving their lives, advancing their interests, and so on. Hence, his applying the test of universalizability need never yield a motive for action that opposes his self-interested motives since it need never transform his opposition to another's self-interested action – particularly one that adversely affects his interests – into opposition to his similarly self-interested actions. It need never transform his complaints about another's double-parking when it blocks his path into self-criticism of his own plan to double-park, even when he realizes that his double-parking will block the paths of those behind him. Of course, when a fair-minded agent applies the test in circumstances like those we are imagining, the application will yield a motive for action that opposes the agent's self-interested inclination to double-park. But – and here I appeal to Mill's methods, specifically the method of difference – we cannot infer that the motive it yields is internal to the cognitive operation that produced it, for this motive may originate in desires that a fair-minded agent has acquired and an egocentric agent has not, in which case it would be external to the operation when the fair-minded agent carried it out and nonexistent when the egocentric agent carried it out.

Perhaps, though, the way the egocentric agent views himself in relation to others implies impaired cognition. Perhaps the egocentric view itself, treated as a kind of policy its agent adopts, fails the test of universalizability. The most carefully constructed and fully developed argument for this latter thesis appears in Alan Gewirth's widely discussed book *Reason and Morality*.[9] The argument has received such thorough criticism that any further examination will now seem like an unnecessary autopsy. So I can afford to be brief. At the same time, much of the criticism has focused on Gewirth's claim to have derived fundamental moral principles from the bare idea of rational agency, and this claim, because it raises the questions of metaethics we have shelved, is beyond the scope of our study. So in shortening Gewirth's argument to its case against the rationality of the egocentric view and fixing it in relation to our study, I'll be looking at a less popular target of criticism and from a new angle. This should prove instructive.

Gewirth's strategy, as I've indicated, is to consider individuals as rational agents in abstraction from their particular aims and desires and their particular circumstances. His argument, in a nutshell, is this. Consider a rational agent, Molly Malloy, to give her a name. Qua rational agent, Ms. Malloy has purposes, which she necessarily thinks are good because, being her purposes, she cares about their fulfillment. Accordingly, she also regards her freedom and well-being as good since being free and tolerably well are necessary to her fulfilling her purposes, which, as we noted, she thinks are good. It follows that

9. Chicago: The University of Chicago Press, 1978, pp. 48–198.

she will oppose interference by others with her freedom and well-being since such interference deprives her of what she needs as a rational agent. She will thus think, again in abstraction from time, place, and other particulars, "Others ought not to interfere with my freedom and well-being." Since her sole reason for this thought is that she is a rational agent, an individual with purposes that are good, she must then acknowledge, on penalty of violating the Principle of Sufficient Reason, that she ought not to interfere with the freedom and well-being of others. They too are rational agents, individuals with purposes that they regard as good, which are facts she cannot deny. Hence, the principle constrains her to adopt a fair-minded view of her relations with others.

Having abstracted away all of the particulars of the agent's circumstances, Gewirth thinks there is now nothing to distinguish one rational agent from another, and hence whatever forbearances an agent demands from others he must accept as forbearances that others would be justified in demanding from him. There is no personal peculiarity, Gewirth would say, that Ms. Malloy could invoke as a relevant difference between herself and others. There is only the fact of her rational agency, which she has in common with others and which is the sole fact on which she bases her opposition to interference by others with her freedom and well-being.

Closer inspection of Gewirth's argument, however, reveals a mistake in this last point. Ms. Malloy does not base her opposition solely on the fact of her rational agency. She also bases it on her judgment that her purposes are good, which is to say, on her interest in fulfilling those purposes. Since she need not have any interest in whether others fulfill their purposes, she need not judge that their purposes are good. She may even judge that they are worthless or evil. Hence, she can invoke a relevant difference between herself and others, for as she views herself in relation to them, she sees that she acts for purposes that are good, and if no one else, as far as she can tell, is acting to advance her purposes, then she may also see that no one else is acting for purposes that are good. Hence, she may, without running afoul of the Principle of Sufficient Reason, think that others ought not to interfere with her freedom and well-being and at the same time think she may interfere with theirs. As she sees things, her freedom and well-being are goods, necessary goods as Gewirth would say,[10] but theirs are not. You might wonder, I suppose, whether this description of her is too fantastic, whether there really could be someone who saw value only in her own purposes and in what contributed to their fulfillment. But remember that the ultimate object of our inquiry is the psycho-

10. Ibid., pp. 52-63.

pathic mind, and as a description of a psychopath's view of himself in relation to others this one should not seem all that far-fetched.[11]

The description does contain one curious feature, though, a riddle, if you will, that arises when one asks, "How can Ms. Malloy have the thought that others ought not to interfere with her freedom and well-being? What could be its basis?" She cannot be thinking, for instance, that others are forbidden by law from interfering with her freedom and well-being, or that morality forbids it, or that some other norms of proper behavior to which others are subject proscribe such interference. Laws, principles of morality, and other norms of propriety are not available to her merely as a rational agent, at least not at this early stage of Gewirth's argument. Nor can she be thinking that others would be well-advised not to interfere with her freedom and well-being, that a policy of noninterference would be to their advantage. Her thought here cannot be that of someone realizing, say, how angry she gets when others interfere with her and worrying about the consequences for them of her belligerence. It is not comparable to the thought "others ought to stay clear of me" that some-one might have who posed a threat to others, owing, say, to a contagious disease. For as someone who cares only about fulfilling her own purposes, Ms. Malloy has no interest in other people's welfare and therefore nothing in her orientation toward others supports her thinking about what would benefit them. There are, of course, interpretations of her thought on which it is not a directive or imperative, but none of these is possible in the context of Gewirth's argument, since on any the question of whether Gewirth had de-rived a principle of right and wrong would not even arise.

To some philosophers, the answer to this riddle is simple. The description of Ms. Malloy I have given is incoherent. Since her thought that others ought not to interfere with her freedom and well-being must be an imperative based on reasons they have to refrain from interfering, she must be using 'ought' ei-ther categorically, in virtue of some authoritative rule to which others are sub-ject, or hypothetically, in virtue of some advantage that others would gain from doing what she thinks they ought to do. That is, she must be assuming that they have either principled reasons not to interfere or reasons based on their interests and desires, if she is using it intelligibly.[12] Yet neither of these al-ternatives makes sense, given that nothing more is true of her than that she is a rational agent, an individual with purposes that she regards as good, and

---

11. See, e.g., Cleckley, pp. 346–348.
12. Statements of this view about the use of 'ought' in practical judgments are found in Philip-pa Foot, "Morality as a System of Hypothetical Imperatives," *Philosophical Review* 81 (1972): 305–316 and Gilbert Harman, "Moral Relativism Defended," *Philosophical Review* 84 (1975): 3–22.

that she acknowledges the existence of other rational agents, other individuals with purposes that they regard as good. The upshot of this answer, then, is that no judgment about what others ought to do can issue from a perspective like hers, the perspective of mere rational agency with which Gewirth's argument starts. His argument goes wrong in that it assumes that the mere rational agent can make such judgments, judgments to which the criterion of universalizability then applies, and my description simply inherits the same error. Thus, according to this answer, the opposition between Gewirth and me over what must follow from applying the criterion of universalizability to Ms. Malloy's judgment about what others ought to do is a mirage. No genuine opposition can arise from applying the criterion to an unintelligible judgment.

The answer is certainly congenial to the immediate point I am making. For it makes no difference to my rejection of Gewirth's argument whether the argument fails for the reason I gave or for the reason this answer furnishes. Still, I think the answer is mistaken, and the mistake does matter to the larger question at hand. There are egocentric uses of 'ought' that a less philosophically driven account of acceptable English should recognize as intelligible.[13] Married life provides familiar examples. Sometimes, when my wife and I are eating out and she is torn between two desserts, she will decide on one and tell me that I ought to order the other. While admittedly her instruction to me is open to various interpretations, an obvious one is that she thinks I ought to order the second dessert because she wants to taste it. At such times she is thinking of me as a helpmate rather than an independent agent, and consequently my own desires and interests do not figure in her calculations. She is not thinking, that is, of what I would like, imagining, for instance, which of the desserts would be tempting to me. Rather, she is thinking of what I can do to help her get what she would like. Her use of 'ought', in this case, is egocentric, but intelligible nevertheless. As she views my circumstances in relation to hers, they merit my ordering the dessert because she desires it.

This sort of case is intelligible because we understand how two people who have shared a life for many years can come, in some situations, to lose sight of the boundaries that separate them as autonomous agents and to regard each other as extensions of themselves. Suppose, then, that Ms. Malloy viewed others in a similar way. Suppose that, though she recognized others as rational agents, individuals who had purposes that they regarded as good, she nonetheless regarded them as instruments of her will. "They may regard their purposes as good," she might say, "but it is my purposes, and not theirs, that truly matter. Hence," she would conclude, "they ought not to interfere with my free-

---

13. Gewirth, p. 79, also argues for the intelligibility of this use of 'ought'. The argument's metaethical premises, though, invite the kind of dispute I mean to avoid.

dom and well-being." And this conclusion, given her view of others as instruments of her will, would be perfectly intelligible.

Of course, if she were to imagine having the purposes that another person has, then she would see how purposes other than her own can matter too. That is, if she regarded these purposes as this other person would, she would then see that they were worth pursuing and, having no reason to count them as less worthwhile than her own, would conclude that she and others ought no more to interfere with his freedom and well-being than he and they ought to interfere with hers. But to arrive at this conclusion requires something besides applying the criterion of universalizability to her own judgment that others ought not to interfere with her freedom and well-being. It requires instead empathy with the person with whose freedom and well-being she judges that others ought not to interfere. Moreover, the empathy it requires must involve not only taking this other person's perspective and imagining the feelings of frustration or anger, say, that he would feel as a result of being interfered with but also understanding his purposes as generating (in conjunction with his circumstances) reasons for action even as one realizes that these purposes and reasons are independent of one's own. Only if this latter condition is satisfied can we say that Ms. Malloy recognizes the other person as a separate, autonomous agent. Only then can we say that she has advanced beyond the egocentric view.

To define the empathy capacity for which implies that one has advanced beyond the egocentric view, it is necessary to distinguish it from emotional identification.[14] Both involve one's taking another's perspective and imaginatively participating in this other person's life. But it is distinctive of empathy that it entails imaginative participation in the other's life without forgetting oneself.[15] The same is not true of emotional identification. Indeed, when such identification is strong and one's own identity weak or budding, the result is likely to be a loss of the sense of oneself as separate from the person with whom one identifies. Thus a boy who so strongly identifies with a favorite

---

14. I adapt here a point Max Scheler made in distinguishing among emotional contagion, fellow feeling, and emotional identification. See *The Nature of Sympathy* (Hamden, Conn.: The Shoe String Press, 1970), pp. 8-36.

15. The word 'empathy', it should be noted, does not have a settled meaning among those who write on the topic. The meaning chiefly varies between a kind of cognitive state and a kind of affective state, and I intend to capture the former in distinguishing it from emotional identification as I do. On the history and current variability of its usage, see Laura Wispé, "History of the Concept of Empathy" in Nancy Eisenberg and Janet Strayer, eds., *Empathy and Its Development* (Cambridge: Cambridge University Press, 1987), pp. 17-37; and Janet Strayer, "Affective and Cognitive Perspectives on Empathy" in Eisenberg and Strayer, pp. 218-444.

ballplayer that every game is an occasion for intense, vicarious ball playing does not manifest an empathic understanding of his hero. Rather, he makes believe that he is this player and loses himself in the process. He takes the latter's perspective and imaginatively participates in the player's trials, successes, and failures, but in doing so he may merely be transferring his own egocentricity from one perspective to another. To empathize with another, by contrast, one must recognize him as separate from oneself, a distinct person with a mind of his own, and such recognition requires that one retain a sense of oneself even as one takes up the other's perspective and imaginatively participates in his life.

At the same time, empathy must involve more than seeing another as a separate site of mental activity and imaginatively participating in that activity if it is to imply an advance beyond the egocentric view. Yet making its involving more a defining condition of empathy would mean that the emergence of empathy in children as they grow older was a later and more abrupt development than it has seemed to those who have studied the phenomena.[16] Consequently, to capture its gradual emergence from early experiences of shared feeling, it is necessary to conceive of empathy instead as taking increasingly mature forms as one's understanding of what it is to be a human being and to live a human life deepens. Accordingly, one's egocentricity will be presumed to begin to weaken at some point as one's capacity for empathy matures, and advancing beyond the egocentric view would then be a matter of developing and exercising more mature capacities for empathy.

What argues for this developmental conception is the general outline of how empathy in children emerges and matures on which recent accounts by developmental psychologists, though they differ on specifics, agree.[17] Children, on these accounts, are capable, even at a young age, of responding in kind or solicitously to the behavior of others that signals their feelings and emotions, and in these responses one can see evidence of the child's early capacities for empathy. Young children, that is, indicate through their behavior, toward companions, for example, that they both share their companions' feelings and recognize that those feelings are distinct from their own. Yet a young child is far from seeing its companion as an autonomous agent or imagina-

16. For a useful survey of relevant studies, see Alvin I. Goldman, "Ethics and Cognitive Science," *Ethics* 103 (1993): 337–360.
17. R. A. Thompson, "Empathy and Emotional Understanding: The Early Development of Empathy," in Eisenberg and Strayer, pp. 119-145; and Martin Hoffman "Interaction of Affect and Cognition in Empathy," in *Emotions, Cognition, and Behavior*, Carroll Izard, Jerome Kagan, and Robert B. Zajonc, eds. (Cambridge: Cambridge University Press, 1984) pp. 103-131 and "The Contribution of Empathy to Justice and Moral Judgment," in Eisenberg and Strayer, pp. 47–80.

tively participating in any more of its companion's life than the events with which it is immediately confronted. Its empathy is thus restricted to the immediate feelings, sensations, and emotions that another is experiencing, a restriction that reflects its limited comprehension of human life. This restriction then eases as the child learns to see people as having an existence that goes beyond the immediate situation in which it finds them. Correspondingly, it becomes capable of a maturer empathy in which the recognition of others as architects and builders, so to speak, of human lives is more pronounced. In taking another's perspective, it sees the purposes that give extension and structure to the other's life and sees those purposes as worthwhile, as purposes that matter. In this way it comes to recognize others as autonomous agents and to participate imaginatively in their separate lives.

Having a developmental conception of empathy is, needless to say, of signal importance to assessing the role of empathy in the deeper knowledge of right and wrong that people, as they mature, normally acquire. Thus, while reflection on characters such as Molly Malloy leads to seeing empathy as having a critical role in this knowledge, it would plainly be a mistake to infer that empathy simpliciter had this role. For the empathic responsiveness of young children to the feelings and emotions of their companions, though it certainly shows the potential for their acquiring deeper knowledge of right and wrong – indeed, it is hard to imagine a program of moral education that did not center on its cultivation and training – is nonetheless consistent with their having as egocentric a view as Ms. Malloy's. What appears to be critical, in other words, is empathy in a maturer form.

The same point applies to the troublesome case of sadistic pleasure. The case is troublesome because the pleasure a sadist gets from, say, assaulting someone is typically increased by his imagining his victim's pain. The sadist thus exhibits empathy inasmuch as he shows that he is taking in his victim's suffering, imagining, say, its course and intensity. Yet the sadist's empathy does not count against his having an egocentric view. The reason is that his empathy, like that of a young child, does not imply a recognition of his victim as an autonomous agent. The sadist, one might say, in getting pleasure from another's pain, fails to take in the whole person. He revels in the pain and suffering he has produced in that person but does not see beyond these particular feelings and emotions to the life his victim is living or the purposes that give it extension and structure. He does not see those purposes as worthwhile, as purposes that matter. How could he, one wants to ask, and still get pleasure from their frustration? He can, to be sure, like Molly Malloy, acknowledge that his victim is an autonomous agent, someone who has purposes and who regards his purposes as worthwhile. But acknowledging that a person regards his purposes as worthwhile is hardly the same thing as seeing from that person's perspective that his purposes are worthwhile. The sadist's empathy, in other words, is not of a form that could be critical to our deeper knowledge of right and wrong. It is not of a mature form.

Suppose, then, that judgments of right and wrong implying this deeper knowledge entail empathy in its mature form and that anyone who has and exercises a capacity for mature empathy makes such judgments. Suppose, that is, a different account of the deeper knowledge of right and wrong one acquires as one comes to understand the reasons for the conventional moral standards of one's community and to comprehend the ideals that give them meaning, an account on which judgments about what it is right to do or what one ought to do follow from one's empathizing with another or others rather than from one's applying the test of universalizability. Would internalism be true of such knowledge on this account, and would it be the internalism of categorical imperatives? Would the account, in other words, give us reason to conclude that psychopaths suffer some cognitive disorder? If it did, then their disorder would be a deficiency in their capacity for empathy, though the deficiency need not be so severe as to render them entirely incapable of empathy. Indeed, given the undoubtedly large intersection of sadists and psychopaths, it could not be that severe. It should be severe enough, however, that it prevented psychopaths from seeing others as autonomous agents, severe enough, that is, that it kept them bound to an egocentric view of their relations to others.

Initially, it may seem as though internalism of some kind must be true of the knowledge of right and wrong that one would exercise in taking up other people's perspectives, seeing their purposes as purposes that matter, and then judging that such and such ought to be done. If Ms. Malloy, for example, as a result of taking another's perspective and thus coming to regard his purposes as purposes that mattered, judged that she ought not to interfere with his freedom and well-being, then her judgment would imply, so it seems, a motive to refrain from such interference, since to see someone's purposes as purposes that mattered is to be inclined to do what would help to accomplish them. In this case, the judgment would seem to follow directly from judgments about what the person whose perspective Ms. Malloy took would want her to do given his purposes and given that these purposes were the focus of her attention. Yet the judgment could not follow *directly* in this way unless Ms. Malloy had either forgotten her own purposes or reflexively subordinated them to those on which she was focused, and on either possibility one can infer that the judgment would not be the result of mature empathy. On either possibility, it would have to be the result of emotional identification.

The reason it would not be the result of mature empathy is that such empathy, while it brings one to see another's purposes as worthwhile, does not necessarily lead one to favor those purposes over other purposes, one's own, in particular, that one also regards as worthwhile. Thus, for Ms. Malloy's judgment to be the result of mature empathy, she would not only have to see the other's purposes as worthwhile but would also have to resolve any conflict between his purposes and hers in favor of his or allow that there was no conflict. Put generally, mature empathy has to be combined with sensitivity to the possibility of conflict among the different purposes one regards as worthwhile and a criterion for resolving whatever conflict among them may arise before it can result in judgments of what one ought to do or what it is right to do. And since many situations call for empathy with more than one person, the possibilities of conflict corresponding to interpersonal differences can be multiple. Any account of our deeper knowledge of right and wrong that made empathy in its maturer forms essential must, therefore, also include a sensitivity to the possibility of interpersonal conflicts and a criterion by which to arbitrate those conflicts. For this reason, it is a mistake to assume that, in exercising this knowledge, one concludes directly from seeing another's purposes as worthwhile and realizing what action would help the person to accomplish those purposes that one ought to do that action.[18]

The question, then, is whether internalism is true of the judgments about what one ought to do that exercising this knowledge yields. This is, moreover, a particularly problematic question when the internalism it concerns is the internalism of categorical imperatives. For the judgments are no longer merely judgments about what one ought to do in order to promote personal purposes, one's own or another's, that one sees as worthwhile. Rather they are judgments about what one ought to do as the best way of handling interpersonal relations in which there is potential for conflict among such purposes. And even on the assumption that these judgments imply some motive to act on them, it is not easy to determine from abstract consideration of the cognitive operations that would yield them whether this motive is internal to those operations or due, say, to an external commitment to an ideal of harmony in interpersonal affairs and relations.

18. This point is well illustrated by the leading accounts of this sort. These are ideal observer accounts, such as R. M. Hare's, and contractualist accounts, such as T. M. Scanlon's. On either, judgments of what it is right to do or what one ought to do mediate conflicting interests and desires that reflect the competing purposes of the various people whose lives one must consider in making these judgments. While empathy is essential to considering these various lives, the judgments follow only after one applies the method of ideal observation or contractualist negotiation to resolve the conflicts among them and thus do not follow directly from judgments of what any of those whose lives one considers would want one to do given his purposes. See Hare, *Moral Thinking* (Oxford: Clarendon Press, 1981) and Scanlon, "Contractualism and Utilitarianism," in *Utilitarianism and Beyond*, ed. by Amartya Sen and Bernard Williams (Cambridge: Cambridge University Press, 1982), pp. 103-128.

At the same time, we might find support for ascribing such internalism to these judgments in a different place. Specifically, we might find that, as a fact of human psychology, to possess and exercise the capacity for mature empathy is to be disposed to accept some criterion for mediating harmoniously among the competing purposes of the many autonomous agents in whose lives one imaginatively participates. We might find, in other words, that, as a fact of human psychology, no one who was capable of taking the perspectives of different individuals and seeing seriatim that different, competing purposes corresponding to these different perspectives each mattered could rest content with the disharmony that this survey would yield or steel himself to the pull of all those purposes that were not compatible with his own. A psychopath, then, might suffer deficiency in empathic powers for either of two reasons: stunted development or regression to an egocentric view out of inability to tolerate the clash of different perspectives with which one in whom the capacity for empathy has matured is presented. Plainly, confirming or falsifying any of these hypotheses is beyond the methods of moral philosophy. It properly falls within those of developmental psychology and cognitive science. At this point, our philosophical study must look to these other disciplines for help in unraveling the mystery of the psychopathic personality.

9

Sidgwick on ethical judgment

British moral philosophy has had two great traditions. Its empiricist tradition, which began with Hobbes and resurged with Hume and the classical utilitarians on whom Hume exercised so much influence, takes ethical judgments to be founded on or to originate in desire or feeling. Its intuitionist tradition, which formed in reaction to Hobbes and continued by way of debate with Hume and the classical utilitarians, takes ethical judgments to be deliverances of reason which subserve neither desire nor feeling and in which one recognizes and affirms morality's fundamental precepts. Within the empiricist tradition several works have supreme importance as alternative statements of its philosophy. Within the intuitionist tradition, by contrast, *The Methods of Ethics*,[1] Sidgwick's masterwork, towers above the others.

The pedigree of Sidgwick's *Methods* is established early in the work when, in the third chapter of its first book, Sidgwick queried the nature of ethical judgment and gave in response a distinctively intuitionist account. He fashioned this account to settle the dispute between intuitionism and empiricism over the proper conception of ethical judgment, and the argument he advanced for his side appears to leave empiricism without a rejoinder. This argument is the subject of the present study. In the first two sections I will set it out as I read it and argue for this reading as against an alternative. Then, in the third and last section, I will critically examine the argument and assess its cogency. My conclusion will be that the argument fails to vindicate intuitionism. The reasons for its failure should prove instructive.

I

Sidgwick's argument proceeds from consideration of two issues: the sense of the words 'right' and 'ought' in expressions of ethical judgment and the role of such judgment in motivating human action. Sidgwick saw an important connection between these issues, and he used this connection to ground the intuitionist conception of ethical judgment on observations of common hu-

---

1. Henry Sidgwick, *The Methods of Ethics*. 7th ed. (London: Macmillan and Co., 1907). Hereafter abbreviated *ME*.

man experience. His argument extends over the whole of Chapter 3 of Book 1. Its crux, however, occurs in the chapter's opening section, where the two issues are joined.

In this section Sidgwick speaks first to the issue concerning the role of ethical judgment in motivating human action. For him, the issue is defined sharply by Hume's thesis that no exercise of reason can alone influence the will. Hume, as we know, used this thesis to great effect in arguing against rationalist ethics. Morality is essentially practical, Hume declared, and this is to say that moral opinion can by itself influence the will. Hence, our moral opinions are not exercises of our reason. Morality, at bottom, is a matter of feeling and not judgment. Sidgwick starts from propositions that contradict this conclusion. Morality is basically a matter of judgment, and the judgments it particularly concerns are judgments of what it is right to do and what one ought to do. On the issue of whether such judgments can by themselves motivate action, then, Sidgwick argues affirmatively by first redefining the issue as that of whether such judgments are reducible to judgments of empirical fact or one's own mental state and, second, asserting that they are not, that to the contrary they involve a fundamental notion, which the words 'right' and 'ought' express and which is "essentially different from all notions representing facts of physical or psychical experience."[2]

The argument's crucial step, obviously, is Sidgwick's redefinition of the first issue. It is here that the two issues are joined. He bases this step, I believe, on the following observations. It is clear, he thinks, from reflection on experiences of the kind we commonly describe, whether correctly or not, as a conflict of reason and passion or reason and appetite that the deliverances of reason in these experiences have influence on the will. These deliverances are judgments of what it is right to do or what one ought to do, and the experiences are those of being strongly inclined by passion or appetite to act against these judgments and of needing to summon the strength of will to resist the inclination. It is also clear, Sidgwick thinks, that some judgments can and do influence the will indirectly in the way Hume supposed. That is, they can influence the will by altering the understanding the agent has of the objects of his already existing desires and the means and obstacles to their attainment. Such judgments, given this description of the indirect way in which they can influence the will, must be either judgments of empirical fact or judgments of one's own mental state; and when reason works in the service of already existing desire to influence the will, it does so by means of them alone. The issue therefore becomes that of whether judgments of what it is right to do or what one ought to do are reducible to judgments of empirical fact or one's own

2. *ME*, p. 25.

mental state. For if they are not, then when they influence the will as they do, for instance, in the experiences of conflict on which Sidgwick bids us to reflect, they must do so directly.

Sidgwick's argument, as I have explained it so far, has three main premises: that morality is a matter of judgment as opposed to feeling; that its special notion is irreducible to physical or psychological notions; and, a central doctrine of Hume's argument, that morality is essentially practical. The first two are evident in my explanation, whereas the last is implicit in the lesson Sidgwick draws from his reflection on the experiences we commonly describe as a conflict between reason and passion. As a set, these three propositions contain the defining elements of Sidgwick's conception of ethical judgment. The first two reveal his commitment to intuitionism. Taken together, they distinguish this position in ethics from noncognitivism, on the one hand, which denies that morality is a matter of judgment, and naturalism, on the other, which denies that morality's special notions are irreducible to physical or psychological notions. The third, then, when conjoined with the other two, yields Sidgwick's singular formulation of intuitionism: An ethical judgment is an exercise of reason whose constitutive notion is not only simple, in Locke's sense, but also practical, in the sense that Hume's doctrine requires.

The singularity of this formulation will be apparent to any student of the metaethical wars that were waged within Anglo-American philosophy during the middle decades of this century. For Hume's doctrine was the chief weapon used against intuitionism by the noncognitivists. They were able to use this doctrine to attack intuitionism and to do so effectively because the leading intuitionists of this period accepted the other central doctrine of Hume's argument, that reason is inert. Specifically, the noncognitivists argued that intuitionism sprang from a mistake: Although its adherents correctly took the terms special to ethics, terms such as 'right' and 'ought', to be indefinable in terms that expressed physical and psychological notions, they mistakenly inferred from the indefinability of these terms that they expressed simple notions. What explained the indefinability of a term like 'right', the noncognitivists maintained, was its essentially practical character, which they then variously specified as its emotive meaning, magnetic effect, prescriptivity, commendatory force, et cetera. By thus making the choice between their position and intuitionism a choice between competing explanations of what makes ethical terms indefinable in terms that express physical and psychological notions, they made their position appear to be a significant advance over intuitionism. After all, that the terms are essentially practical seems a more powerful explanation - richer and more easily verified - than that they express simple notions. Sidgwick, as we've seen, rejected Hume's doctrine of the inertness of reason, and this rejection was then reflected in the way he defined ethical judgment and characterized the fundamental notion it involved. As a result, his formulation of intuitionism avoids the issue of competing explanations that the noncognitivists pressed to such advantage. It falls, therefore, outside the range of their attack.

The distance between Sidgwick's formulation and that of the leading twentieth-century intuitionists, Prichard and Ross, can be seen in their different relations to Kant. For Prichard and Ross, unlike Sidgwick, broke with Kant on the question of moral motivation.[3] They attributed such motivation to a desire to do what is right that is independent of ethical judgment. Sidgwick, by contrast, agreed with Kant in taking ethical judgment to be the source of such motivation. Indeed, as the vocabulary and distinctions he borrowed from Kant indicate, he followed Kant's general views on the nature of ethical judgment. In particular, he characterized ethical judgments as imperatives or dictates of reason. "[W]hen I speak of the cognition or judgment that 'X ought to be done' – in the stricter ethical sense of the term ought – as a 'dictate' or 'precept' of reason to the person to whom it relates, I imply that in rational beings as such this cognition gives an impulse or motive to action."[4] In words relevant to current philosophical debate, for Sidgwick, as for Kant, a rational agent, in recognizing that it is right to do a certain action or that it ought to be done, recognizes a reason for doing it.

One question, however, that arises from this debate is whether the cognition that it is right to do a certain action or that it ought to be done of which Sidgwick speaks here is a cognition of a duty to do it. Put differently, the question is whether the notion of duty falls within the scope of the fundamental notion of ethics that Sidgwick intended his argument to capture and that he identified with the stricter ethical sense of the words 'right' and 'ought'. And to fully understand Sidgwick's account of the nature of ethical judgment we must address this question.

II

The debate that gives rise to the question concerns the use of 'ought' to express moral judgments, specifically, judgments of duty. On one side of the debate are the internalists, philosophers who hold that this moral use of 'ought' implies a reason for action. On their view, to say that a certain action ought to be done, meaning that it is one's duty to do it, implies that one has a reason to do it. On the other side are the externalists, philosophers who deny in-

3. See H. A. Prichard, "Duty and Interest," in Prichard, *Moral Obligation and Duty and Interest: Essays and Lectures* (Oxford: Oxford University Press, 1968), pp. 223-225; and W. D. Ross, *The Right and the Good* (Oxford: Oxford University Press [Clarendon Press], 1930), pp. 157-158.
4. *ME*, p. 34.

ternalism. On their view, one can say that a certain action ought to be done, meaning that it is one's duty to do it, without thereby implying that there is a reason to do it. Since Sidgwick's argument, as I have so far explained it, if sound, would show only that some judgments about what it is right to do or what ought to be done imply reasons for action irrespective of any desire or feeling, it remains pertinent to ask whether his argument places him on either side of this debate.

It would be surprising, of course, if the argument turned out to place him on the side of the externalists. Yet, recently, David Brink, in an essay on Sidgwick's famous quandary over the relation between egoism and utilitarianism, has proposed an interpretation that places Sidgwick squarely on this side.[5] Brink's principal interpretative interest is in explaining the dualism of practical reason to which Sidgwick was led by his conclusion about the equal and independent tenability of egoism and utilitarianism. On the received interpretation, the dualism represents Sidgwick's failure to reconcile completely the fundamental principles of morality, specifically, the axioms of prudence and rational benevolence on which egoism and utilitarianism, respectively, are founded. On the interpretation Brink proposes, which he appropriately dubs "the externalist reading," the dualism represents Sidgwick's failure to solve the traditional problem of finding compelling reasons to be moral. Accordingly, in view of Sidgwick's firm belief in utilitarianism as the correct theory of duty, Brink reasons that Sidgwick must at least implicitly have regarded egoism as the correct theory of reasons for action. And once it is assumed that Sidgwick, at least implicitly, distinguished between these two domains of study, that of duty, on the one hand, and rationality as regards action, on the other, and took egoism rather than utilitarianism to be the correct theory of the latter while taking utilitarianism rather than egoism to be the correct theory of the former, it follows that, on his view, judgments of duty do not necessarily imply reasons for action. In other words, on Brink's externalist reading, the notion of duty falls outside the scope of the fundamental notion of ethics that the argument of Book 1, Chapter 3, is intended to capture. Further consideration of the argument, however, shows that this result is not a happy one. It shows, that is, that Sidgwick, as we would expect and as far as this chapter goes, sided with those philosophers who think judgments of duty necessarily imply reasons for action.

5. David O. Brink, "Sidgwick's Dualism of Practical Reason," *Australasian Journal of Philosophy* 66 (1988): 291–307. Brink's complete view, I should note, is more complicated than I have indicated. He thinks Sidgwick's text admits of both an internalist and an externalist reading, but he favors the latter over the former as the reading that best captures the text's philosophical import. See Brink's "Sidgwick and the Rationale for Rational Egoism," in *Essays on Henry Sidgwick*, Bart Schultz, ed. (Cambridge: Cambridge University Press, 1992), pp. 199–240 for a concise statement of his view.

That Sidgwick held this view is first signaled at the point in the argument where he reflects on experiences of the kind we commonly describe as a conflict between reason and passion. He offers there two examples: the experience of judging, while in the grip of anger, that the act one's emotion prompts would be unjust or unkind; and the experience of judging, while subject to some strong bodily appetite, that the act one's appetite inclines one to do would be imprudent. And he indicates that the judgment in the first example concerns duty whereas the judgment in the second concerns self-interest. Hence, in view of the former, it is clear that Sidgwick regarded judgments that one has a duty to do a certain act as belonging to the class of ethical judgments (i.e., those judgments that the words 'right' and 'ought' in their stricter ethical sense are used to express), since he meant the former to be an example of a judgment that can influence the will but is irreducible to judgments of empirical fact or one's own mental state.

Subsequently, for the purpose of further examining this question of the irreducibility of ethical judgments, Sidgwick explicitly distinguished two kinds of ethical judgment, moral and prudential, according as the judgment concerns duty or self-interest. The passage in which he made this distinction is worth quoting, since the distinction is not unproblematic.

In considering this question it is important to take separately the two species of judgment which I have distinguished as 'moral' and 'prudential'. Both kinds might, indeed, be termed 'moral' in a wider sense. . . . But in ordinary thought we clearly distinguish cognitions or judgments of duty from cognitions or judgments as to what is 'right' or 'ought to be done' in view of the agent's private interests or happiness: and the depth of the distinction will not, I think, be diminished by the closer examination of these judgments we are now to enter.[6]

The problem the distinction creates is one of uncertainty. Does it import into Sidgwick's account of the nature of ethical judgment a different sense of the terms 'right' and 'ought' from the one he called the stricter ethical sense and identified with the fundamental notion of ethics? This problem is particularly urgent because if the distinction did import into Sidgwick's account two different senses of these terms, a moral sense and a prudential one, and if the moral sense differed from Sidgwick's stricter ethical sense, then the notion of duty that the terms 'right' and 'ought' expressed when used in this moral sense would fall outside the scope of the fundamental notion and Sidgwick's argument would thus be thrown into confusion. This possibility may then give some hope to the externalist reading, inasmuch as that reading offers a way out of the confusion. But consideration of how Sidgwick used the distinction to advance his argument for the irreducibility of ethical judg-

6. *ME*, p. 25–26.

ments and how that argument proceeds argues against the possibility and so dampens this hope.

Briefly, as he implied in the passage quoted above, he thought the best way to see the irreducibility of ethical judgments was to examine separately specific types of such judgment, and the distinction thus served to separate the relevant types. He then proceeded to examine and make the case for the irreducibility of moral judgments before examining and making the case for the irreducibility of prudential judgments. Finally, in making the latter case, he divided it into two parts and based one of them on the results of the former. Both this ordering of the two cases and his basing part of the latter on the former indicate that Sidgwick regarded the former as the principal or at least the clearer case. Hence, they indicate that Sidgwick took moral judgments to be the primary or clearest examples of what he meant by an ethical judgment and, correspondingly, that he took the notion of duty to be the primary or clearest representative of what he meant by the fundamental notion of ethics. The way the argument proceeds, therefore, rules out the idea that the distinction he drew between the two types of judgment imports into his account a notion of duty that falls outside the scope of the fundamental notion. The idea, then, cannot be the start of an externalist reading. Indeed, the externalist reading seems at this point at greatest odds with Sidgwick's argument. For, given what the irreducibility of an ethical judgment signifies in this argument, we can say that, for Sidgwick, moral judgments represented the primary or clearest examples of inherently motivational judgments or, in other words they represented the primary or clearest examples of when in recognizing that it is right to do a certain action or that it ought to be done one recognizes a reason to do it.

All of this notwithstanding, the distinction Sidgwick drew between moral and prudential judgments remains a problem, and until we get to the bottom of it the externalist reading will continue, I think, to have some hold on our imagination. The source of the problem becomes apparent in the last section of Chapter 3, where Sidgwick made the case for the irreducibility of prudential judgments. This case, as I mentioned, is divided into two parts. In the first part, prudential judgments are understood to be judgments about what it is right to do or what one ought to do in view of one's interest in one's own happiness, and the end in view of which these judgments are made, one's own happiness, is then assumed to be unconditionally prescribed by reason. In the second part, the same understanding of prudential judgments holds, but the end in view of which they are made is assumed to be given by a desire that is not itself the product of reason. Taking our cue from Sidgwick, we can say that the first part proceeds on the assumption that prudential judgments presuppose an unconditional dictate of reason, a categorical imperative, to adopt

187

as one's end one's own happiness. They are thus analogous to moral judgments that presuppose a categorical imperative to adopt as one's end some such universal end as the general happiness, and the argument of this part consists in an appeal to this analogy. By contrast, the second part proceeds on the assumption that no categorical imperative lies behind prudential judgments but rather that their validity is determined relative to an end that one has adopted but that reason has not prescribed. They are thus all mere hypothetical imperatives, and the argument of this part consists in an attempt to show that even a mere hypothetical imperative is irreducible to judgments of empirical fact or one's own mental state. What emerges, then, in effect, is a distinction between alternative accounts of the validity conditions of prudential judgments, and it is this distinction that creates the problem. The ambiguity it fosters makes it uncertain whether Sidgwick's earlier distinction between moral and prudential judgments imports into his account a different sense of 'right' and 'ought' from their stricter ethical sense. For the answer arguably depends on which account of the validity conditions one follows.[7]

On the first, the account according to which prudential judgments presuppose a categorical imperative, the sense of the terms 'right' and 'ought' when they are used to express prudential judgments is the same sense as the one they have when they are used to express moral judgments. So the distinction between the two types of judgment does not introduce any new sense of these terms. Indeed, to distinguish between the two types as Sidgwick did is, on this account, misleading since prudential judgments form only a subclass of moral judgments. They concern self-regarding duty, the duty to promote one's happiness, and consequently the opposition between duty and what is 'right' or 'ought to be done' in view of one's private interests or happiness, on which Sidgwick's distinction between the two types of judgment turns, is illusory. On the second account, the account according to which prudential judgments are mere hypothetical imperatives, the sense of 'right' and 'ought' when used to express prudential judgments is arguably different from the sense they have when used to express moral judgments. So the distinction between the two types of judgment, one could argue, introduces a new sense. At the same time, because this new sense, assuming the distinction introduces one, attaches to 'right' and 'ought' when they are used to express *prudential* judgments, its introduction does not affect our earlier conclusions about moral judgments or their constitutive notion of duty. It does not, in other words, give renewed hope to an externalist reading.

What is more, Sidgwick's distinction between the two types of judgment is,

---

7. Sidgwick himself thinks that same sense is expressed in either case. The difficulty into which this view leads him is discussed below in Section 3.

on this account too, misleading. For unless psychological egoism holds – and Sidgwick went on to demolish it in the next chapter – prudential judgments form only a proper subclass of mere hypothetical imperatives, and there is nothing about the members of this subclass to warrant distinguishing them and not other mere hypothetical imperatives from moral judgments. Thus, contrary to what Sidgwick said in the passage in which he explicitly distinguished between moral and prudential judgments, the distinction loses its depth upon closer examination. It does not, despite what one might easily suppose, represent a deep fissure in Sidgwick's thought that divides morality from practical reason. And the absence of such a fissure in Sidgwick's thought tells against the externalist reading.

A quick review should make this last point clear. The heart of the reading, as Brink presents it, is the thesis that Sidgwick's conclusion about the dualism of practical reason represents an admission of failure to solve the traditional problem of finding compelling reasons to be moral, and to render Sidgwick's interest in reconciling utilitarianism and egoism as an interest in solving this traditional problem requires supposing that Sidgwick divided the field of his study into two domains, morality and rationality as regards action, and took egoism rather than utilitarianism to be the correct theory of the latter and utilitarianism rather than egoism to be the correct theory of the former. Accordingly, it requires supposing that the distinction between morality and prudence is deeply embedded in Sidgwick's thought, since egoism, in being the theory of rational self-interest, is a theory of prudence.[8] Yet, as we've seen, closer examination of Sidgwick's distinction between moral and prudential judgment proves otherwise. Specifically, reflection on the ambiguity in Sidgwick's understanding of prudential judgment shows that either the distinction corresponds to a distinction of one species of moral judgment from the entire genus, in which case it would make no sense to distinguish egoism as a theory of morality from ego-

8. Brink, for instance, makes this supposition when he takes Sidgwick to be seriously concerned with answering the questions of whether and to what extent duty opposes self-interest and advances this concern as one of the main grounds for an externalist reading. See Brink, "Sidgwick's Dualism of Practical Reason," pp. 303-304. Brink cites several parts of the text as evidence of this concern, but none of them is decisive. The most important is Chapter 5 of Book 2, where Sidgwick considers whether egoism could look to the common rules of morality as the proper guides for achieving happiness. This chapter appears to contain discussion of conflicts between duty and self-interest that would entail a basic distinction between moral and prudential judgment, but a close reading shows that Sidgwick is careful to quality his use of the term 'duty' so that it does not express a notion that falls within the scope of the fundamental notion of ethics. Thus, he says at the outset that examining the question that the chapter concerns necessitates using the received notions of duty, and he indicates in his subsequent argument that the duties in question are the duties of conventional morality. Hence, no conflict between duty and self-interest of the kind that would support an externalist reading is under consideration in this chapter.

THE SOURCES OF MORAL AGENCY

ism as a theory of rationality as regards action, or it corresponds to a distinction between a species of mere hypothetical imperatives and the entire genus of moral judgments, in which case it would make no sense to single out egoism from all other coherent systems of mere hypothetical imperatives as the more rationally justified. Hence, either case opposes the externalist reading.

Sidgwick, of course, did not treat egoism as a system of mere hypothetical imperatives. He did, however, recognize the possibility. Thus, corresponding to his distinction between alternative accounts of the validity conditions of prudential judgments is a distinction he made between alternative views of egoism regarded as a system of ethics. On one view, egoism is a system founded on a categorical imperative. Its foundational imperative is that one ought to adopt one's own greatest happiness as the ultimate end of one's actions. On the other view, egoism is a system of mere hypothetical imperatives and, to quote Sidgwick, "does not properly regard the agent's own greatest happiness as what he 'ought' to aim at: but only as the ultimate end for the realization of which he has, on the whole, a predominant desire."[9] The first view is the one Sidgwick took in the bulk of his treatise, but the second, as he remarked in a subsequent footnote, "is admissible."[10] And he further implied that one could similarly distinguish alternative views of utilitarianism. These distinctions between alternative views of egoism and utilitarianism suggest a division of ethics into two domains, the domain of systems founded on categorical imperatives and the domain of systems of mere hypothetical imperatives. This division, to be sure, is not the same as the one the externalist reading implies. But the latter, it is plausible to suppose, is the misconstruction of the former that results from seeing the distinction between morality and prudence as deeply embedded in Sidgwick's thought, and the naturalness of this misconstruction would then explain the attraction of the externalist reading.

At the same time, correcting the error would not revive the reading's prospects. For with regard to neither of the domains that the former division defines can one interpret Sidgwick as taking egoism to be the correct theory of that domain. Thus, one cannot interpret Sidgwick as having taken egoism as the correct system of mere hypothetical imperatives, because such a view would entail holding that reason required one to adopt one's own happiness as the ultimate end of one's actions, and in taking egoism to be a system of mere hypothetical imperatives, one assumes that the ultimate end is not an end that reason prescribes. Nor can one interpret Sidgwick as having taken egoism as the correct system among those founded on categorical imperatives, because such a view would be the same as taking egoism as the correct theory

9. *ME*, p. 36.
10. *ME*, p. 98 n. 1.

of duty. In sum, the division of domains that the externalist reading implies corresponds to a misconception of how the distinction between morality and prudence figures in Sidgwick's thought, and the division that corresponds to the correct conception of how the distinction figures in Sidgwick's thought does not fit the externalist reading.

Having affirmed an internalist reading of Sidgwick's argument, we may now turn to its assessment.

III

Let us begin our assessment by gently probing the oddity of Sidgwick's willingness to consider systems of mere hypothetical imperatives as among the methods of ethics. Such willingness is sure to seem out of place in an intuitionist account of the nature of ethical judgment. Systems of mere hypothetical imperatives, after all, are a standard product of empiricist moral philosophy. So, presumably, the conception of ethical judgment they presuppose conflicts with the intuitionist conception. This oddity, however, can be resolved. The key to its resolution lies in the second part of Sidgwick's case for the irreducibility of prudential judgments.

Recall that for this part of the case Sidgwick assumes that prudential judgments are mere hypothetical imperatives. He then argues that the 'ought' that is used to express such judgments has the same sense as when it is used to express categorical imperatives. That is, he holds and defends the thesis that the fundamental notion of ethics is a constituent of mere hypothetical imperatives as well as categorical ones, the difference in their validity conditions notwithstanding. Yet, clearly, he could not hold this thesis unless he was willing to consider systems of mere hypothetical imperatives as among the methods of ethics. At the same time, though, the thesis counters the presumption that the conception of ethical judgment such systems presuppose conflicts with the intuitionist conception. Hence, considering such systems as among the methods of ethics does not spoil the uniformity of his account. A method of ethics, according to Sidgwick, is a rational procedure whose application yields dictates of reason that qualify as ethical judgments, and on Sidgwick's account these dictates include both hypothetical and categorical imperatives.

Although Sidgwick is thus able to maintain his view of hypothetical imperatives despite the proprietary claims of empiricism, in doing so he deviates significantly from Kant. As we noted earlier, Sidgwick took a dictate of reason that qualifies as an ethical judgment to be a "cognition [that] gives an impulse or motive to action,"[11] and it follows then that he regarded hypothetical as

---

11. *ME*, p. 34.

well as categorical imperatives as inherently motivational. Both, on his account, are sources of purely rational motives. Kant, by contrast, held that only
categorical imperatives are a source of such motives. Indeed, in Kant's ethics,
the only purely rational motive, the only one that originates in the operations
of reason alone, is the motive of duty. Consequently, for Kant, judgments of
duty, which is to say, categorical imperatives, exhaust the class of inherently
motivational judgments. The difference between Sidgwick's account and
Kant's comes therefore to this: On Sidgwick's account purely rational motivation comprehends more than moral motivation (narrowly defined by the motive of duty), whereas on Kant's account the two are identical.

Sidgwick's view of hypothetical imperatives thus puts him at odds with
both the empiricists and the followers of Kant. Both, that is, would object to
his construing all hypothetical imperatives as, in his sense, dictates of reason,
though of course their objections would take different forms. Still, their common opposition suggests this view as the place to look if one suspects weaknesses in Sidgwick's account. The view represents middle ground, so to speak,
between these two camps, and as such it is an inviting target for suspicions of
weakness. What is more, additional probing of Sidgwick's argument confirms
these suspicions.

The argument's main point is that prudential judgments, even when conceived of as mere hypothetical imperatives, are irreducible to judgments of
empirical fact or one's own mental state. For Sidgwick, following the argument of the opening section of Chapter 3, takes this point as sufficient for
showing that the word 'ought' has the same sense whether it is used to express
a hypothetical or a categorical imperative. That is, he takes it as sufficient for
showing that the fundamental notion of ethics is a constituent of prudential
judgment even when such judgment is conceived of as a mere hypothetical
imperative. The brunt of the argument then is to substantiate its main point,
and to accomplish this Sidgwick turns to an example:

> When (e.g.) a physician says, "If you wish to be healthy you ought to rise early," this is
> not the same thing as saying "early rising is an indispensable condition of the attain-
> ment of health." This latter proposition expresses the relation of physiological facts on
> which the former is founded; but it is not merely the relation of facts that the word
> 'ought' imports: it also implies the unreasonableness of adopting an end and refusing
> to adopt the means indispensable to its attainment.[12]

Yet Sidgwick's concentration on substantiating this point is misplaced. A
prior question, which he does not address, is much more troublesome. Specifically, one could first challenge Sidgwick's argument by asking whether the ar-

12. *ME*, p. 37.

gument of the opening section even applies to prudential judgments conceived of as mere hypothetical imperatives, and Sidgwick, I think, would be hard pressed to come up with a satisfactory answer. The reason for the difficulty is that the earlier argument proceeds from reflection on experiences we commonly describe as a conflict of reason and passion or reason and appetite, and no such conflict seems to arise when reason is only issuing hypothetical imperatives in the service of what Sidgwick calls nonrational desires, by which he means desires that originate independently of any dictate of reason.

As we noted before, Sidgwick divides the experiences from reflection on which the argument of the opening section proceeds into two classes, which he then treats as separate cases. On the one hand, there is the experience of conflict in which a moral judgment represents what the common description denotes as the side of reason. On the other, there is the experience of conflict in which a prudential judgment represents what the common description denotes as the side of reason. One could then say that the thrust of the entire chapter was to confirm the correctness of the common description of these experiences in either case and that, in the opening section, Sidgwick argued for the controlling thesis that the description would be correct if the moral or prudential judgment in question were irreducible to judgments of empirical fact or one's own mental state. It would seem, though, that the irreducibility of a prudential judgment could not have this implication if the judgment were a mere hypothetical imperative. For such an imperative, by our very understanding of it, is the product not of reason alone but rather of reason operating in the service of some nonrational desire, and consequently any conflict between the impulse to act as it directs and some passion or appetite would seem to be correctly described as a conflict between two nonrational desires and not as a conflict between reason and passion or reason and appetite. Hence, it would seem that prudential judgments, when conceived of as mere hypothetical imperatives, lie beyond the reach of the argument of the opening section.

Evidently, then, this argument proves too much. A mere hypothetical imperative seems more aptly construed as a counsel of reason than a precept or dictate, and the role of reason in the issuance of such imperatives is more aptly explained as that of a guide than that of a mover. In this refrain empiricism would reassert its proprietary claim on systems of mere hypothetical imperatives. The question, then, is where the argument goes wrong; and the answer must lie in its crucial step, the step at which Sidgwick redefines the issue of whether an ethical judgment can by itself motivate action as that of whether it is irreducible to judgments of empirical fact or one's own mental state. Empiricists need not regard mere hypothetical imperatives as reducible to such judgments.

When Sidgwick takes this step, he carefully describes how some judgments motivate action indirectly in the way Hume supposed. He states, in effect, that every judgment of this sort is either a judgment about the means to attaining the object of an already existing, nonrational desire or a judgment that further or more specifically characterizes the object of such a desire. The judgment, then, is either identical or reducible to a judgment of empirical fact or one's own mental state since it amounts to either a judgment about causal relations or a judgment about the character of certain experiences. In addition, Sidgwick takes the time to point out that, although he calls the desires these judgments serve nonrational and even irrational – the latter term being reserved for times when they appear to conflict with reason – their impulses are commonly modified and directed by these judgments and so commonly prompt intelligent action. And as he describes the process by which such action typically comes about, it occurs without the intervention of any judgment that it is right to do that action or that it ought to be done.

Where then do hypothetical imperatives fit in? Let us consider Sidgwick's example of the judgment that one ought to rise early. This would be a hypothetical imperative if its validity required that the action it prescribed be an indispensable means or the fittest means to some end the agent had in fact adopted. In Sidgwick's example this end is one's own health. Moreover, since he intends this to be an example of a mere hypothetical imperative, we are to assume that the adoption of this end is not something reason has prescribed. Rather, so we are to assume, it follows from some nonrational desire, the love of life, say, or the desire for the pleasures of vigorous activity. He also, obviously, intends it to be an example of a judgment that can motivate action, and consequently we must regard it as a judgment that the agent addresses to himself. We must regard it, that is, as the judgment "I ought to rise early." The key point to note, then, is that the consideration on which the agent bases this judgment is the same as the consideration on which he would be acting if he got up early from a desire to retain or improve his health and without the intervention of any hypothetical imperative in the process that leads from the desire to the action. In either case, the relevant consideration is that early rising is essential to good health, and in the latter case this thought brings him to focus his desire for good health on getting up early without his first passing through the hypothetical imperative that prescribes such actions. Consequently, the occasions when he would make the judgment "I ought to rise early" must be occasions when the action is not immediately forthcoming, either because it cannot be done in the circumstances he faces or because some conflicting desire causes him to vacillate. And indeed, even when he makes the judgment in circumstances in which the action cannot be done, he must be somewhat unsure about whether he will in fact do it when the right circumstances arise, for otherwise he would simply decide to do it. That is, he would simply conclude "I will do it" rather than "I ought to do it." A hypothetical imperative, therefore, represents to the agent the act it would be rational for him to do relative to some end he has adopted, follows from the same consideration on which he would do the act or decide to do it if nothing deterred or distracted him, and is issued when the agent is to some extent disengaged from taking immediate action or making a firm decision.

Clearly, on this account, the motivational force we attribute to a hypothetical imperative has the same genesis and explanation as the motive we would attribute to an agent who acted on the same consideration as the one from which the imperative follows or who decided so to act on the strength of that consideration. Hence, if the motive behind the action or decision could be traced to some nonrational desire, then the imperative's motivational force originates in that desire; and if the action or decision would have sprung from some nonrational desire because of a judgment that taking the action is the only or best way to attain that desire's object, then the imperative derives its motivational force from this desire by virtue of that judgment. In short, the same type of explanation applies to mere hypothetical imperatives as applies to certain actions and decisions.

Accordingly, mere hypothetical imperatives no more represent reason's conative power than do the actions and decisions that have the same type of explanation. This type of explanation fits Hume's account of the way some judgments motivate action indirectly and thus illustrates how reason sometimes influences the will by subserving desire. Mere hypothetical imperatives, then, likewise result from reason's subservience to desire. Consequently, one can affirm that such imperatives are irreducible to the considerations on which they are based, or any other judgments of empirical fact or one's own mental state for that matter and at the same time deny that their motivational force originates even in part independently of any nonrational desire.

Sidgwick's error in thinking otherwise should now be apparent. It is due to a faulty assumption on which the crucial step of his argument in the opening section depends, the assumption that when reason influences the will by subserving desire it does so solely by altering the understanding the agent has of desire's objects and of the means and obstacles to their attainment. In other words, the step depends on the assumption that when a judgment, a deliverance of reason, has influence on the will in virtue of its relation to some preexisting desire it derives that influence *solely* through a partnership with that desire. This assumption, however, as the foregoing discussion reveals, does not hold of mere hypothetical imperatives. Their influence on the will comes from being the products of such partnerships rather than being partners themselves. Hence, though their irreducibility to judgments of empirical fact

THE SOURCES OF MORAL AGENCY

or one's own mental state implies that they are unsuitable for the kind of partnership Sidgwick had in mind, their being unsuitable for partnerships of this kind does not imply that their influence on the will originates independently of any nonrational desire. Sidgwick's error consists, then, in his thinking, mistakenly, that such unsuitability carries this implication.

Sidgwick's error may, nevertheless, seem to pertain only to his treatment of prudential judgments conceived of as mere hypothetical imperatives. It may therefore seem removable. In fact, though, his failure to fit these judgments when they are so conceived to his account of the nature of ethical judgment spells defeat for the entire argument of Chapter 3. For it shows that a judgment's irreducibility to judgments of empirical fact or one's own mental state does not have the significance Sidgwick ascribed to it. The words 'right' and 'ought' when used in expressions of ethical judgment may indeed express a unique and fundamental notion, but its being unique and fundamental does not mean that the judgments of which it is a constituent can influence the will independently of any nonrational desire. It does not mean that these judgments are dictates of reason in Sidgwick's sense. Hence, the force that the notion has when applied in ethical judgment may not originate in the operations of reason. It may, instead, originate in the impulses of appetite and passion. Contrary to intuitionism, then, the fundamental notion of ethics may not be entirely a creature of reason, and ethical judgments may not be deliverances of reason that subserve neither desire nor feeling.

Of course, the defeat of Sidgwick's argument in Chapter 3 does not entail the demise of his intuitionist conception of ethical judgment. It only leaves the latter ungrounded. And it might then be said in Sidgwick's defense that, despite the error of the argument's crucial step, the argument does succeed in refuting any empiricist program of reducing ethical judgments to judgments of physical and psychical fact, and this refutation is sufficient for Sidgwick's purposes. For it narrows the question to one of deciding between Sidgwick's intuitionist conception and a conception according to which ethical judgments are mere hypothetical imperatives, and the decision is sure to go in Sidgwick's favor once attention is turned from prudential judgments to moral judgments. The latter, after all, are for Sidgwick the clearest if not the primary case of ethical judgment, and careful and well-focused reflection on transparent examples of them, like the common example of judging, in circumstances in which it would be highly advantageous to lie, that one ought to tell the truth, will confirm their categorical character and so confound any conception of them as mere hypothetical imperatives. Sidgwick, admittedly, read too much into the irreducibility of judgments of what it is right to do or what one ought to do, and he erred in failing to distinguish between the sense that the words 'right' and 'ought' have when used to express categorical impera-

tives and the sense they have when used to express mere hypothetical imperatives. But starting with the more restricted implication of an ethical judgment's irreducibility to judgments of physical or psychical fact and then, with
respect to this distinction between the two senses of 'right' and 'ought', reflecting carefully on which of the two senses applies to transparent examples
of moral judgment will bring one to the same result as the argument Sidgwick
gave. These considerations, so this defense of Sidgwick would conclude, will
serve to vindicate intuitionism as he formulated it.

This defense plainly depends on the probative force of careful and well-focused reflection on transparent examples of moral judgment. It assumes that
we can be confident in the conclusions of such reflection. Yet this assumption
is unwarranted. Reflection on such examples for the purpose of discerning the
nature of moral judgment is liable to two mistakes, and there is no way to
prove that one has avoided both. In particular, no one who concludes from reflection on these examples alone that moral judgments are categorical imperatives can acquit himself of the charge of having made one or the other of
these two mistakes. Thus, on the one hand, one might mistake for a moral
judgment a mere affirmation of some standard of conventional morality.
Such an affirmation is categorical, to be sure, but it need not have any influence on the will. Sidgwick himself cautions against making this mistake when
he distinguishes moral judgments that are ethical judgments, strictly speaking
(i.e., that contain the fundamental notion of ethics), from "judgments resem-
bling moral judgments in form, and not distinguished from them in ordinary
thought, in cases where the obligation affirmed is found, on reflection, to depend on the existence of current opinions and sentiments as such."[13] On the
other hand, having guarded against making this first mistake by fixing one's
attention on judgments of whose influence on the will one was certain, one
might then mistake reason for the source of this influence. Hume cautioned
against making this mistake when he famously diagnosed the fallacy of rationalist moral philosophy, both ancient and modern, as the confusion of reason
with calm passion. We cannot, solely from reflection on our experiences of
moral judgment, however clarifying and sharp our introspective powers, know
the true source of its influence on the will. To insist, to the contrary, that we
can, that our powers of reflection on such matters are fundamentally probative, and that their testimony is self-evident, is to make an appeal of the sort
characteristic of intuitionism and largely responsible for its eclipse.

Sidgwick, to his credit, offered an argument instead.

13. *ME*, p. 30. See also Philippa Foot, "Morality as a System of Hypothetical Imperatives," *Philosophical Review* 81 (1972): 305–316, for a discussion of this distinction.

10

Reason and ethics in Hobbes's *Leviathan*

Hobbes's ethics teaches the ways of self-preservation. Its lessons are arranged in a system of rules that Hobbes understood to be the laws of nature. These two themes, self-preservation and natural law, have inspired opposing interpretations of Hobbes's text. The historically dominant and still prevailing interpretation, which develops the former theme, is that Hobbes's ethics is a form of egoism. A later and less popular interpretation, which develops the latter theme, is that his ethics is a system of absolutes, "a strict deontology."[1] These two interpretations represent a dispute between what I will call orthodoxy and dissent in Hobbes scholarship. The dispute chiefly turns on two questions: What is the basis of Hobbes's ethics, and how stringent are the rules it comprises?[2]

Orthodoxy takes Hobbes's ethics to be based on his moral psychology, specifically, his theory of motivation. That theory, on the orthodox reading, is thoroughly egocentric. It holds that all voluntary action springs from self-interest.[3] Hence, on this reading, one can attribute to Hobbes the view that a person's well-being, since it is the ultimate end of all voluntary action, is the

1. A. E. Taylor, "The Ethical Doctrine of Hobbes," *Philosophy* 13(1938): 406–424, esp. p. 408.
2. One can find the orthodox interpretation in Henry Sidgwick's *Outline of the History of Ethics*, 2nd ed. (London: Macmillan and Company, 1902), pp. 163–170, and there are no doubt earlier statements of it. Recent statements include David Gauthier, *The Logic of Leviathan* (Oxford: Oxford University Press, 1969), pp. 27–98; and Jean Hampton, *Hobbes and the Social Contract Tradition* (Cambridge: Cambridge University Press, 1986), pp. 27–57. The principal statements of the dissent's interpretation are found in the article by A. E. Taylor cited in the previous footnote and Howard Warrender, *The Political Philosophy of Hobbes* (Oxford: Clarendon Press, 1957), pp. 1–102. An excellent review and assessment of the controversy, which offers an extensive list of recent essays on the topic, is given in Edwin Curley, "Reflections of Hobbes: Recent Work on His Moral and Political Philosophy," *Journal of Philosophical Research*, 15(1990), 169–250, esp. pp. 187–194.
3. Some recent orthodox interpretations, e.g., Hampton, pp. 19–24, qualify this statement of Hobbes's egoism. Their use of decision theoretic models to explain Hobbes's arguments makes the question of whether Hobbes took all voluntary action to spring from self-interest no longer crucial to their showing that Hobbes's ethics is based on his moral psychology. Accordingly, they characterize Hobbes's theory of motivation as largely or predominately egoistic. These qualifications, however, as will become clear, are incidental to the tenets of the orthodox position that I examine in this essay. For an excellent discussion of these issues see Gregory S. Kavka, *Hobbesian Moral and Political Theory* (Princeton: Princeton University Press, 1986), pp. 44–41.

only end at which it makes sense for that person to aim. Accordingly, the laws of nature are to be understood as rules for achieving this end. They specify the fittest means in the conduct of life to promoting personal well-being, and consequently they represent the derivation of morality from prudence. That is, their derivation exemplifies the exercise of reason in the service of the desire for personal well-being, and given how precarious Hobbes thought our social environment was, their derivation especially exemplifies the exercise of reason in the service of the desire for self-preservation. The laws of nature, therefore, on the orthodox interpretation, are valid relative to this desire or the more general desire to promote one's good. Their validity is conditional on the operation within the agent of these desires and on his being in unexceptional circumstances, unexceptional, that is, in the sense that he could not better promote his good by ignoring the laws. In sum, orthodoxy does not regard the laws of nature as unconditionally valid. It regards them as advisory, so to speak, rather than binding.

Dissent denies this last result. Indeed, this denial is its point of departure. Relying on passages where Hobbes characterizes the natural law as obligatory even in the state of nature, dissent's interpretation represents Hobbes's ethics as a system of law that imposes binding duties on human beings. Since law, as Hobbes defines it, implies a legislator, one whose will is supreme relative to those under its governance, it follows, on this interpretation, that the laws of nature in Hobbes's system issue from a will that is supreme relative to human beings. In short, they issue from God's will. Hence, dissent interprets Hobbes's ethics as a form of the divine command theory of morality, whose precepts are grounded in the necessity of God's will rather than the contingencies of human experience. The laws of nature, in other words, are valid absolutely. Their exposition exemplifies the exercise of disinterested reason, reason, that is, unhinged from desire. Dissent thus takes Hobbes's ethics to be logically independent of his moral psychology. Thanks to modus tollens, one might say, its opposition to the orthodox interpretation is complete.

Dissent's two main positive theses, that Hobbes took the natural law to impose obligations on human beings generally, and not solely in civil society, and that his ethics is a form of the divine command theory of morality, have not stood up well to close examination of the relevant texts.[4] At the same time, its main negative thesis, that Hobbes's ethics is logically independent of his moral psychology, has not received similar scrutiny. The thesis has escaped separate treatment, perhaps, because its fate has been thought to rest with the fate of dissent's positive theses. One can treat it separately, however. The positive theses raise questions about the authority and substance of Hobbes's

4. See Curley, p. 190.

ethics. The negative thesis raises questions about its structure. In particular, since Hobbes conceives of the laws of nature as rules of reason, it raises the question of the role of reason in his ethics: Does reason, in the deductions of these rules, follow the lead of desire or does it proceed independently of desire? This question, moreover, remains open even if one denies that Hobbes's ethics is a form of the divine command theory, indeed, even if one affirms that it is a form of egoism. One can address it, then, while leaving undecided the kind of ethical theory Hobbes held. In doing so, one undertakes a study of the structure of Hobbes's ethics apart from questions about its substance. This essay represents such a study. My hope is that it will uncover facts about the structure of Hobbes's ethics that studies that have proceeded on assumptions about the kind of theory his ethics is or have concentrated on proving which kind it is, egoism or strict deontology, have obscured.

I will restrict the study to Hobbes's *Leviathan*, which I regard as the best statement of his philosophy.[5] I ignore what he wrote in his other works because I believe that to understand his ethics one should start with *Leviathan* and be guided first by the idea of its integrity.[6] This requires waiting until one has come to see the extent to which its thought is unified before considering passages from his other works. While consideration of them would no doubt help to strengthen one's understanding of his ethics, this essay will not go beyond the first stage of this procedure.

I

Given an interest in finding clues to Hobbes's views in *Leviathan* about the role of reason in ethics, a single passage would appear to be the right place to start digging. The passage I have in mind is the famous reply to the Fool.[7] Since the Fool's position is that injustice is not always contrary to reason, Hobbes's argument against the Fool should tell us a good deal about what Hobbes thought the role of reason was in ethics. A sound interpretation of this argument, both in regard to its internal organization and in regard to its relation to the surrounding text, should then move us fairly far toward determining whether Hobbes thought reason, when exercised in the deductions of

5. All references will be to the Cambridge edition, Richard Tuck ed. (Cambridge: Cambridge University Press, 1991); hereafter abbreviated with the letter L. I have modernized some of the spelling and punctuation.
6. I particularly regard as methodologically suspect the common enterprise of ransacking Hobbes's corpus for pieces of text that one can then excise and stitch together to support an interpretation of his thought, abstractly conceived, as if the various works he produced over many years exhibited the kind of constancy and unity of thought that one has trouble realizing in a single work produced in a comparatively short time.
7. L, pp. 101-103.

the laws of nature, operated as an independent faculty or under the direction of desire. Certainly, it should tell us whether one can profitably study the structure of Hobbes's ethics apart from its authority and substance.

At first blush, Hobbes's reply to the Fool appears to support strongly the orthodox view of the relation of Hobbes's ethics to his moral psychology. You could not find a more instructive passage, some would say, on the erroneousness of dissent's negative thesis. The Fool's view represents unbridled self-interest, after all, and what Hobbes criticizes in this view is the lack of a bridle and not the call for self-interested action. Specifically, what the Fool maintains is that, since it can never be against reason to aim at that which best promotes one's good and since sometimes practicing injustice best promotes one's good, sometimes reason counsels injustice. And Hobbes's reply, then, consists in criticizing the Fool's reasoning while leaving both of his premises undisturbed. No maxim or strategy of action, Hobbes argues, follows from these premises. Indeed, Hobbes maintains, contrary to what they seem to imply, an unwavering allegiance to justice is a surer way to promote one's good. Thus his reply appears to be intended to vindicate justice as a rule of self-interest and on that account a moral virtue. The reply, in other words, if it in fact has this intention, shows Hobbes to be recommending justice as a moral virtue on the grounds of its value to self-interested pursuits. Firmer support for interpreting him as basing his ethics on his moral psychology would be hard to find.

Yet this reading of Hobbes's reply glosses over the crucial issue. One cannot show that the reply supports the orthodox view just by highlighting Hobbes's acceptance of the Fool's premise that it can never be against reason to aim at that which promotes one's own good. His acceptance of this premise may well signal his subscription to ethical egoism, but ethical egoism, as we know from Sidgwick's account of the theory, need not rest on doctrines about human motivation.[8] Its fundamental principle could be a dictate of reason. Indeed, this is how Sidgwick understood it. Hence, while Hobbes's acceptance of the Fool's premise may imply answers to questions about the substance of his ethics, it leaves open the very question about the structure of his ethics that concerns us. We are asking whether Hobbes based his ethics on his moral psychology, and the issue that is crucial to answering this question is whether he accepted the Fool's premise because he thought reason, in reaching moral conclusions, always followed the lead of desire and all desire was at bottom egoistic or because he thought reason, without recourse to desire, dictated the pursuit of one's own good above all others or at least condoned its pursuit regardless of the other pursuits available to one.

---

8. Henry Sidgwick, *Methods of Ethics*, 7th edition (London: Macmillan and Company, 1907), pp. 119-122.

This point is worth making in another way. Typically, when philosophers ask whether reason, in issuing moral judgments, operates without recourse to desire, they are asking, in effect, whether reason, in issuing such judgments, determines the proper ends of action as well as the best means to achieving the agent's ends. For if reason's contribution to moral judgment is restricted to determining the best means to the ends set by the agent's desires, then it can only follow the lead of desire; whereas if its contribution to moral judgment includes determining the proper ends of action, then it can reach moral conclusions without recourse to desire. Thus one could take our question about the role of reason in Hobbes's ethics as a question about Hobbes's view as to whether reason determines the proper ends of action or is restricted to determining the best means to the ends set by the agent's desires. Knowing that he accepts the Fool's premiss that it is never against reason to aim at that which promotes one's own good does not answer this question. It tells us that Hobbes agrees with the Fool in regarding one's own good as always a proper end of action, but it does not tell us whether he agrees because he thinks reason has determined that one's own good is always a proper end or because he thinks self-interested desires are ever-present and restricts the role of reason to determining means to the satisfaction of one's desires. Indeed, nothing in Hobbes's reply, taken by itself, settles this crucial issue.

In light of this result, I propose that we make a fresh start on trying to unearth from the reply answers to our question about the role of reason in Hobbes's ethics. The first thing to do is to place the reply within the larger project to which it belongs. That project, carried out in Chapters 14 and 15 of *Leviathan*, is Hobbes's exposition of the laws of nature that pertain to the maintenance of social order. In keeping with his well-known admiration of geometry, his belief that it supplies the right model for organizing the knowledge gained in a branch of science, Hobbes represents this body of natural law as having an axiomatic structure. He calls the first law "the fundamental law,"[9] and it is therefore natural to assume that he understands this first law as a postulate in relation to which the other eighteen laws he expounds are theorems. This assumption is further strengthened both by what he says in deriving the other eighteen laws and by how he derives them. He introduces the second law, for instance, by saying it follows from the first and introduces the third by saying it follows from the second. Similarly, his argument for them and each of the remaining sixteen, with one or two exceptions, consists in demonstrating that disobedience to it is either directly or indirectly contrary to the fundamental law. Thus his exposition of the second through the nineteenth law displays an understanding of them as consequences of the fundamental law.

9. L, p. 92.

The reply to the Fool occurs in the course of Hobbes's discussion of the third law, the principle of honoring covenants. Immediately upon introducing this law, Hobbes presents its derivation from the two laws that precede it. He argues, in effect, that the validity of the second law guarantees the validity of the third, for, as he points out, unless the principle of honoring covenants were a valid law of nature, the second law would not follow from the first, which contradicts what he has already shown. Then, after briefly explaining the third law's status as the first principle of justice, Hobbes sets out the contentions of the Fool followed by his reply.

Since he has already derived the third law from the first and the second, one might easily suppose that the exchange between him and the Fool is a digression from his exposition of the laws of nature. This supposition, however, would be a mistake. The exchange extends Hobbes's argument for incorporating the principle of honoring covenants into the body of natural law. The Fool's contention that reason does not always condemn injustice constitutes an objection to taking the principle of honoring covenants as a law of nature, and the objection must be defeated, lest the derivation be overturned. Hobbes's reply, then, is meant to remove this objection.

To see that the Fool's chief contention constitutes such an objection one need only connect it to Hobbes's conception of the laws of nature as rules of reason. At the beginning of Chapter 14, Hobbes defines a law of nature as "a precept, or general rule, found out by reason, by which a man is forbidden to do that, which is destructive of his life...,"[10] and a paragraph later he introduces the fundamental law of nature by describing it as "a precept, or general rule of reason."[11] Thus, when the Fool contends that reason does not always condemn injustice, he is to be understood as denying that the principle of honoring covenants is a precept of reason and therefore denying that it is a natural law. That Hobbes means his reply to justify, in answer to this objection, incorporating the principle of honoring covenants into the natural law is then confirmed by what he says in concluding it. "Justice therefore," he writes, "that is to say, keeping of covenant, is a rule of reason, ... and *consequently* a law of nature."[12] The reply, we may therefore conclude, is Hobbes's defense of incorporating the principle of honoring covenants into the natural law against the traditionally powerful objection, the spokesman for which in *Leviathan* is the Fool, that injustice is not always contrary to reason.

---

10. L, p. 91. The full definition is "a precept, or general rule, found out by reason, by which a man is forbidden to do, that, which is destructive of his life, or taketh away the means of preserving the same; and to omit that, by which he thinketh it may be best preserved." As a convenience, I will repeat only the first part of the definition and let that stand for the whole.
11. L, pp. 91–92.
12. L, p. 103 (emphasis added).

In disputing whether the principle of honoring covenants is a rule of reason, Hobbes and the Fool agree on the relevant criterion a principle of action must meet to qualify as a rule of reason. What they disagree on is whether the principle of honoring covenants meets that criterion. The relevant criterion is whether noncompliance with the rule invites self-destruction, and it is contained in Hobbes's definition of a law of nature. To repeat the core of that definition, a law of nature is "a precept, or general rule, found out by reason, by which a man is forbidden to do that which is destructive of his life." The question of whether reason always counsels just action, which is to say, honoring covenants, is therefore settled by determining whether injustice, reneging on covenants, tends to self-destruction. The Fool, since he speaks for the view that sometimes a man best promotes his good by reneging on his covenants, implicitly holds that such a practice need not tend to self-destruction. He implicitly denies, that is, that the third law of nature meets the criterion for a principle's being a rule of reason. Hence, his view threatens to invalidate the third law as such a rule. Hobbes then, in his reply, addresses this implication of the Fool's view and argues against it. The details of his argument, for our purposes, do not matter. What does matter, though, is its importance: Hobbes must disprove the Fool's view about reason's counsel, else his own account of the laws of nature as rules of reason will succumb to the threat the view represents.

It may now appear that we can definitively answer our question about the role of reason in Hobbes's ethics. For having seen that the issue that divides Hobbes and the Fool is whether the principle of honoring covenants is a rule of reason and that Hobbes settles it by applying the *material* criterion he introduces into his definition of a law of nature, we may be tempted to conclude that Hobbes accepts a material criterion of reason and accordingly takes reason by its very nature to determine the proper ends of action as well as the best means to achieving one's ends. A material criterion of reason, after all, if it applies to the exercise of reason in practical matters, carries this implication. We would be jumping to conclusions, however, if we yielded to this temptation. Hobbes defines reason in chapter five of *Leviathan* as a faculty whose operations are entirely formal. "Reason, in this sense, is nothing but reckoning (that is adding and subtracting) of the consequences of general names...,"[13] he declares after pointing out that we not only add and subtract numbers in arithmetic but also add and subtract lines and figures in geometry

---

13. L, p. 32. Note the sentence preceding the definition makes clear that the phrase 'in this sense' is meant to specify the sense of reason as a faculty of the mind in contradistinction to the sense that it has in the term 'right reason' and that Hobbes specifies in the next paragraph. Reason in the sense of right reason is, according to Hobbes, like arithmetic, an "infallible art."

and words and sentences in logic. His definition clearly excludes material criteria from the concept of reason, and nowhere in the subsequent chapters does he expressly take it back or modify it. Inconsistency, of course, is possible, but before attributing it to Hobbes, we should see whether his definition of reason in Chapter 5 can be squared with his using a material criterion to determine whether the principle of honoring covenants is a rule of reason.

Hobbes proceeds from his definition of reason to an account of the right use of reason, and from there to a characterization of science as the knowledge that comes from using reason rightly. Reason, when used rightly, according to Hobbes, begins with well-defined general terms.[14] It then combines these terms into well-formed sentences and the sentences into well-formed deductive arguments. Scientific knowledge, Hobbes says, comes from extending these arguments further and further so as to capture increasingly remote consequences of the notions that the definitions of the general terms with which one began express. Science, then, is the knowledge of the consequences of these definitions; and each branch of science is distinguished from the others by its subject matter, which means by the general terms whose definitions are the starting points of the knowledge it yields. The definitions, in other words, are the basic premises of that branch of science, and the consequences of these premises are its theorems, which is the name Hobbes gives them after first identifying them as general rules.[15]

Could Hobbes, in defining a law of nature as a general rule found out by reason, mean nothing more than that a law of nature is a theorem of a branch of science? If he did, then we can easily interpret the dispute between him and the Fool as a dispute over the deliverances of reason as it is defined in Chapter 5. On this interpretation, the relevant science is ethics, and the question being disputed is whether the third law of nature is a theorem of this science. Accordingly, when the Fool contends that reason does not always condemn injustice, he is to be understood as contending, in effect, that the third law does not follow as a theorem from the definition or definitions that are the basic premises of ethics. And since the chief consideration, that of whether noncompliance invites self-destruction, is, as we have seen, built into the definition of a law of nature, the Fool is to be understood as contending, in effect, that one cannot validly derive the third law from this definition. Hobbes's reply, then, is to be taken as directed against this thesis, the refutation of which would show that the third law qualified as a rule of reason. This interpretation has the great virtue of preserving consistency in Hobbes's use of the term 'reason'. Rather than represent him as accepting a material criterion of reason

14.   Ibid. See also the contrast Hobbes draws between reasoning and deliberation in ch. 6; L, p. 45.
15.   L, p. 34.

and thus abandoning the definition of reason he gives in Chapter 5, it represents him as applying a formal criterion, whether the third law follows as a theorem of a branch of science, and thus remaining faithful to that definition.

Let us take stock of the three different interpretations of Hobbes's reply to the Fool that have now surfaced in our study. The first is the one favored by orthodoxy. On this interpretation, the dispute between Hobbes and the Fool concerns the deliverances of reason when reason is exercised in the service of self-interest, that is, when its exercise consists in determining the fittest means to achieving the ends set by egoistic desires. Such an exercise falls outside the definition of reason that Hobbes gives in Chapter 5. It exemplifies strategic or means-to-ends thinking and not deduction. Indeed, it corresponds to what Hobbes, in Chapter 3, defines as seeking and attributes to the faculty of invention.[16] Seeking, according to Hobbes, is mental discourse regulated by some desire or design, and it is plain that he meant to distinguish seeking and invention from reason.[17] Hence, the first interpretation implies that Hobbes, in expounding the laws of nature, went back on the notion of reason that he defined in Chapter 5. It implicitly attributes a fundamental inconsistency to Hobbes's philosophy.

The same is true of the second interpretation, according to which Hobbes introduced a material criterion of reason into his definition of a law of nature. This interpretation would be favored by dissent, given the role of reason in the divine command theory dissent ascribes to Hobbes.[18] On this interpretation, the dispute between Hobbes and the Fool concerns the deliverances of reason when reason is exercised by applying the criterion Hobbes introduced to the question of honoring one's covenants. Such an exercise, given that the criterion is material and understood to be essential to reason, also falls outside Hobbes's definition. Thus, the second interpretation, like the first, implicitly

16. L, pp. 21–22. To be more exact, Hobbes attributes the perception that a certain action or operation is a means to an end to the faculty of invention. He attributes the evaluation of alternative means to a given end (by which one determines which of the alternatives is the best) to the faculties of judgment and prudence. But this complication does not affect the general point, for Hobbes also holds that these latter faculties are distinct from reason. The relevant passages are contained in the first fifteen paragraphs of ch. 8, where Hobbes distinguishes natural from acquired wit, classifies judgment and prudence as species of the former, and identifies reason as the only species of the latter. See L, pp. 50–53.
17. L, p. 21–22.
18. See Warrender, pp. 80–81 and 309–311; but cf. pp. 251–252. The thesis that the notion of reason Hobbes applies in expounding the natural law includes a material criterion is also put forth by Bernard Gert. Gert's general interpretation of Hobbes's ethics, however, differs from the interpretations of both orthodoxy and dissent. See his "Hobbes's Account of Reason and the Passions," *Thomas Hobbes de la Metaphysique a la Politique*, Martin Bertman et Michel Malherbe (Paris: J. Vrin, 1989), pp. 83–92; and "The Right of Nature," published in French as "Le Droit de Nature," *Le Pouvour et let Droit: Hobbes et les fondements de la Loi*, Textes reuis par by Louis Roux et Francois Tricaud, 1992, pp. 27–48.

attributes a fundamental inconsistency to Hobbes's philosophy. Only the last of our three interpretations avoids this problem since it represents the deliverances of reason over which Hobbes and the Fool dispute as conclusions of the faculty as he defined it in Chapter 5. Yet this interpretation unfolded on the assumption that Hobbes understood the laws of nature as, by definition, theorems of a branch of science, and we have left hanging the question of whether he in fact understands them in this way. It must now be addressed.

II

That Hobbes regarded the laws of nature as theorems of a branch of science is most clearly shown when he summarizes his exposition of the natural law toward the end of Chapter 15. "[T]he science of [the laws of nature]," he says, "is the true and only moral philosophy,"[19] and soon after making this remark, he identifies the nineteen laws he has expounded as "theorems concerning what conduces to [our] conservation and defense."[20] Unfortunately, one could also argue that his derivations of the laws of nature, which make up the bulk of his exposition, show that he did not regard them as theorems of a branch of science. One could make this argument because his conception of a science requires that its theorems follow as consequences of the definitions that are its starting points, and the premises of these derivations include more than definitions. They include as well propositions to the effect that such and such action promotes warfare or hinders peace-making. Consequently, to hold that Hobbes conceived of the laws of nature as theorems of a branch of science, one must explain this disparity between conception and exposition.

One possible explanation, of course, is that Hobbes simply failed to appreciate the importance of factual premises to his derivations. A better explanation, though, lies in the distinction he drew in Chapter 9 between scientific knowledge and factual knowledge.[21] The former, he remarked, is conditional, the latter absolute. Since the exposition of Chapters 14 and 15 combines both kinds of knowledge, it is plausible to suppose that Hobbes in these chapters meant to be at once presenting the science of the laws of nature and applying it to the facts of the human condition. After all, *Leviathan*'s larger aim is to convince its readers that their interests lay in obedience to their sovereign, and suppressing the conditionalized propositions that would qualify the exposition as a purely scientific presentation would be an obvious expedient to realizing this aim. Thus, to avoid the tedium of first presenting these propositions and then applying them to statements of fact so as to obtain the conclu-

19. L, p. 110.
20. L, p. 111.
21. L, p. 60.

sions about obedience he wanted to propagate, Hobbes, we may suppose, compressed these two stages of his enterprise into one. Arguably, he saw little difference between this expedient and that of physicists who applied geometry to the facts of the world in presenting the science of body and motion.[22]

Accepting this second and better explanation, let us take Hobbes's exposition of the laws of nature to exemplify his conception of science as modified by this expedient. We can then use this modified conception to specify further what I earlier described as the exposition's axiomatic structure. Accordingly, the structure has at its base a set of propositions that precede the laws of nature and consist of definitions and factual premises. The former are the major premises of the laws' derivations, and the latter, which would drop out if the science were presented as pure science, are thus eliminable. Clearly, then, the fundamental law is not, despite our initial supposition, a postulate or basic premiss. Rather, it is, like the other eighteen laws, a theorem. At the same time, since Hobbes derives these other laws from the fundamental law, the set of definitions and factual statements from which he derives the latter must contain the basic premises on which his science of the laws of nature, which is to say, his ethics, rests.

Of these premises, the main one is his definition of a law of nature. Indeed, Hobbes may have regarded it as the only premiss that is essential to grounding the natural law; for at the close of his exposition in Chapter 15, he speaks of self-destruction as "contrary to the ground of all laws of nature,"[23] and it is not hard to see in this remark reference to the clause of his definition that makes forbidding self-destructive acts a condition of a precept's being a natural law. On this reading, each law of nature qualifies as such because to violate it is to invite self-destruction, or what comes to the same thing, because to comply with it is to promote one's efforts at self-preservation. And since Hobbes conceives of every law from the second through the nineteenth as a consequence of the fundamental law, showing that he grounded the latter in this way should be sufficient to confirm this reading. The relevant passage occurs almost immediately after Hobbes puts forth the definition of a law of nature.

---

22. A further point in favor of this explanation can be seen from comparison with F. S. McNeilly's resolute attempt to reconstruct the arguments of Hobbes's *Leviathan*, including the derivations of the laws of nature, so that they all conform to Hobbes's conception of science. McNeilly's aim is to represent Hobbes's system as consisting entirely of propositions knowable a priori, and to achieve it he has to introduce definitions that Hobbes never gave. As a result, his reconstructions go beyond the text in ways that it doesn't plausibly support. No such ad hoc additions to or extensions of Hobbes's exposition are necessary on the explanation I've proposed. See McNeilly, *The Anatomy of* Leviathan (London: Macmillan, 1968), esp. pp. 183–212. See also Kavka, pp. 171–178 for instructive criticism of McNeilly's program.
23. L, p. 110.

And because the condition of man, (as hath been declared in the precedent chapter) is a condition of war of every one against every one; in which case every one is governed by his own reason; and there is nothing he can make use of, that may not be a help unto him, in preserving his life against his enemies; it followeth, that in such a condition every man has a right to every thing; even to one another's body. And therefore, as long as this natural right of every man to every thing endureth, there can be no security to any man, . . . of living out the time, which nature ordinarily alloweth men to live. And consequently it is a precept or general rule of reason, *that every man, ought to endeavour peace, as far as he has hope of obtaining it; and when he cannot obtain it, that he may seek, and use, all helps, and advantages of war.* The first branch of which rule, containeth the first, and fundamental law of nature; which is, *to seek peace, and follow it.* The second, the sum of the right of nature; which is, *by all means we can, to defend ourselves.*[24]

The passage makes clear that Hobbes did not regard the fundamental law as an underived principle of his system but rather drew it as a conclusion from considerations of the deadly conflict that confronts individuals who live in a state of nature. Such conflict, he maintained, in the preceding chapter, inevitably results when men are not ruled by a common power, which is the defining property of a state of nature. Each man, living in such a state, thus finds himself at war with every other, and to preserve himself he must find a way out of this war and into peaceful relations with others. Hence, provided that the search for peace is not hopeless, the principle of seeking peace follows as a law of nature, for to make war when there is hope for peace is to hasten one's demise. Although not every step of this argument is expressed in the passage, its outline can readily be made out from the steps that are. The passage therefore supports reading Hobbes as basing his ethics on his definition of a law of nature.[25]

The reading, however, generates a problem about whether Hobbes really did regard the laws of nature as theorems of ethics. For if ethics is based on a definition, then the laws of nature are not, strictly speaking, its theorems. No law of nature, after all, can follow from one or more definitions alone, since no set of declarative sentences that merely explain equivalences of meaning can yield an imperative. The theorems of Hobbes's ethics, rather, are propositions of the form 'X is a law of nature', where X ranges over principles such as keep peace and honor one's covenants. This feature appears at the beginning of Hobbes's exposition of the natural law, where he establishes the precept of keeping peace as the fundamental law, and it appears again in his reply to the Fool, where he brings the precept of honoring covenants directly under the definition itself. At

---

24. L, p. 91-92 (emphasis original).
25. The passage does not support this reading unequivocally, however. See pp. 220-221 below, for a different reading.

these points he expressly proves that a certain precept is a law of nature. But the feature is otherwise suppressed in the exposition, since most of its proofs consist in showing only that a subsidiary law is a consequence of the fundamental law. Perhaps, then, Hobbes simply failed to see that the real theorems of ethics were propositions about which principles are laws of nature and not the laws themselves. Alternatively, we can understand him as speaking loosely, when he calls the laws theorems. He speaks this way, let us suppose, because for him proving that a principle is a law of nature is as good as proving the principle itself. It is like proving that a proposition is true. That is, just as one can assert a proposition once one has proved it is true, so one can assert a principle of action once one has proved it is a law of nature. Either possibility leaves the reading intact, and the latter suggests that Hobbes's characterization of the laws as theorems is an inaccuracy of no consequence to his conception of ethics. We can therefore discount the inaccuracy as at most a minor problem for this reading if not for Hobbes's conception of ethics.

A more serious problem, which may be a problem either for the reading or for Hobbes's conception of ethics, concerns the actual arguments Hobbes gives to show that honoring covenants and keeping peace are laws of nature. The original motive for interpreting Hobbes as basing his ethics on definitions, it should be recalled, was to avoid representing him as having abandoned his definition of reason when, in replying to the Fool, he defended the principle of honoring covenants as a rule of reason. According to this interpretation, he remains faithful to that definition because his reply consists in arguing that the principle follows by correct inferences from well-formed definitions. Unfortunately, a problem of circularity arises if the only definition from which the principle follows is the definition of a law of nature. For the principle meets this definition only if it is found out by reason, yet it is supposed to qualify as a rule of reason because it follows from this definition.

The same problem can be seen in Hobbes's derivation of the fundamental law when that derivation is cast as an attempt to ground the fundamental law on the definition of a law of nature. Close inspection of the passage that we just considered shows that Hobbes characterizes the principle of seeking peace as a rule of reason before he identifies it as the first law of nature. If this characterization is consistent with his definition of reason, then the principle must follow from definitions. But if the definition from which it follows is the definition of a law of nature, then its following from this definition cannot without circularity be used to qualify it as such a law. The question, then, of whether Hobbes understood the laws of nature as, *by definition*, theorems of a branch of science, whether in defining them as precepts or general rules found out by reason he meant to be using 'reason' as he had defined it in

REASON AND ETHICS IN HOBBES'S *LEVIATHAN*

Chapter 5, is complicated by the problem of circularity in which this way of taking 'reason' lands him.

The source of the problem is Hobbes's definition of a law of nature. It is not well-formed if its reference to reason is glossed according to the way Hobbes defined reason in Chapter 5. To be specific, this gloss makes it an impredicative definition.[26] The definition violates the general principle that a term is well-defined only if it is defined by terms that are themselves well-defined, and the specific violation consists in the use of the term 'precept or general rule found out by reason' to define 'a law of nature' when that term itself cannot be well-defined until 'a law of nature' is well-defined. That the well-definedness of the former depends on that of the latter should be clear once the former is translated, in accordance with Hobbes's definition of reason, as 'theorem of a branch of science'. For the term 'theorem of a branch of science' is well-defined only if the definition enables one to determine the term's extension, yet one cannot determine its extension unless one is already able to determine the theorems of the various branches of science, including, in particular, the theorems of ethics. These of course are the laws of nature, and consequently, the term 'theorem of a branch of science' is well defined only if 'law of nature' is well defined. In this way one can trace the circularity that appears in Hobbes's derivation of the fundamental law and in his reply to the Fool to the impredicativeness of his definition of a law of nature.

It turns out then that none of the interpretations of Hobbes's reply to the Fool that we have considered renders Hobbes's system free of internal problems. What is more, the major problems we have uncovered are complementary. Removing the circularity from Hobbes's definition of a law of nature entails introducing a fundamental inconsistency into Hobbes's understanding of reason, and, conversely, enforcing consistency in his understanding of reason insures circularity in his definition of a law of nature. Hence, citing either problem as indirect evidence for an interpretation that avoids it does not by itself help to settle the question of which is the most plausible interpretation, for the evidential weight of each problem counterbalances that of the other. What we must do is to evaluate, with respect to each problem, the evidence against attributing it to Hobbes's system. And since the problems are complementary, this amounts to weighing the evidence for and against attributing in-

26. The term is from Henri Poincaré, who held that impredicative definitions were the source of the antinomies of set theory the discovery of which cracked the foundations of mathematics at the end of the nineteenth century. Bertrand Russell's vicious circle principle expressed the same idea. From Alonzo Church's lectures in philosophy of mathematics, UCLA, February 11, 1975, private notes. See Poincaré, *Science and Method*, Francis Maitland, trans. (London: Thomas Nelson and Sons, 1914) pp. 189–190.

consistency to Hobbes's understanding of reason. The question then is whether the evidence, on balance, favors or opposes this attribution.

III

It would of course simplify things if all the evidence fell on one side of this question. But it would be unreasonable to expect to find such uniformity in a work as long and involved as *Leviathan*. Nonetheless, the evidence against attributing inconsistency to Hobbes is substantially greater than the evidence for the opposite view. The latter consists of isolated pieces of text in Chapters 14 and 15 that support reading Hobbes as having used in his exposition of the laws of nature a notion of reason that conflicts with the one he explicitly defined in Chapter 5. The former consists chiefly in the extent of the incoherence this reading creates between the account of our mental life that Hobbes gives in *Leviathan*'s early chapters and the exposition of natural law in the later chapters. In addition, the text in and around the exposition, though it contains the recalcitrant passages mentioned above, also contains positive evidence of continuity with the early chapters. This evidence removes any residual doubt about whether Hobbes intended 'reason', as he used it in his exposition, to have the meaning he gave it. in Chapter 5, and combining this evidence with the incoherence yields a very strong case against the attribution of inconsistency. In this section, I will describe the extent of the incoherence that the attribution creates. In the following section, I will first describe the positive evidence of continuity and then, at the end, briefly discuss the evidence on the other side.

To see how extensive the incoherence is, we must connect the notion of reason Hobbes defines in Chapter 5 with his accounts of thought and speech that lead up to it. In *Leviathan*'s first three chapters, Hobbes describes the faculties of sensation and thought native to human beings. Having surveyed these faculties, he declares at the close of Chapter 3, and without having yet introduced reason into human psychology, that his survey is complete.

There is no other act of man's mind, that I can remember, naturally planted in him, so as to need no other thing, to the exercise of it, but to be born a man, and live with the use of his five senses. Those other faculties, of which I shall speak by and by, and which seem proper to man only, are acquired, and encreased by study and industry; and of most men learned by instruction and discipline; and proceed all from the invention of words, and speech. For besides sense, and thoughts, and the train of thoughts, the mind of man has no other motion, though by the help of speech, and method, the same faculties may be improved to such a height, as to distinguish men from all other living creatures.[27]

27. L, p. 23.

Hobbes's mentioning of other faculties that he plans to speak of by and by is obviously a veiled reference to reason, and hence it is evident from this passage that Hobbes means to exclude reason from the class of innate powers.[28] It is instead, in his system, a power human beings acquire by learning to speak.

The innate powers are, on the one hand, those through the exercise of which thoughts originate in the mind and, on the other, those through the exercise of which the mind regulates its trains of thoughts. The former are the five senses, which Hobbes covers in Chapter 1. The latter are memory, foresight, and invention, which he discusses in Chapter 3. The thoughts that originate through the exercise of the five senses are, needless to say, sensations, and their residues are then referred, in Chapter 2, either to memory or to imagination. These residual thoughts, while they could occur in isolation, typically occur in a sequence or train, which when made by design is made through the exercise of memory, foresight, or invention and out of a desire to recapture the past, see into the future, or achieve some end. A train of thoughts, which Hobbes also calls mental discourse, is thus a sequence of images. The images are images of particular things, and memory, foresight, and invention enable their possessor to make useful connections of one particular with another.

The abilities to keep these connections in the mind for more than a few moments, to recall them when needed, and to extend their reach are then vastly improved by the invention of names for these particulars. Names, and more generally, speech, is the subject of Chapter 4, and its subtext is that the invention of speech elevates human beings above other animals and is the vehicle for the acquisition of those powers without which human beings could not form political societies.[29] While the argument for this latter thesis must await Chapters 13 through 17 to be completed, the argument for the former is wholly contained in Chapter 4 and can be quickly summarized. With the invention of names, verbal discourse replaces mental discourse as the preferred form of regulated trains of thoughts: "By this imposition of names, ... we turn the reckoning of the consequences of things imagined in the mind, into a reckoning of the consequences of appellations."[30] This replacement radically transforms man's cognitive powers. It turns them into rational faculties, the possession of which distinguishes human beings from other an-

28. He makes the same point in distinguishing reason from prudence in chs. 5 and 8. See L, pp. 35 and 52-53.
29. "[T]he most noble and profitable invention of all other, was that of speech, consisting of names or appellations, and their connection; whereby men register their thoughts; recall them when they are past; and also declare them one to another for mutual utility and conversation; without which there had been amongst men, neither commonwealth, nor society, nor contract, nor peace, no more than amongst lions, bears, and wolves." L, p. 24.
30. L, p. 26.

imals.[31] The reckoning of appellations is, we should note, Hobbes's definition of reason.

This transformation comes about because speech has certain features that characterize nothing else. The invention of names brings common names as well as singular names, and common names, which collect particulars under a single marker according to how the particulars resemble each other, are the media of universals. It is through them and them alone that universals come into the world and reside in it.[32] Similarly, connections of names through predication are the media of truth and falsity. Truth and falsity are borne by affirmations, in which one name, the predicate, is joined to another, the subject, and they are borne by nothing else.[33] Truth, for Hobbes, is a matter of the inclusion of all the things collected under the latter, the subject, among the things collected under the former, the predicate, and falsity a matter of the absence of this relation between the two collections.[34] Mastery of these features means that one has the ability to add names together to form affirmations and to make appropriate substitutions, one name for another, where the things collected under one name are the same as or (in the case of an affirmation's subject-term) a subset of the things collected under the other. These operations are what Hobbes means by the reckoning of names, their addition and subtraction, and hence human beings acquire reason by mastering speech. Anticipating the definition of reason he will give in Chapter 5, Hobbes writes in the chapter on speech, which precedes it,

Subject to names is whatsoever can enter or be considered in an account; and be added one to another to make a sum; or subtracted one from another, and leave a remainder. The Latins called accounts of money *Rationes*, and accounting *Ratiocinatio*: and that which we in bills or books of account call items, they called *Nomina*, that is names: and thence it seems to proceed that they extended the word *Ratio*, to the faculty of reckoning in all other things. The Greeks have but one word, *logos*, for both speech and reason; not that they thought there was no speech without reason; but no reasoning without speech.[35]

To suppose, then, that Hobbes's exposition of the natural law incorporated a notion of reason that conflicted with the one he defined in Chapter 5 is to

31. Hobbes does not take speech and reason to be the only powers distinctive of human beings. In ch. 3, he writes that, while human beings are not the only animals who seek the causes of things, they are the only ones who seek effects. See L, p. 21. And in ch. 6, he defines curiosity as the "desire, to know why, and how, ... such as in no living creature but *man*: so that man is distinguished, not only by his reason; but also by this singular passion, from other *animals*." L, p. 42 (emphasis original). See also L, p. 76.
32. "There being nothing in the world universal but names; for the things named are every one of them individual and singular." L, p. 26.
33. "For *true* and *false* are attributes of speech not of things." L, p. 27 (emphasis original).
34. Ibid.
35. L, p. 29.

set the later chapters in which this exposition occurs at war with the early chapters, which contain his definition of reason and the accounts of thought and speech that are essential preliminaries to its introduction. To suppose, for instance, with orthodoxy, that what Hobbes meant by reason in these later chapters was means-to-ends thinking is to contradict a doctrine that Hobbes plainly constructed the early chapters to uphold, the traditional doctrine that human beings alone, among animals, possess reason. For Hobbes includes means-to-ends thinking in his survey of the faculties native to human beings, mentions it as one that human beings share with other animals, and implies at the close of this survey that the faculties traditionally (and as far as he can tell rightly[36]) regarded as setting human beings apart from other animals are those that men acquire by learning to speak.[37] To suppose then, instead, with dissent, that what Hobbes meant by reason was a faculty that operated according to material as well as formal criteria is to run afoul of Hobbes's nominalist metaphysics. For a material criterion of reason implies either universal concepts that inhere in the human mind or a world of universals that exists independently of any particulars and is accessible to reason alone, and either implication contradicts Hobbes's thesis that nothing universal exists independently of speech. Similarly, a material criterion of reason implies propositions whose truth is a matter either of the structure of the human mind or of relations among universals existing independently of particulars, and either implication contradicts Hobbes's thesis about the nature of truth. None of these contradictions should come as a surprise, however. Hobbes surely would not have put forth his account of how human beings acquire reason by learning to speak if he thought there were more to reasoning than formal operations on signs and symbols.

These contradictions make clear that the incoherence resulting from the attribution of inconsistency to Hobbes's understanding of reason is extensive, so much so that an interpretation that entails it effectively cuts off the argument of Chapters 14 and 15 from the arguments of the first five chapters. The incoherence in this case is theoretical. Different parts of Hobbes's theory fail to mesh. In addition, the attribution results in incoherence that is practical, for it results in inconsistencies between Hobbes's statements about the proper method of science, of the philosophical search for truth, and his actual conduct of such a search. It therefore represents Hobbes as having grossly failed to

36. "Understanding being nothing else, but conception caused by speech. And therefore if speech be peculiar to man (as for ought I know it is), then is understanding peculiar to him also." L, p. 30.
37. That Hobbes distinguished means-to-ends thinking from reason does not imply that he excluded the former from his determination of the laws of nature. Rather it implies that he did not take its contribution to the determination of those laws to be what qualified them as rules of reason. On this point see Section IV below.

practice what he preached. This too is a kind of incoherence, and one can get a good sense of its gravity by noting the many places in Chapters 4 and 5 where Hobbes preaches the lesson that, on the attribution of inconsistency, he fails to practice.

The lesson is that in any pursuit of truth and scientific knowledge one must begin with definitions of the terms one will use. This is the first principle of the proper method of reasoning or science as Hobbes understands it. Thus, in Chapter 4, he says about geometry, his model science, that in it "men begin at settling the significations of their words; which settling of significations, they call *definitions*; and place them in the beginning of their reckoning."[38] And he concludes, from this illustration and subsequent considerations of difficulties that the failure to begin with definitions creates, that "in the right definition of names lies the first use of speech; which is the acquisition of science."[39] In Chapter 5 he writes, "The use and end of reason, is not the finding of the sum, and the truth of one, or a few consequences, remote from the first definitions, and settled significations of names; but to begin at these; and proceed from one consequence to another."[40] Further, to underscore the importance of this principle, Hobbes repeatedly warns of the nonsense and false conclusions that its neglect causes. "In wrong or no definitions," he declares in Chapter 4, "lies the first abuse [of speech]; from which proceed all false and senseless tenets."[41] And earlier in the same chapter he describes this first abuse of speech as "inconstancy in the signification of [one's] words"[42] and warns that a thinker who does not take the right steps to avoid it, which is to say, who does not begin with definitions, "will find himself entangled in words, as a bird in lime-twigs; the more he struggles the more belimed."[43] In Chapter 5 one finds more of the same: "The first cause of absurd conclusions I ascribe to want of a method; in that they begin not their ratiocination from definitions; that is from settled significations of their words."[44] Et cetera, et cetera.

In view of all this harping by Hobbes on the necessity of beginning with definitions and of avoiding ambiguity in the use of one's terms, it would be an astonishing lapse on his part if he were to use 'reason' throughout any of *Leviathan*'s central arguments in a sense he nowhere defined and in conflict with the sense he explicitly defined. Of course, we have to examine later chapters to confirm that he did not lapse in this way, and in the next section I will

38. L, p. 28.
39. Ibid.
40. L, p. 33.
41. L, p. 28.
42. L, p. 25.
43. L, p. 28.
44. L, p. 34.

consider the most important of these. Still, that Hobbes generally appears to take great care to apply his method in the central arguments of *Leviathan's* philosophical parts already attests to the unlikelihood of our finding anything more than an occasional slip. Even on minor matters, he appears to be sensitive to the method's requirements, which makes the inconsistency in the understanding of reason that both orthodoxy and dissent must attribute to him all the more curious.[45] In sum, the incoherence that results from attributing to him this inconsistency is not only extensive but occurs on distinct levels, and on either level it gravely disrupts the unity of thought in the first part of *Leviathan*.

IV

This disruption notwithstanding, the incoherence will not weigh heavily against attributing this inconsistency to Hobbes unless one is able to locate within these later chapters the notion of reason he defined in Chapter 5. In other words, if this notion were alien to these later chapters, one could acknowledge the incoherence and still argue for attributing this inconsistency. Such an argument would certainly be attractive to orthodoxy, which assumes that Hobbes's derivations of the laws of nature are essentially exercises in means-to-ends thinking, for Hobbes could not have regarded the laws of nature as essentially the products of such thinking and, at the same time, excluded this sort of thinking from what qualified the laws as rules of reason. The text in and around the chapters that contain the derivations, however, does not support this assumption. To the contrary, it shows that Hobbes understood exercises of reason, in the sense he defined in Chapter 5, to be no less essential to his derivations than means-to-ends thinking. Hence, it shows sufficient continuity between *Leviathan's* early chapters and these later ones to render the incoherence that results from attributing inconsistency to Hobbes's understanding of reason both strong and unrebuttable evidence against the attribution.

To describe the evidence for this continuity, let us use, as Hobbes did, 'natural wit' to refer to means-to-ends-thinking and 'acquired wit' to refer to reason as he defined it in Chapter 5. The evidence is of two kinds. First, there are passages in the chapters that surround and contain Hobbes's derivations indicating that he viewed acquired wit as making a distinct contribution to the determination of the laws of nature. Second, there are the derivations them-

---

45. In ch. 2, for example, he is careful to distinguish two senses of 'understanding', though neither is important to subsequent arguments. The distinction, in fact, parallels the distinction between two senses of 'reason' that the orthodox interpretation implicitly finds in the text, leaving one to wonder why, if orthodoxy is right, Hobbes didn't draw it explicitly.

selves, in which one can distinguish the work of acquired wit from that of natural wit and therefore show that the former notion is at home in the chapters containing the derivations. The first kind of evidence is the easiest to describe. Its earliest instance occurs in Chapter 13.

Consider, then, what Hobbes says at the beginning and end of this chapter. At the beginning, he exempts men's acquired wit from any role in the chapter's famous argument for the inevitable degeneration of a state of nature into a state of war. In presenting his initial premises about human equality in the state of nature, he writes,

And as to the faculties of mind, (setting aside the arts grounded upon words, and especially that skill of proceeding upon general and infallible rules called science, which very few have and but in few things, as being not a native faculty born with us nor attained (as prudence) while we look after somewhat else), I find yet a greater equality amongst men than that of strength.[46]

The equality he finds is that of natural wit, specifically, prudence.

For prudence is but experience, which equal time equally bestows on all men in those things they equally apply themselves unto.[47]

Then, at the end of the chapter, having demonstrated that life outside of political society would be hell, Hobbes brings in reason as the faculty that, together with the passions that "incline men to peace," shows the way out of this living hell.

And thus much for the ill condition, which man by mere nature is actually placed in, though with a possibility to come out of it, consisting partly in the passions, partly in his reason.[48]

This possibility, Hobbes believes, is realized through the determination of the laws of nature, which he characterizes at the end of Chapter 13 as "convenient articles of peace" suggested by reason. By inserting reason at this point, having first exempted it from complicity in the conspiracy of circumstances that leads a state of nature to degenerate into a state of war, Hobbes implies that reason promises instruction that one cannot get from prudence alone. And because Hobbes takes prudence to be means-to-ends thinking that is made swift and inventive by experience, the implication is that reason promises instruction that one cannot get from means-to-ends thinking alone. The instruction, as we have just noted, consists in the determination of the laws of nature. So the concluding paragraphs of this chapter, when read in view of the opening ones, indicate that Hobbes, in attributing the laws of nature to the

46. L, p. 87.
47. Ibid.
48. L, p. 90. Compare passage cited in fn. 29 above.

REASON AND ETHICS IN HOBBES'S LEVIATHAN

work of reason, understood reason to be distinct from means-to-ends thinking and a faculty whose operation was essential to determining those laws.

The same point is then reiterated in Chapter 14. After opening the chapter with a definition of the right of nature, Hobbes immediately stipulates that men will use both judgment and reason in exercising this right. He had earlier, in Chapter 8, defined judgment as the faculty within natural wit by which one detects differences between one thing and another that are useful in advancing one's ends.[49] Hence, one should read him as specifying at this point distinct faculties, judgment and reason, which correspond to natural and acquired wit. Since what follows is his exposition of the laws of nature, one can infer that Hobbes viewed the derivation of these laws as the joint work of both faculties if not the sole work of reason. In other words, the chapter's opening passages and the way they segue into the derivations of the first two laws imply that Hobbes in this chapter continued to regard reason as distinct from means-to-ends thinking and as a faculty whose operation was essential to the determination of the laws of nature.

Finally, it may be worth noting that Hobbes again pairs judgment and reason in Chapter 17, though the pairing is less perspicuous. It lies in his comparison of humans to bees and ants.[50] Hobbes describes the latter as possessing judgment but lacking reason. He then remarks that these creatures are able to live together peaceably in a natural society because their private ends naturally coincide with the common good. In men, Hobbes maintains, no such coincidence between private ends and common good exists absent a state whose power can artificially create such coincidence. Therefore, by implication, Hobbes bids us to conclude that judgment alone is insufficient to enable human beings to live together peaceably in civil society, that human beings must use reason as well if not instead.

Looking next at Hobbes's derivations themselves, which supply the second kind of evidence for continuity between the early and later chapters, one can easily distinguish the work of reason from that of judgment by tracking the source and consequences of the two kinds of premisses the derivations contain, definitions and statements of fact. The latter originate in exercises of judgment; the former initiate exercises of reason. Through an exercise of judgment, for instance, one recognizes that certain acts will cause others to be angry with one or distrustful of one. One recognizes, that is, that certain acts would, in the state of nature, reinforce the hostility and wariness with which others behave toward one. Judgment, in this case, produces a link between ideas in mental discourse, which when encoded in words yields a statement

49. L, 50–51. See also fn. 14 above.
50. L, pp. 119–120.

that some act X arouses the enmity and distrust of others. Applying the definition of 'war', one then can infer that Xing prolongs war, which yields, once one applies the definition of 'peace', that Xing violates the fundamental law of nature. Hence, a principle proscribing Xing is a law of nature that derives from the fundamental law. The fourth and eighth laws, those proscribing ingratitude and contempt, are examples of laws whose derivations, more or less, fit this scheme,[51] and similar reconstructions of other derivations are not hard to produce. In all of them, the notion of reason as acquired wit is clearly exemplified.

Both kinds of evidence, then, show positive continuity between *Leviathan*'s early chapters and the later ones containing the exposition of the laws of nature. Both show that the notion of reason as acquired wit resides comfortably within these later chapters, and consequently, the case for reading them as incorporating a conflicting notion of reason is unpromising. The chapters do contain a few passages that one could easily read as expressing such a notion, and these passages constitute the evidence for attributing to Hobbes inconsistency in his understanding of reason. In only one of them, however, is the inconsistency incontrovertible. The passage is worth noting, both for this reason and because of its fundamental importance to the exposition. It represents the principal piece evidence in favor of the attribution.[52]

The passage in question is the one containing the derivation of the fundamental law, which I quoted earlier.[53] While this passage can, in the way I have argued, be used to support interpreting Hobbes as basing his ethics on the definition of a law of nature, it also expresses a notion of reason that is at odds with that of acquired wit, which makes its support of that interpretation problematic. The problem arises because the derivation, as Hobbes lays it out, is a two-stage proof. At the first stage, Hobbes derives a compound rule, which he calls a precept or general rule of reason. Then, at the second stage, he identifies this rule's first clause as the fundamental law. Hobbes thus brings in his definition of a law of nature at this second stage. At the first stage, though, it plays no role. Hence, the compound rule he derives at that stage qualifies as a rule of reason independently of this or, it would appear, any definition. Therefore, to characterize it, as he does, as a precept or general rule of reason is to apply a notion of reason that conflicts with that of acquired wit. And to the

---

51. See L, p. 105 for the derivation of the fourth law and L, p. 107 for that of the eighth.
52. In the other passages Hobbes uses 'reason' loosely or metaphorically in ways suggesting a conflicting notion of reason. But because the language is loose or figurative it can also be rendered consistent with the idea acquired wit. Examples are "reason suggesteth convenient articles of peace," L, p. 90; "glorying to no end, is vainglory, and contrary to reason; and to hurt without reason, tendeth to the introduction of war." L, pp. 106–107.
53. See p. 13 above.

extent that Hobbes thought it important to construe the compound rule and, particularly, its second clause, which specifies the right of nature, as a rule of reason, the passage counts in favor of attributing to him inconsistency in his understanding of reason. Still, on balance, the evidence weighs heavily against this attribution.

V

Let us return to the question of the relation of Hobbes's ethics to his moral psychology with which our study began. That question is whether, in Hobbes's ethics, reason follows the lead of desire in its deductions of the laws of nature or proceeds independently of desire. We sought the answer in Hobbes's reply to the Fool and the search yielded three distinct interpretations of this reply, one favored by orthodoxy, one favored by dissent, and a third that does not immediately fit into either of these schools and differs from its rivals in that it avoids attributing inconsistency to Hobbes's understanding of reason. The argument of the last two sections has established this third inter- pretation as the most plausible one. So we should turn to it for the answer to our question. Since its leading thesis is that Hobbes based his ethics on his de- finition of a law of nature, we should find the answer in the criterion in virtue of which Hobbes thought this definition was correct.

That Hobbes thought there was a distinction to be drawn between correct and incorrect definitions is clear from what he says in Chapters 4 and 5 about the importance of definitions to good reasoning. In those chapters, he speaks of right and wrong definitions,[54] as we have seen, describes the proper method of reasoning as beginning with apt definitions,[55] and advises those who seek truth "to examine the definitions of former authors and ... to correct them where they are negligently set down."[56] He gives no explicit criterion, unfortu- nately, for distinguishing right definitions from wrong ones, but he does say enough to give the reader a fair sense of the criterion he is using.

Thus he speaks on two occasions of words being ordained to convey certain conceptions. At one point, he criticizes metaphorical speech as using words "in [an]other sense than that they are ordained for",[57] and at another point, he explains a man's understanding someone's speech as his having the "thoughts which the words of that speech ... were ordained and constituted to signify."[58] From these and other suggestive remarks we can safely surmise

54. L, p. 28.
55. "Reason is ... attained by industry; first in apt imposing of names." L. p. 35.
56. L, p. 28.
57. L, p. 26.
58. L, p. 30.

that, with respect to definitions from which reasoning properly engaged in begins, Hobbes took a correct definition to be one that expressed in equivalent terms the same thought that the term being defined was customarily used to convey, and we can also surmise that he understood this thought to be the thought of an object that is typical of the particulars that made up that term's extension. As shorthand, let us say that Hobbes took a correct definition to be one that captured the customary meaning of the term being defined. Presumably, then, Hobbes believed that knowledge of a term's customary meaning came from competency as a speaker of the relevant language, though he evidently also believed that how other equally competent speakers used the term provided evidence of whether one's definition was correct.

Be this as it may, to the question of the criterion in virtue of which Hobbes thought his definition of a law of nature was correct, the answer must be the term's customary meaning. This answer may at first seem puzzling in light of Hobbes's often cited remark at the very end of Chapter 15 that the rules he has shown to be laws of nature are improperly called 'laws'.[59] How could Hobbes believe he was giving the customary meaning of the term as its definition and at the same time say that the term implies something else? The puzzle, however, disappears once we bring back into view the thesis about what words signify for which we are using the expression 'customary meaning' as shorthand. On this thesis, the term 'law of nature', to be a significant expression, must convey a thought of some particular object. Yet if it conveyed the thought of a law, it would then have to convey the thought of a lawgiver. For Hobbes defines a law as a command,[60] and the thought of a command entails the thought of a commander. In the case of a law of nature, though, the commander would be God, and Hobbes did not think one could have a thought of God.[61] Hence, to make 'law of nature' a significant expression he had to find a way to define it that did not imply that the laws of nature were, strictly speaking, laws.

His solution was to use what he regarded as the laws' common content, the common subject of their instruction. He believed, that is, that the laws instructed men and women on how best to preserve themselves and that by defining a law of nature as he did, he had succeeded in collecting under the term the same rules that would be counted as laws of nature by those who as-

59. "These dictates of reason, men use to call by the name of laws, but improperly." L, p. 111.
60. E.g., ibid., "[L]aw, properly is the word of him, that by right hath command over others," and in ch. 26, "And first it is manifest, that law in general, is not counsel, but command." L, p. 183.
61. In ch. 3, "And therefore the name of *God* is used, not to make us conceive him; (for he is *incomprehensible*; and his greatness, and power are unconceivable;) but that we may honor him." L, p. 23 (emphasis original).

serted that such laws were general commands of God. Whether or not he succeeded is not here to the point, of course. What is to the point is that what would make the definition correct, in Hobbes's view, are facts about the linguistic usage of competent speakers and not facts about human desire. Consequently, his derivations of the laws of nature do not represent operations of reason in which reason follows desire's lead. Hobbes's ethics, in other words, if it is based on his definition of a law of nature, is logically independent of his moral psychology. This result confirms dissent's negative thesis.

At the same time, the result does not support either of dissent's positive theses. As should now be apparent, an interpretation of Hobbes's ethics that applies his conception of science to his exposition of the laws of nature lies outside the dispute between orthodoxy and dissent. Hence, its confirming dissent's negative thesis does not have the import that proving the thesis would have within that dispute. Within the dispute, proving the thesis would mean that Hobbes conceived of reason as including the power to determine the ends one ought to pursue as well as the best means to achieving the ends one is inclined to pursue, for both sides assume of Hobbes's ethics that, if it is not based on his moral psychology, then the proper ends of human action are determined by reason rather than passion. This is because both sides assume that Hobbes's derivations of the laws of nature represent exercises of practical reason. The issue then that divides them is whether practical reason, as represented by these derivations, includes the determination of proper ends or is restricted to the determination of the best means to achieving ends the agent is already inclined to pursue. By contrast, if one interprets Hobbes's ethics by applying his conception of science, his derivations do not represent either form of practical reason. Instead, they represent the exercise of reason by a scientist to determine which principles of action qualify as natural laws. Indeed, on this definitivist interpretation, there is no issue about the nature of practical reason, because Hobbes does not recognize any distinction of form between practical and theoretical reason. For Hobbes, reason is practical only in its content, not in its form, and to assume otherwise is just to make the attribution of inconsistency examined above.

Hobbes's implicit denial of practical reason as a distinct form of reason reflects a feature of his ethics noted earlier, that, strictly speaking, its theorems are not principles of action themselves but propositions about such principles.[62] The difference between types of ethical system this feature implies makes even clearer the gap between the definitivist interpretation and the interpretations of orthodoxy and dissent. The latter take Hobbes's ethics to be a system whose theorems are principles of action. On these interpretations, the

62. See above, pp. 209-210.

principles follow directly from the ultimate end of right action, self-preservation, for either that end is specified in an unstated first principle, a material criterion of reason, which one could cash out as a dictate and which is axiomatic relative to the laws of nature, or it is given in some brute desire the existence of which is the condition of each law's validity. Using Kant's terms, though not with his exact meaning, such a system is either a system of categorical imperatives or a system of hypothetical ones. These alternatives show the dispute between dissent and orthodoxy to be a dispute over whether Hobbes's ethics is founded on truths of reason or objects of desire. By contrast, on the definitivist interpretation, Hobbes embeds the ultimate end of right action in a definition, and it then serves as a criterion for qualifying principles of action as laws of nature. His ethics is thus neither a system of categorical imperatives nor one of hypothetical imperatives. It is founded neither on truths of reason nor on objects of desire.

The definitivist interpretation takes seriously Hobbes's express understanding of ethics as a science and his conception of science as proceeding by deductive inferences from definitions. This understanding and conception secure the logical independence of his ethics from his moral psychology, given Hobbes's view as to what makes a definition correct. His ethics is logically independent in that its theorems have no other ground than the definition on which it is based. That is to say, justifying its theorems does not require looking beyond this definition to theorems and basic premises of some other science. It does not follow, however, that Hobbes's ethics has no relation to his moral psychology. Because science is a product of speech and speech a human activity, the psychology supplies explanations of the science's development. On the general points about speech, Hobbes's views are clear. Human beings invent names and settle on their meanings to advance their individual and common interests, and the same motives explain their use of words in verbal discourse to record, extend, and share their trains of thoughts.[63] They are thereby enabled to turn the wisdom of mere experience in the pursuit of the ends that most preoccupy them in daily life into rational and scientific ways of living.[64] A science of morals, perhaps more than any other science, is therefore likely to show in its basic notions and major theorems strong traces of the interests it serves, and for Hobbes the predominant interest for human be-

---

63. L, p. 25.
64. "As, much experience is *prudence*; so, is much science, *sapience*. . . . [T]o make their difference appear more clearly, let us suppose one man endued with an excellent natural use, and dexterity in handling his arms; and another to have added to that dexterity, an acquired science, of where he can offend, or be offended by his adversary, in every possible posture, or guard: The ability of the former, would be to the ability of the later, as prudence to sapience; both useful; but the later infallible." L, pp. 36–37 (emphasis original).

ings, the predominant desire in our lives, is that of self-preservation. His moral psychology, then, while not a source of justification in ethics, is a source of explanation: it explains the construction and teaching of a system of rules compliance with which is every one's best answer to the question, How can I preserve myself? The orthodox interpretation, which ties Hobbes's ethics to his psychology, may thus be faulted not so much for having tied the two sciences together too tightly as for having tied them together in the wrong way. Its error is that it confuses a causal relation in Hobbes's philosophical system for a structural one.

11

Shame and self-esteem:
A critique

Twenty-five years ago the psychoanalyst Gerhart Piers offered what remains the most influential way of distinguishing shame from guilt. Reformulated without terms special to psychoanalytic theory, Piers's distinction is that shame is occasioned when one fails to achieve a goal or an ideal that is integral to one's self-conception, whereas guilt is occasioned when one transgresses a boundary or limit on one's conduct set by an authority under whose governance one lives. Succinctly, shame goes to failure, guilt to transgression. Shame is felt over shortcomings, guilt over wrongdoings.[1]

More recently, writers who have addressed themselves to the way shame differs from guilt, notably, among philosophers, John Rawls, have characterized shame as an emotion one feels upon loss of self-esteem and have analyzed self-esteem and its loss in a way that bears out Piers's influence.[2] Rawls plainly is in Piers's debt. He explains self-esteem in terms of the goals and ideals one incorporates into one's life plans, and he makes this explanation central to his account of our moral personality, in particular, our capacity to feel shame.

A characterization of shame like Rawls's, when set in the context of distinguishing shame from guilt, we are likely to find intuitively appealing. And we may feel a further pull in its direction when we think of shame in comparison with other emotions to which it is thought similar – for instance, embarrassment. For we associate both shame and embarrassment with an experience of discomfiture, a sudden shock that short-circuits one's composure and self-possession; yet we would agree, I think, that embarrassment is an experience of discomfiture that, unlike shame, does not include a diminishment in one's sense of worth. An experience of shame, by contrast, strikes at one's sense of worth. Here we may be reminded of times when things were going well and we were somewhat inflated by the good opinion we had of ourselves, when sud-

---

1. Gerhart Piers and Milton B. Singer, *Shame and Guilt: A Psychoanalytic and a Cultural Study* (Springfield, IL: Charles C. Thomas, 1953), pp. 11–12.
2. John Rawls, *A Theory of Justice* (Cambridge, Mass.: Harvard University Press, 1971), pp. 440–446. For similar views see Helen Merrell Lynd, *On Shame and the Search for Identity* (New York: Harcourt Brace & Co., 1958), pp. 23–24; Robert W. White, "Competence and the Psychosexual Stages of Development," in *Nebraska Symposium on Motivation 1960*, ed. Marshall Jones (Lincoln: University of Nebraska Press, 1960), pp. 125–127; and David A. J. Richards, *A Theory of Reasons for Action* (Oxford: Clarendon Press, 1971), pp. 250–259.

denly, quite unexpectedly, we did something that gave the lie to our favorable self-assessment, and we were shocked to see ourselves in far less flattering light. Such are the circumstances for shame, and the positive self-image that disappears in these circumstances and is replaced by a negative one spells loss of self-esteem.

These contrasts between shame and guilt and shame and embarrassment present the bare outlines of a characterization of shame, which, when filled out, appears rather attractive. It is the topic of this chapter. My thesis is that this characterization, though attractive at first appearance, is unsatisfactory. It represents, I contend, a misleading conception of shame. In particular, I mean to challenge its central idea that shame signifies loss of self-esteem.

The chapter is divided into three parts. In the first I lay out what I will call the Rawlsian characterization of shame – Rawlsian in that I retain the controlling thesis and overall structure of Rawls's account but do not concern myself with its specifics, an exact rendering of Rawls being unnecessary for my purposes. Though my approach here is largely uncritical, my aim is to set up a well-defined target for subsequent criticism. In the second, then, I begin that criticism. I set forth a case of loss of self-esteem and some cases of shame that pose problems for the characterization. By themselves these cases stand as counterexamples to it, but my hope is that they will have a more illuminating effect, that they will produce a sense or spark an intuition that its central idea is problematic. Accordingly, in the third part I complete the criticism. I draw from the cases two lessons about shame intended to give definition to the intuition I hope will already have been sparked. Each lesson points to a key feature of shame that the characterization leaves out or misrepresents, its central idea being implicated as the source of these failures. Thus, while the criticism of this third part is aimed at the target set up in the first, the force of the criticism should lead us to consider rejecting the idea at the target's center.

I

We need at the start to fix our understanding of self-esteem, since the concept is at the base of the Rawlsian characterization. To this end I will present some considerations leading up to a definition of self-esteem, from which an explanation of its loss will follow directly. This will then yield the characterization of shame we seek. Let us begin with the general idea that self-esteem relates to what one makes of oneself or does with one's life. One has self-esteem if one's spirits are high because one believes that one has made or will make something of oneself, that one has been or will be successful in one's life pursuits. Conversely, one lacks self-esteem if one is downcast because of a judgment that one has failed to make or never will make something of oneself, that one

227

doesn't or won't ever amount to much. Something of this idea is suggested in William James's equation that sets self-esteem equal to the ratio of one's successes to one's pretensions.[3]

The first thing to note in this general idea is that self-esteem connects up with the condition of one's spirits. We speak of vicissitudes of self-esteem: highs and lows. One's self-esteem can plummet. It can also be boosted or bolstered. Indolence and languishing in doldrums are signs that one's self-esteem is at a low ebb. Enthusiasm for and vigorous engagement in activities in which one chooses to participate are signs of an opposite condition. We also describe persons in these conditions as having or lacking self-esteem. And though subtle differences may exist between a person's having self-esteem and his self-esteem's being high and between his lacking self-esteem and his self-esteem's being low, I will treat the two in each pair as equivalent.

A second point of note, which is corollary to the first, is that self-esteem goes with activity. But to assert that having self-esteem requires that one be active would be an overstatement. We should allow that the esteem a person has for himself is relative to that period in his life with which he identifies for the purpose of self-assessment. Thus, a person may retain his self-esteem after having retired from active life if he looks back on his endeavors and accomplishments with pride while content to take it easy. He maintains a high opinion of himself while leading a rather leisurely and unproductive life because his self-assessment proceeds from recollections of an earlier period when he was active and successful. Or, to take the viewpoint of a youth looking forward in time, he may have esteem for himself in view of the life he aspires to lead if he believes in the accuracy of the picture he has of his future. He identifies, for the purpose of self-assessment, with the person he believes he will become, his present self having little bearing. Consequently, he may even at the time be leading an altogether easygoing and frivolous life while exuding self-esteem. I mention these possibilities only to set them aside. We simplify our task of explaining self-esteem if we restrict the discussion to self-esteem had in view of one's current doings and development.

Besides this simplifying restriction, we must also add a qualification to the statement that being active is a condition of having self-esteem. As a third point, then, one's actions, if they are signs of self-esteem, must have direction. They must be channeled into pursuits or projects and reflect one's goals and ideals. A wayward vagabond does not present a picture of someone who has self-esteem. Nor do we ascribe self-esteem to someone who, having no settled conception of himself, tries on this and that trait of personality, as he would

3. William James, *The Principles of Psychology*, 2 vols. (1890; reprint ed., New York: Dover Publications, 1950), vol. 1, p. 310.

sunglasses of different styles, to see which gives him the most comfortable look. Self-esteem is had by persons whose lives have a fairly definite direction and some fairly well-defined shape, which is to say that self-esteem requires that one have values and organize one's life around them.

One's values translate into one's aims and ideals, and a settled constellation of these is necessary for self-esteem. Specifically, we may take this as a precondition of self-esteem. For, arguably, someone who had no aims or ideals in life, whose life lacked the direction and coherence that such aims and ideals would bring, would be neither an appropriate object of our esteem nor of our disesteem. We would understand his behavior as the product of primitive urges and desires that impelled him at the time of action. Having given no order or design to his life, he would act more or less at random or for short-lived purposes. We should recognize in him a figure who frequents recent philosophical literature on human freedom: the man assailed by a battery of desires and urges, who is helpless to overpower them because he lacks a clear definition of himself.[4] Such a man is impelled in many directions at once but moves in no particular one for any great distance. Frustrated and disoriented by inner turmoil, he lapses into nonaction. He would, were we ever to encounter his like, properly evoke in us pathos indicating abeyance of judgment rather than scorn indicating low esteem for him.

By contrast, when a person has aims and ideals that give order and direction to his life, counterpoint between primitive forces that impel him and his wanting to fulfill those aims and ideals becomes possible. Thus, at those times when he acts in conflict with his aims and ideals, he may declare that he was caught in the grip of some emotion or was overpowered by some urge or desire. He would then convey the idea that he had been acted upon or compelled to act as opposed to doing the act or choosing to act. Undeniably, the emotion, urge, or desire is attributable to him; but by such declaration he disowns it and so disclaims authorship of the act it prompted. Authorship, not ownership, is the key notion here, that is, authorship in the general sense of being the originator or creator of something. When one has a settled constellation of aims and ideals, then one distinguishes between the acts of which one is the author and those in which one serves as an instrument of alien forces.[5] Without any such constellation, one is never the author of one's actions,

4. See Joel Feinberg, "The Idea of a Free Man," in *Educational Judgments: Papers in the Philosophy of Education*, ed. James Doyle (London: Routledge & Kegan Paul, 1975), pp. 148-149; Harry Frankfurt, "Freedom of the Will and the Concept of a Person," *Journal of Philosophy* 68 (1971): 5-20; Wright Neely, "Freedom and Desire," *Philosophical Review* 83 (1974): 32-54; and Gary Watson, "Free Agency," *Journal of Philosophy* 72 (1975): 205-220.
5. I have drawn here from Harry Frankfurt, "Identification and Externality," in *The Identities of Persons*, ed. Amélie Rorty (Berkeley: University of California Press, 1976), pp. 239-251.

though many times the instrument of alien forces that act on one, triggered by external events.

It is in view of this contrast that I suggest we take one's having a settled constellation of aims and ideals as a precondition of self-esteem. When one is the author of one's actions, one is an appropriate object for esteem or disesteem; when one is only an instrument of alien forces, one is not. We can then look to this precondition for the defining conditions of self-esteem. So while we would have said, loosely speaking, that self-esteem came from one's having a good opinion of oneself, we may now say more strictly that it comes from a good opinion of oneself as the author of one's actions, more generally, one's life. Accordingly, this opinion comprises a favorable regard for one's aims and ideals in life and a favorable assessment of one's suitability for pursuing them. Lacking self-esteem, one would either regard one's aims and ideals as shoddy or believe that one hadn't the talent, ability, or other attributes necessary for achieving them. Either would mean that one lacked the good opinion of oneself that makes for self-esteem, and either would explain the dispirited condition that goes with one's lacking self-esteem.

These considerations then yield an understanding of self-esteem as requiring that two conditions jointly obtain. This we can formulate as a definition. Specifically, one *has self-esteem* if, first, one regards one's aims and ideals as worthy and, second, one believes that one is well suited to pursue them.[6] With reference to the first we say one has a sense that one's life has meaning. With reference to the second we speak of a confidence one has in the excellence of one's person. And this combination of a sense that one's life has meaning and a confidence in one's ability to achieve one's ends gives one impetus to go forward.

Turning then to loss of self-esteem and, in particular, the sudden loss taken on the Rawlsian characterization to be explicative of shame, we obtain immediately from the foregoing definition an account of this experience. One loses self-esteem if, because of a change in either one's regard for the worthiness of one's aims and ideals or one's belief in one's ability to achieve them, a once favorable self-assessment is overturned and supplanted by an unfavorable one. The loss here is the loss of a certain view of oneself. One had self-esteem and correspondingly a good opinion of oneself: one viewed oneself as having the attributes necessary for successfully pursuing worthy ends around which one had organized one's life. The change in judgment about the worthiness of one's ends or the excellence of one's person destroys that view. One's good opinion of oneself gives way to a poor one. This constitutes loss of self-esteem.

The Rawlsian characterization has it that shame is the emotion one feels

6. The definition matches Rawls's (see p. 440).

when such loss occurs. Moreover, shame is to be understood as signifying such loss. Shame on this characterization is the shock to our sense of worth that comes either from realizing that our values are shoddy or from discovering that we are deficient in a way that had added to the confidence we had in our excellence. Either is a discovery of something false in the good opinion we had of ourselves, and such self-discovery spells loss of self-esteem.

Of course, self-discovery of this sort does not figure in every experience of shame, for a person who has a poor opinion of himself is nonetheless liable to feel shame when the very defect that is his reason for the poor opinion is brought to his notice. Thus, as a last point, we must say something about shame felt by someone whose self-esteem is already low. While a schoolboy, Philip Carey, in Maugham's novel *Of Human Bondage*, feels shame innumerable times over his clubfoot. His feelings do not involve loss of self-esteem, since his self-esteem is low to begin with, nor, obviously, do they reflect any act of self-discovery. But it would be uncharitable to object to the Rawlsian characterization on the ground that it does not cover such cases, for they can be treated on analogy with cases it does cover. Philip does not always have his crippled foot on his mind. There are plenty of times when he is forgetful of it. On these occasions, especially when he is comfortable with himself, he is liable to feel shame when made conscious of his "freakish" condition, when, as it were, he rediscovers it. Then, while he does not lose any self-esteem, his being comfortable with himself is certainly lost to him.

II

In this section I will set forth a case of loss of self-esteem and some cases of shame that present real problems for the Rawlsian characterization. I begin with the former. The case itself is quite straightforward. We have only to think of someone who suddenly loses self-esteem because he discovers that he lacks the ability to achieve some aim he has set for himself, who is crestfallen, dispirited, and deeply disappointed with himself, but owing to circumstances or a philosophical temperament, does not feel shame. And such a case is not hard to construct.[7]

Imagine, for example, some youth who is indisputably the best tennis player in his community. He defeats all challengers; he wins every local tournament; and he has recently led his high school team to a first-place finish in a league consisting of teams from the high schools of his and the neighboring towns. His coach rates him the most promising player to come along in a

7. Examples similar to this first case were suggested to me by Herbert Morris and Rogers Albritton.

231

decade, and he is highly touted by other tennis enthusiasts in the area. Quite naturally, he comes to have a high opinion of his ability and visions of winning tournaments on the professional tour. At some point early in his high school years, he makes professional tennis a career goal and devotes much time to improving his game. In truth, though, the grounds for his high opinion of his ability and for his decision to make tennis a career are shaky. The competition in his and the neighboring towns is rather poor. They are rural and isolated from urban centers. And the aging coach's hopes have distorted his judgment of his star player's talents. Thus, when this young player enters his first state tournament, he quickly discovers that his skills are below those of the top-seeded players. His first defeat need not be humiliating, just convincing. And though he will surely lose some self-esteem, we need not suppose that he feels any shame.

One explanation of his losing self-esteem but not feeling shame is this: the first defeat is sufficiently convincing that it alters his view of himself as a tennis player, and given his aims, this means loss of self-esteem. But just as others close to him would respond that his defeat is nothing to be ashamed of, so his own attitude toward it may reflect such judgment. Accordingly, he would be deeply disappointed with himself but not ashamed. This possibility becomes even more vivid if we suppose that he has gone to the tournament alone or with friends who, unlike him, have only a passing interest in tennis. For then he does not find himself having to face someone like his coach before whom feeling some shame would be natural, though even here the presence of the coach does not necessitate the emotion. This case thus broaches the question of what distinguishes those cases of loss of self-esteem whose subjects feel shame from those whose subjects feel disappointment but no shame. The inability of the Rawlsian characterization to answer this question implies that the understanding of shame it gives is, at best, incomplete.

Let us next take up cases of shame. The first comes from an observation, made by several writers, that shame is commonly felt over trivial things. One writer mentions experiences of shame had on account of "one's accent, one's ignorance, one's clothes, one's legs or teeth."[8] Another, to illustrate the same point, mentions shame felt over "an awkward gesture, a gaucherie in dress or table manners, ... a mispronounced word."[9] To be sure, none of these examples poses a threat to the Rawlsian characterization, since each of the things mentioned could be for someone a shortcoming the apprehension of which would undercut the confidence he had in the excellence of his person. This

---

8. Stanley Cavell, *Must We Mean What We Say?* (Cambridge: Cambridge University Press, 1976), p. 286.
9. Lynd, p. 40.

would certainly be true of someone who consciously subscribed to ideals the achievement of which required that he not have the shortcoming. For then, though others would disparage these ideals as superficial or vulgar and accordingly think the shortcoming trivial, to him it would still appear as a serious flaw in himself.

Naturally, the more interesting case is that in which the subject also thinks the shortcoming trivial and is surprised at having felt shame on its account. This case too can be understood as coming under the Rawlsian characterization. For one need not fully realize the extent to which one places value on certain things, and one may even deceive oneself about one's not being attached to certain ideals. We need, then, to distinguish between, on the one hand, what one would declare were one's aims and ideals and would list as one's important attributes if one were asked to describe oneself and, on the other, one's self-conception as it is reflected by one's behavior apart from or in addition to any explicit self-description. By one's self-conception I mean the aims and ideals around which one has organized one's life together with the beliefs one has about one's ability to pursue them. And what we understand is that these aims, ideals, and beliefs can guide one's behavior without one's being conscious of having subscribed to them. Consequently, a person who feels shame over crooked teeth or the slurping of soup, though he would have thought himself unconcerned with appearance and proper form, shows by his emotion that a pleasant-looking face or good table manners are important to him, that he subscribes to ideals of comeliness or social grace. Hence, we can easily understand his shame as signifying loss of self-esteem.

At the same time, such examples invite us to look for things over which someone might feel shame though he did not believe they made him ill suited to pursue his ends. Shame one feels over something one could not believe affected one's excellence, say, because one could not regard it as a fault in oneself, would present a problem for the Rawlsian characterization. Thus, consider shame felt over a humorous surname. The example comes from Gide. He describes to us the experience of a young French girl on her first day of school, who had been sheltered at home for the first ten years of her life, and in whose name, Mlle Péterat, something ridiculous is connoted, which might be rendered in English by calling her Miss Fartwell. "Arnica Péterat – guileless and helpless – had never until that moment suspected that there might be anything laughable in her name; on her first day at school its ridicule came upon her as a sudden revelation; she bowed her head, like some sluggish waterweed, to the jeers that flowed over her; she turned red; she turned pale; she wept."[10]

---

10. André Gide, *Lafcadio's Adventures*, trans. Dorothy Bussy (New York: Alfred A. Knopf, 1953), p. 100. The rendering of her name in English is suggested by the translator.

With this example we move from attributes that one can regard as minor flaws and insignificant defects to things about a person that leave him open to ridicule, though they do not add to or detract from his excellence. The morphemes of one's surname do not make one better or worse suited for pursuing the aims and ideals around which one has organized one's life. Hence, shame in this example, because it is felt over something that lies outside its subject's self-conception, opposes the Rawlsian characterization.

The second case of shame is cousin to the first. One finds oneself in a situation in which others scorn or ridicule one or express some deprecatory judgment of one, and apprehending this, one feels shame. Given only this general description, such a case presents no real problem for the Rawlsian characterization. It serves to remind us that one's self-esteem depends to some extent on the esteem others accord one – certain others, anyway – and the greater that dependency the more readily one will feel shame in response to any deprecatory judgments they express. This can be understood by way of the amount of confidence one has in one's own independent judgments about the worthiness of one's aims and one's ability to fulfill them, for this, we might say, varies inversely with the strength of the dependency of one's self-esteem on the esteem of others. That is, the greater that dependency, the less one's confidence will be in independent judgments one makes about oneself and, concomitantly, the more accepting one will be of the judgments others make about one. Consequently, given a strong enough dependency, if they criticize or ridicule one for some fault, one accepts their criticism and thus makes the same judgment about oneself, where before one did not notice the fault or it did not much matter to one. This arouses shame inasmuch as the judgment issues in an unfavorable self-assessment that replaces a favorable one, that is, in loss of self-esteem. We have then an account of the case that is fully in line with the Rawlsian characterization.

But we must also admit cases of shame felt in response to another's criticism or ridicule in which the subjects do not accept the other person's judgment of them and so do not make the same judgment of themselves. And these cases do present a problem for the Rawlsian characterization. Consider Crito and his great concern for what the good citizens of Athens will think of him for failing to deter Socrates from meeting his demise. "I am ashamed," he says in vainly trying to argue Socrates out of accepting his fate, "both on your account and on ours, your friends'; it will look as though we had played something like a coward's part all through this affair of yours."[11] And though

---

11. Plato, *Crito* 45d-e. Quoted from the Hugh Tredennick translation, *The Collected Dialogues of Plato*, ed. Edith Hamilton and Huntington Cairns (Princeton, N.J.: Princeton University Press, 1961), p. 30.

Crito is in the end convinced that Socrates' course is the right one and knows all along that he has done everything one can expect of a friend, we still have, I think, no trouble picturing this good-hearted but thoroughly conventional man feeling ashamed when before some respectable Athenian, who reproaches him for what he believes was cowardice on Crito's part. Examples like this one demonstrate that shame is often more, when it is not exclusively, a response to the evident deprecatory opinion others have of one than an emotion aroused upon judgment that one's aims are shoddy or that one is deficient in talent or ability necessary to achieve them.

The third problematic case of shame is this. We commonly ascribe shame to small children. Shaming is a familiar practice in their upbringing. "Shame on you" and "You ought to be ashamed of yourself" are familiar admonishments. And, setting aside the question of the advisability of such responses to a child's misdemeanors, we do not think them nonsensical or incongruous in view of the child's emotional capacities. Furthermore, close observers of small children do not hesitate to ascribe shame to them. Erik Erikson, writing about human development, observed that children acquired a sense of shame at the stage when they began to develop muscular control and coordination.[12] Charles Darwin, writing about blushing, noted that small children began to blush around the age of three and later remarked that he had "noticed on occasions that shyness or shamefacedness and real shame are exhibited in the eyes of young children before they have acquired the power of blushing."[13]

But it would certainly be a precocious child who at the age of four or five had a well-defined self-conception, who organized his life around the pursuit of certain discrete and relatively stable aims and ideals and measured himself by standards of what is necessary to achieve them. In other words, a child at this age, though capable of feeling shame, does not have self-esteem. Hence, the shame he experiences does not signify loss of self-esteem.

Finally, a fourth problematic case of shame emerges once we juxtapose the orientation of an aristocratic ethic and that of an achievement ethic. The Rawlsian characterization with its emphasis on making something of oneself, being successful in one's life pursuits, is tied to the latter. The experiences of shame it describes are at home in a meritocratic society, one in which social mobility is widespread, or, at any rate, the belief that it is constitutes a major article of faith. On the other hand, some experiences of shame reflect an aristocratic ethic; one feels shame over conduct unbecoming a person of one's rank or station. The experiences are better suited to a society with a rigidly

12. Erik Erikson, *Childhood and Society*, 2d ed. (New York: Norton, 1963), pp. 251-254.
13. Charles Darwin. *The Expression of the Emotions in Man and Animal* (1872; reprint ed., Chicago: University of Chicago Press, 1965), p. 331.

stratified social structure like a caste society. And, as we shall see, they stand in marked contrast to experiences the Rawlsian characterization is designed to fit.

The contrast is this. With shame reflective of an achievement ethic, the subject is concerned with achieving his life's aims and ideals, and he measures himself against standards of excellence he believes he must meet to achieve them. So long as he regards his aims and ideals as worthy, they define for him a successful life, and accordingly he uses the standards to judge whether he has the excellence in ability or of character necessary for success. He is then liable to shame if he realizes that some of his aims and ideals are shoddy or that he has a defect portending failure where previously he had ascribed to himself an excellence indicating success. And this fits nicely the idea that shame signifies loss of self-esteem. On the other hand, with shame reflective of an aristocratic ethic, the subject's concern is with maintaining the deportment of his class and not necessarily with achieving aims and ideals that define success in life. He is concerned with conforming to the norms of propriety distinctive of his class, and conformity to these is neither a mark of achievement nor an excellence that forecasts achievement. In the usual case one is born into one's class and conforms to its norms as a matter of course. Failure to conform, that is, failure to deport oneself as becomes a member of one's class invites comparison to persons of lower classes on whom the members of one's class look down. Thus, someone from a social class beneath which there are other classes may be liable to shame over such failure: someone well-born may be liable to shame if he behaves like the vulgar. And such shame does not fit the Rawlsian characterization. For the subject neither realizes that his aims and ideals are shoddy nor discovers a defect in himself that makes him ill suited to pursue them. In other words, given the analysis we have laid out, he does not lose self-esteem.

But, one might ask, can't we say of someone who feels shame over conduct unbecoming a member of his class that he too has ideals that regulate his actions and emotions? After all, with his class we associate a way of life, and this implies an ideal or set of ideals. To feel constrained to act as becomes a member of one's class is to feel pressed to conform to its ideals, and conduct unbecoming a member is, in other words, conduct that falls short of an ideal. Granted, one doesn't so much achieve these ideals as conform to them, which shows perhaps that the conception of self-esteem on which the Rawlsian characterization is built must be modified. But supposing we make whatever modification is needed, isn't it sufficient to bring the experience under the Rawlsian characterization that we can redescribe it as shame felt over one's falling short of an ideal?

Something, however, gets lost in this redescription. When we redescribe the experience as shame felt over falling short of ideals around which one's life is organized, our focus shifts from who one is to how one conducts one's life. The subject's identity as a member of a certain class recedes into the background. We see it as the source of his ideals but do not assign it any further part. This, I think, is a mistake. In this experience the subject has a sense of having disgraced himself, which means he has an acute sense of who he is. We do not have an understanding of shame otherwise.

It is revealing that on the Rawlsian characterization this shift in focus does not register. For the characterization recognizes no distinction between questions of identity and questions of life pursuits, between who one is and how one conducts one's life. From its viewpoint, a person says who he is by telling what his aims in life are and what ideals guide him through life.[14] This makes it an attractive characterization of the shame felt by persons who are relatively free of constraints on their choice of life pursuits owing to class, race, ethnic origins, and the like. For such persons tend more to regard their aims and ideals as constituting their identity and their ancestry, race, class, and so forth as extrinsic facts about themselves. So the characterization explains the shame they feel as including an acute sense of who they are. But because it restricts a person's identity to his aims and ideals in life, it fails to explain as including this sense the shame someone, living in a rigidly stratified society, feels when he does not act as befits a member of his class or the shame someone, living in a multiethnic society, feels when he acts beneath the dignity of his people. Granted, such a person recognizes that his conduct falls short of ideals members of his class or culture are expected to follow, but these ideals do not constitute his identity. Another, a pretender for instance, could have the same ideals as he but not the same identity, just as a tomboy has the ideals of a boy but not the identity of one. Hence, we fail to account for such shame if we describe it as being felt over one's having fallen short of ideals that regulate one's life.

Thus, about the following experience, which Earl Mills, a Mashpee Indian, relates, a defender of the Rawlsian characterization will insist that sometime during the episode Mills must have embraced the ideals of an Indian way of life or, alternatively, that he must have realized, though he nowhere suggests this, that the ideals he was then pursuing were shoddy. But ignoring the Rawlsian characterization, we can explain Mills's feeling shame without importing either of these assumptions: his having, in the circumstances he describes, to acknowledge his ignorance of Mashpee traditions disgraced him as an Indian, made him betray, as it were, his Indian identity, and this aroused shame. This explanation accepted, his experience directly opposes the Rawlsian characteri-

14. See Rawls, p. 408.

zation, for it suggests that, despite the aims and ideals around which a person organizes his life, circumstances may arise that make him, because of an identity he has that is independent of those aims and ideals, liable to experience shame.

When I was a kid, I and the young fellows I ran around with couldn't have cared less about our Indian background. We never participated in any of the tribal ceremonies, we didn't know how to dance, and we wouldn't have been caught dead in regalia. We thought anyone who made a fuss about our heritage was old-fashioned, and we even used to make fun of the people who did. Well, when I came back from the Army in 1948, I had a different outlook on such matters. You see, there happened to be two other Indians in my basic training company at Fort Dix. One of them was an Iroquois from Upper New York State, and the other was a Chippewa from Montana. I was nineteen years old, away from Mashpee for the first time in my life, and, like most soldiers, I was lonely. Then, one night, the Iroquois fellow got up and did an Indian dance in front of everyone in the barracks. The Chippewa got up and joined him, and when I had to admit I didn't know how, I felt terribly ashamed.[15]

III

Before drawing any lessons about shame from the discussion of Section II, I should say something to allay doubts about the import of the cases of shame presented there. Such doubts naturally arise because one might think that some, if not all, of those cases exemplify experiences of the emotion the subjects of which one could criticize for being irrational or unreasonable. That is, while agreeing that many persons are liable to such experiences, one might wonder whether they ought to be so liable and then note that a case's force as a counterexample lessens if it only describes an experience of irrational or unreasonable emotion. The first and last cases of shame are especially in point. To feel shame over one's surname and because of conduct unbecoming a person of one's class seem good examples of shame one ought not to experience. For one is not responsible for one's parentage and thus ought not to judge oneself according to facts wholly determined by it. Inasmuch as shame in these cases reflects such judgment, they exemplify experiences to which one ought not to be liable.

These doubts arise under the assumption that, in giving a characterization of an emotion, one specifies those conditions in which the emotion is experienced reasonably or rationally. Such an approach to characterizing an emotion requires that one regard as its standard cases those in which the subjects

15. Paul Brodeur, "A Reporter at Large: The Mashpees," *New Yorker* 54 (November 6, 1978): 62-150, p. 103.

are fully rational individuals and not at the time of the experience in any irrational frame of mind. But we ought to question this requirement. Why should we restrict the class of standard cases to these? While there is, for instance, something absurd in the familiar picture of an elephant terrified at the sight of a mouse, why should this absurdity lead us to regard the elephant's terror as any less important a case to be considered in characterizing that emotion than the terror a lynch mob strikes in the person on whom it takes revenge? To be sure, the elephant is not a creature capable of bringing its emotions under rational control, whereas a human being, if sufficiently mature, is. And for this reason there is a point in criticizing the emotional experiences of human beings, whereas making similar criticisms of an elephant's emotional experiences is altogether idle. But this provides no reason to regard the class of rational or reasonable experiences of a given emotion as privileged for the purposes of conceptual inquiry. To have brought one's emotions under rational control means that the range of one's emotional experiences has been modified through development of one's rational capacities: one no longer responds with, say fear, to certain sensory stimuli that before the development provoked fear, and conversely. But far from instructing us to discount the elephant's or the toddler's emotions in our conceptual inquiries, this bids us to examine emotional experiences had in response to sensory stimuli unmediated by rational thought as well as experiences the occurrence of which we explain by reference to rational thought.[16]

Similar points, then, apply to characterizing shame. To focus primarily on cases the subjects of which one would not criticize for being irrational or unreasonable is to risk introducing distortion into the characterization. Indeed, one might be well advised to examine closely those cases in which such criticism is forthcoming on the grounds that they may display more prominently than others certain characteristic features of the emotion. Thus, one might be well advised to examine closely the shame typical of *Homo hierarchicus*, even though one thought that rigid, hierarchical social structures lacked rational foundations (i.e., even though one thought that the emotion indicated an irrational attachment to social class), on the grounds that in such shame one sees more clearly than in shame typical of persons living in an egalitarian society those parts of the subject's self-conception in virtue of which he is liable to the emotion. Moreover, though the resultant characterization rendered shame an emotion that, from the perspective of an egalitarian or meritocratic ethic, one never had good reason to feel, this would not in itself show the characterization to be faulty: no more than that gentlefolk like the Amish, be-

16. I have developed these points elsewhere. See my "Cognitivism in the Theory of Emotions," *Ethics* 104 (1994): 824–854.

cause of certain theistic beliefs, regard resentment as an emotion one never has good reason to feel shows that they harbor misconceptions about resentment. Since we are capable of bringing our emotions under rational control, we may regard our feeling a specific emotion as incompatible with our moral principles and so try to make ourselves no longer liable to it. Alternatively, we may regard this emotion as essential to our humanity and so revise our principles. The conflict makes evident the importance of having a correct understanding of such emotions. At the same time we should see that altering the understanding one has in order simply to avoid such conflict or the criticism of irrationality would be misguided.

Turning then to lessons that come out of our discussion of the problematic cases, I will draw two. The first is that a satisfactory characterization must include in a central role one's concern for the opinions of others. This is really a lesson in recall. From Aristotle onward, discussions of shame have focused attention on the subject's concern for the opinions others have of him.[17] Aquinas, Descartes, and Spinoza each incorporated this concern into his definition of shame.[18] And latter-day writers, Darwin and Sartre in particular, took the experience of shame before another as key to an understanding of the emotion.[19] Consequently, we should not be surprised to find that the Rawlsian characterization founders, since it regards such concern as not internally related to shame.

Its failure, however, is not due to neglect. The characterization, through emphasis on the dependency of one's self-esteem on the esteem of others, can accord the concern an important role in an overall understanding of shame.[20] But this makes the concern part of a mechanism that induces shame rather than part of our conception of shame. A mechanism exists which, when put into operation, transforms high self-esteem into low; part of that mechanism is the concern one has for the opinion of others; and one way in which the mechanism gets going is when others on whose good opinion one's self-esteem depends deprecate one and one apprehends this. In this way, the characterization gives one's concern for the opinion of others an important role. But it is only a supporting role and not the central one I think it deserves. And this is one reason for its failure.

Each of the first three problematic cases bears out this last point. It is evident

---

17. For Aristotle's view see *Rhetoric*, bk. 2, ch. 6.
18. For Aquinas's definition see *Summa Theologiae* la2ae, 41,4. For Descartes's see *The Passions of the Soul*, pt. 2, art. 66. For Spinoza's see *The Ethics*, pt. 3, definition 31.
19. See last chapter of Darwin. Sartre's view is found in *Being and Nothingness*, trans. Hazel E. Barnes (New York: Philosophical Library, Inc., 1956), pp. 252–302.
20. See, e.g., Rawls's discussion of the companion effect to the Aristotelian principle, pp. 440–441.

in the second and third cases, where the subjects feel shame but do not lose self-esteem. In the third case shame is felt directly in response to another's scorn or reproach. Thus, an expressed low opinion of the subject induces in him shame without affecting his self-esteem. In other words, the mechanism is not engaged, though the subject's concern for the opinion of another is clearly operative. In the second, Mlle Péterat, even apart from the context in which she feels shame – jeering classmates – feels the emotion because of something about herself that is laughable. It invites deprecatory responses. Thus she may feel ashamed because of it, even though it is not a deficiency. It is not a ground for reassessing her excellence, though, of course, the whole experience could cause her to think less of herself. Here, too, there is shame reflecting a concern for the opinion of others without the mechanism's being engaged.

We can also mine the first case to bring out the point that the Rawlsian characterization has misconstrued the role one's concern for the opinion of others has in shame. Consider again our young tennis phenom. In the circumstances described, he loses self-esteem, is disappointed with himself, but does not feel shame. On the other hand, as we noted, if the circumstances had been different, if he had had, say, to face his coach after the defeat, then his feeling shame would have well been imaginable. There would then have been someone at courtside whose look he could not meet. He would have averted his eyes, lowered his head, gulped to fight back tears. That the coach's presence could spell the difference between disappointment and shame cannot be explained by reference to the player's losing self-esteem, for the loss occurs in either case. The mechanism would be in operation whether or not the subject felt shame, so it would not account for the role his concern for the coach's opinion would have had in his experiencing shame. We can therefore conclude from these three cases that one's concern for the opinion of others has a role in shame apart from the way in which their opinion can support or bring down one's self-esteem.

The second lesson is about our sense of worth. The Rawlsian characterization yields an understanding of a person's sense of worth according to which it has two sources. One is the person's conviction that he has given meaning to his life. The other is the confidence he has in his own excellence as a person. The first comes from his regarding his aims and ideals in life as worthy. The second comes from his belief that he is well suited to pursue them. Thus, according to the Rawlsian characterization, shame, since it is felt either upon a judgment that one's aims or ideals are shoddy or upon a judgment that one is deficient in a way that makes one ill suited to pursue them, is aptly described as a shock to one's sense of worth. One experiences a diminishment in one's sense of worth since either one's sense of having given meaning to one's life or one's confidence in one's excellence has been struck down.

There is difficulty in this, however, because, while the description of shame as a shock to one's sense of worth is apt, the account of the various ways in which the sense gets shocked is, at best, too meager. The reason for this is that the characterization omits important sources of our sense of worth. The point is directly evident in our last two cases. The child of four who feels shame over some misdemeanor has not given meaning to his life and does not have confidence in his excellence as a person. Hence, he has a sense of worth the source of which the characterization does not acknowledge. Similarly, we recognize in an aristocrat who feels shame over behaving like a plebeian or in an American Indian who feels shame over betraying his Indian identity a sense of worth the source of which is neither a conviction about the worthiness of his ends nor a belief about his suitability to pursue them. A sense of worth that comes from knowledge that one is a member of the upper class or a noble people also lies beyond the sight of the Rawlsian characterization. To put the point generally, the Rawlsian characterization fails to recognize aspects of our identity that contribute to our sense of worth independently of the aims and ideals around which we organize our lives.

We should note here the structural, as well as the substantive, difference between the sense of worth the Rawlsian characterization recognizes and the one it excludes. We can get at this structural difference by looking at the theory of worth that underlies the characterization. That theory is based on a conception of us as the authors of our actions. We are authors in the sense discussed in Section I, that is, in virtue of having a constellation of aims and ideals according to which we live our lives. We have worth on this theory in accordance with the value of our lives, such as they are and such as they promise to be. An author has worth in view of his work, completed or in progress, and our lives, so to speak, are our work. This analogy can be pressed. Our work has value to the degree that it is the kind of thing that when well made has value and is itself well made. So we have worth to the degree that we produce such things or have directed our energies toward producing them and possess the talents and skills that augur successful production. Our lives, conceived as our work, thus have value to the degree that the ends that give them order and direction define a kind of life that has value and those ends have been realized. And we have worth as authors of our lives to the degree that we live lives of value or have directed our energies toward living such lives and possess the attributes that promise success

In capsule form, what might be called the auteur theory of worth is that what a person does with his life, how well he directs it, determines his worth. On this theory, then, we attribute different degrees of worth to someone depending on how valuable we deem the kind of life he lives and how successful we think he has been in living it or how suitable we think he is for it. In other

242

words, we attribute to him more or less worth according to how well or badly he conducts his life. Contrast this with attributions of worth made because of one's class or culture. Judging from these attributions, we might say that a person's worth is determined by his status in the context of some social hierarchy. The salient feature here is that one's status, and so one's worth, is fixed independently of one's conduct. To be sure, one can change classes through marriage or cultures through immigration, but short of this the general conduct of one's life, that is, however well or badly one conducts it, does not increase or decrease the worth that is attributed to one because of one's status. And pretty much the same holds of worth that is attributed to human beings because of their species or to persons because of the kind of beings they are conceived to be: rational ones, say, spiritual ones, or autonomous ones. That is, worth attributed to one because of one's essential nature is, like worth attributed to one because of one's status, fixed independently of how one conducts one's life.

Consequently, the dynamics of the sense of worth that comes from knowing the worth that goes with one's status or essential nature, that is, the understanding we give to augmentations and diminishments in that sense, are altogether different from those of the sense of worth the auteur theory recognizes. Statically, both kinds of sense correspond to the degree of worth one attributes to oneself. But an augmentation in one's sense of worth, as is experienced in pride, or a diminishment in it, as is experienced in shame, is not, if this sense originates in a recognition of one's status or essential nature, to be understood in terms of an attribution to oneself of greater or lesser worth than one attributed to oneself before the experience.[21] A college boy who wears his fraternity pin with pride does not regard himself as having greater worth for having worn it, and a man who feels ashamed of having eaten like a pig does not regard himself as having less worth than is attributed to human beings as such. This contrasts with the way the auteur theory would have us understand augmentations and diminishments in one's sense of worth. In particular, it would have us understand a diminishment in one's sense of worth, as is experienced in shame, as amounting to loss of self-esteem and so corresponding to an assessment of oneself as having less worth.

On the auteur theory, a sense of worth reflects concern with one's real worth, and one takes one's conduct and appearance as evidence of or, more strongly, as the grounds for attributing to oneself that worth. By contrast, a sense of worth that comes from knowing one's status or essential nature reflects concern with the congruency between one's conduct or appearance and

---

21. Of course there are exceptions to this, e.g., a white supremacist who discovers he has a black ancestor.

one's real worth. Here, we could say, one's concern is with the relation between appearance and reality. If one's status is high relative to that of others or one's nature is noble, then conduct that is congruent with one's worth and so displays it is occasion for pride, and conduct that is at variance with it and so gives appearance of lesser worth is occasion for shame.

This model better accommodates the idea that to have a sensibility to shame means that one is prepared to restrain oneself when one verges on the shameful and to cover up the shameful when it comes into the open. We speak in this regard of having shame as opposed to having no shame, and we connect this with modesty, particularly sexual modesty, which involves a sensibility to shame in matters of decorum. Having shame, that is, having a sensibility to shame, can be understood here as self-control that works to restrain one from giving the appearance of lesser worth and self-respect that works to cover up shameful things that, having come to light, give one such appearance.[22]

This suggests that we should conceive of shame, not as a reaction to a loss, but as a reaction to a threat, specifically, the threat of demeaning treatment one would invite in giving the appearance of someone of lesser worth. Its analogues then are, not grief and sorrow, but fear and shyness.[23] Like fear, shame serves to protect one against and save one from unwanted exposure. Both are in this way self-protective emotions. Fear is self-protective in that it moves one to protect oneself against the danger one senses is present or approaching. From fear one draws back, shields oneself, or flees. Of course, it may also render one immobile, thereby putting one in greater danger, so the point does not hold without qualification.[24] Still, the general idea is clear. Shame, too, is self-protective in that it moves one to protect one's worth.[25] Here the general

22. On these points, see Carl D. Schneider, *Shame, Exposure and Privacy* (Boston: Beacon Press, 1977), pp. 24-27.
23. Whether to pattern shame after grief and sorrow or after fear and shyness is an issue a review of the literature reveals. One often finds in the writings of those offering definitions of shame use of one or the other of these emotions as analogues, sometimes even as a generic emotion of which shame is defined as a specific type. For definitions of shame as a type of grief or sorrow see Hobbes (*Leviathan*, ch. 6) and Descartes (*Passions*, pt. 3, art. 205) (though the passage is equivocal since he also says there that shame is a species of modesty). For definition of shame as a type of fear see Aquinas; it is also suggested in Plato's *Euthyphro* 12a-d. In connection with this issue see Havelock Ellis's "The Evolution of Modesty," in *Studies in the Psychology of Sex*, 2 vols., 3d ed. (New York: Random House, 1942), vol. l, p. 36, n. 1. Ellis himself appears to hold that shame is a kind of fear (see pp. 36-52, 72).
24. I owe this point to John T. MacCurdy, "The Biological Significance of Blushing and Shame," *British Journal of Psychology* 21 (1930): 174-182.
25. The idea is one of the central themes of Max Scheler's essay "Über Scham und Schamgefühl," in *Gesammelte Werke*, ed. Maria Scheler and M. S. Frings, 11 vols. (Berne: Franke Verlag, 1954), vol. 10, pp. 65-154.

idea is not so clear, though a trope may be useful. Shame inhibits one from
doing things that would tarnish one's worth, and it moves one to cover up
that which through continued exposure would tarnish one's worth. Less figu-
ratively, we might say that the doing or exposure of something that makes one
appear to have less worth than one has leaves one open to treatment appropriate only to persons or things that lack the worth one has, and shame in in-
hibiting one from doing such things and in moving one to cover them up
thus protects one from appearing to be an unworthy creature and so from the
degrading treatment such appearance would invite.

This idea that shame is a self-protective emotion brings together and explains two important features: first, that a liability to shame regulates conduct
in that it inhibits one from doing certain things and, second, that experiences
of shame are expressed by acts of concealment. The second is crucial. Covering one's face, covering up what one thinks is shameful, and hiding from others are, along with blushing, the most characteristic expressions of shame. Stu-
dents of shame commonly note them. A quote from Darwin is representative,
"Under a keen sense of shame there is a strong desire for concealment."[26]
Moreover, etymology reinforces the point. According to many etymologists, a
pre-Teutonic word meaning 'to cover' is the root of our word *shame*.[27]

Now the Rawlsian characterization, since it conceives shame as a reaction to
a loss, can explain, on the model of fear of loss, how one's liability to shame
regulates one's conduct. Where it has trouble is in explaining shame's moving
one to cover up and to hide. For it does not have in itself the materials needed
to construct such an explanation. Because it conceives of shame as a reaction
to the loss of something one prizes, it yields an account of the emotion as at
first giving way to low spirits and dejection and eventually moving one to attempt to recover what one lost, that is, to regain through self-improvement
one's good opinion of oneself and so one's self-esteem.[28] Acts of concealment,
however, are nowhere implicated in this account. Hence, if one adheres to the
characterization, one must make use of supplementary materials to explain
them. One must go outside the characterization by, say, citing certain fears associated with shame: fear of ridicule or rejection by those upon whose good
opinion of one one's self-esteem depends.[29] But such an explanation would
not be adequate, for it fails to explain acts of concealment as expressions of

26. Darwin, p. 320.
27. See Oxford English Dictionary, s. v. "shame"; also Ernest Klein, *A Comprehensive Etymologi-
cal Dictionary of the English Language* (Amsterdam: Elsevier, 1967).
28. See Rawls, p. 484; Lynd, pp. 50-51; and Richards, p. 256.
29. See Piers and Singer, p. 16; and Rawls, p. 445. White, however, expresses reservations against
connecting shame to such fears (pp. 125-127).

THE SOURCES OF MORAL AGENCY

shame. Instead, it takes these as expressions of fears associated with shame. And the same objection would hold for any explanation one constructed from materials found outside the characterization. The characterization, in other words, is unable to explain, as expressions of shame, these acts. And this should tell us that something has gone wrong.

The adherent to the Rawlsian characterization therefore appears to be in an untenable position. We would dismiss any suggestion that covering up and hiding were not really among shame's natural expressions. Reflection on shame, particularly shame concerning sexual improprieties, alone suffices to rule this out. And we should reject any characterization of an emotion that misrepresents its natural expressions. Faced with these objections, the adherent might retreat to a weaker thesis by proposing that the characterization gives an adequate account of some, but not all, experiences of shame. But this thesis is no more defensible than the original. For our adherent, as we saw from the first problematic case of Section II, has the burden of showing how the emotion the characterization describes is distinguishable from disappointment with oneself. Since he admits on this weaker thesis that some experiences of shame elude the characterization, he has, in other words, the burden of showing that the experiences of emotion the characterization captures are classifiable with these as shame. What reason could he give to show this? That they have the same feeling tone is itself questionable, insistence on the point being question begging. That they involve a shock to one's sense of worth is insufficient. For the characterization identifies this shock with one's suffering loss of self-esteem, and this by itself does not qualify an experience as one of shame. The trouble with this proposal, I think, is that it would, in effect, divide shame into disparate kinds, one kind having fear as its analogue, the other grief. That is, we should suspect of any conception of shame the proposal spawned that it covered a mismatched set of experiences.

We can trace the characterization's problems back to the understanding it gives to the sense of worth that makes one liable to shame and ultimately to the auteur theory of worth, which grounds that understanding. On that theory one attributes to oneself worth according to how one conducts one's life, and so perceptions of that conduct determine one's sense of worth. Shame then, since it is felt upon discovery of shortcomings in oneself that falsify the worth one thought one had, includes a sense that one lacks worth. And this proves problematic because it leaves unexplained how shame motivates acts of concealment. By contrast, when we conceive of shame as including a sense that one has worth, we can readily explain its motivating such acts: one covers up because one senses that the worth one has is threatened. This speaks in favor of the understanding of the sense of worth the idea that shame is a self-

246

protective emotion entails, which understanding is grounded on a conception of worth that opposes the one the auteur theory yields. Consequently, we should suspect that the conception of worth the auteur theory yields is the wrong one for explaining the sense of worth that makes one liable to shame, and, because the Rawlsian characterization presupposes that conception, we should give up the view of the emotion it represents.

Index

249

INDEX

Locke, John, 183
love, xii, 5-6, 42-44, 47-48, 60-61, 88-89;
  of child for parents, 6n, 54-57, 61-62;
  v. self-love, 152-154. *See also* ambivalence in Freud's theory; friendship;
  identification, and introjection
Lupino, Ida, 161
Lynd, Helen Merrell, 226n, 232n, 245n

MacCurdy, John, 244n
Mackie, J. L., 2n
Masters, Roger D., 40n
materialism, xiii, 117
McNeilly, F. S., 208n
McTaggart, J. M. E., 29
meaningfulness of life, 230-231,
  236-237, 241-242
Melden, A. I., 35n
mental disorder, 133-134, 144-145. *See
  also* psychopathy
metaethics, 163-164, 183-184
Mill, John Stuart, viii-ix
mind, 91-92, 117-118; conscious and unconscious parts of, xii, 115, 120-124
  (*see also* psychoanalysis, topographical
  v. structural model)
Moberly, Walter, 18n
moral agency, ix, xii-xiii, 117-119,
  126-131, 134-136, 161-163; and ret-
  ributive justice, 18, 21-22, 24, 27-28
moral development, 5-6, 39-41, 53-64,
  128-129, 165, 176-177. *See also* conscience, child's acquisition of
moral education, 1, 128-129
morality: and fellowship, 2, 11-12, 32,
  40-44, 52, 63; authority of, 47, 51, 60,
  63, 103, 109-111, 114n, 118; based on
  feeling, 181-183; contrary to reason,
  13-16, 97-98, 102, 104, 185, 189 (*see
  also* Fool, argument with); customary,
  1-3, 14, 165, 189n, 197; essential prac-
  ticality of, 182-183; secular v. religious
  foundations of, 95-96, 98-99,
  108-112, 198-199; social function of,

viii-ix, 1-3, 6-13, 29, 40, 46-47, 49,
  98-99, 101-102; supremacy of, x-xii,
  13-17, 103, 114n, 131, 199
moral ideas and principles: fundamental,
  118-119, 127, 130; primitive, 79-80,
  123-124
moral judgment, ix-xi, 1, 15-16; and
  moral motivation, 127-130, 163-164,
  178-180, 184-185, 196-197; v. prudential judgment, 186-190
moral personality, 116; well-integrated,
  ix-x, xii, 30-31, 34, 36, 85
moral psychology, ix-x, 39; in relation to
  ethics, 199, 201, 221, 223-225; naturalism v. rationalism in, xii-xiii,
  114-122, 126-131
moral regeneration. *See* conscience, and
  moral integrity
moral sensibilities, 67-68, 81-82, 93. *See
  also* justice, sense of
Morris, Herbert, 18n, 19-28, 30n, 31n,
  37n, 41n, 43, 46n, 47n, 231n
motivation. *See* feelings and emotions;
  reason, conative power of
Murphy, Jeffrie, 18n, 19n, 162-163

Nagel, Thomas, x, 135-152, 154-159,
  164n
narcissism, 71, 126n, 130, 146n, 153-154
naturalism, 113-115. *See also* ethical naturalism; moral psychology, naturalism
  v. rationalism in
Neely, Wright, 229n
neurosis, 65, 77; obsessional, 95-96
Nietzsche, Friedrich, 74, 77

Oedipus complex, 75-78, 111n
'ought', usage of, 173-174, 194-195. *See
  also* rightness, concept of

pardon, 24-25, 34-35. *See also* forgiveness
parricide, 79-80, 83, 86-90, 123
peace and war, 207, 209, 218-220
Perlmutter, Martin, 18n
personality. *See* moral personality